TRUE COLOURS

TRUE COLOURS
CAROLINE PAIGE

My Life as the First Openly Transgender Officer in the British Armed Forces

\Bᵇ\

Biteback Publishing

First published in Great Britain in 2017 by
Biteback Publishing Ltd
Westminster Tower
3 Albert Embankment
London SE1 7SP
Copyright © Caroline Paige 2017

ISBN 978-1-78590-132-4

10 9 8 7 6 5 4 3 2 1

A CIP catalogue record for this book is available from the British Library.

Set in Adobe Caslon Pro

Printed and bound in Great Britain by
CPI Group (UK) Ltd, Croydon CR0 4YY

CONTENTS

To have a dream is a cause to live, to live is to have a dream

PROLOGUE

A blanket of cloud robbed the sky of its only natural light; there would be no comfort from the company of stars. With the Faroe Islands behind us, there was nothing but black sky and black sea. No boundaries; either way could be up. The only lights the faint green glow of my radar screen, discreetly adding to the radiance of the dimmed-down flight instruments in front of me. Without the radar, we would be blind. 'Where is it now?' asked Brian, his tightly clamped oxygen mask muffling his voice. I focused on the radar picture in front of me, passing bearings and range, orienting the target. 'Twenty-five degrees right, five up, 400 yards.' It enabled him to focus his eyes into the right place in the void surrounding us. What was it? What was it doing out here in the early hours of a Saturday? Why was it showing no lights? I directed us closer, carefully. Closer, closer, slowly, nervously close now as we slowed to match its speed. It was there, we just couldn't see it yet.

An hour ago we had been 500 miles south, sleeping restlessly, our fully armed fighter interceptor in the cold, grey corrugated metal shed next door, prepared for war, ready to go in an instant. A buzzing alarm had interrupted our sleep. 'Scramble!' it shouted. A dance-craze of arms and legs followed, zipping into G-suits, bending and squeezing into survival suits, fastening up life jackets, pulling on helmets and gloves, hopping on unlaced boots. Seven minutes after waking, we were climbing at 500 mph in the pitch-black of the early morning sky. And now we were tucked in behind this aircraft that didn't want to be seen. Gotcha! There it was, a soft shadow, but a soft shadow with shape now, a Soviet long-range bomber.

I felt some affinity with this intruder, feeling its way along in the dark, trying not to be seen for what it truly was. I was hiding my true identity, keeping a secret in the dark, and I had been for a lifetime now. Women weren't allowed to fly combat aircraft – and, worse, discovery of my secret would bring derision, disgrace and embarrassment to my family. I was finding it more and more difficult to endure this deception.

It all began in 1959. On a cold winter's night in Germany, a young British soldier waited excitedly for news from home. His wife was in the UK, due to give birth to their first child. Soon a telegraph message was delivered into his hands, shaking with excited anticipation. 'Congratulations, Daddy, it's a boy!' he shouted out excitedly; it was the news he had longed for. And so I came into the world. Although I was totally unaware of the implications at the time, everything became blue. The decision had been made: I was a boy. A decision based on my outward naked appearance. It wasn't until my own mind matured and I became self-aware that I would get any choice in this matter, though it wouldn't be realisable for many years to follow. And so the doll my mother had bought was cast aside, and my future was decided for me.

It is rare that anyone has to question their gender. The vast majority of people never will – and why would they? You were a girl or a boy and you knew that, everyone knew that, you never had to ask, you just were and you were quite happy with that. Your gender was a given and you just got on with life. Children may experiment with gender values; it is considered a normal part of the growing up process. There may even be times when cross-gender play worries those around them. It matters not to the child, but parents may worry that their young son seems happy pushing a toy pram (though a young daughter playing with toy cars is acceptable, and why not?). However, a child who is uncomfortable with their gender, who challenges it, is wrong. To parents, it can be embarrassing, perhaps abhorrent. What does a young child know about gender anyway? After all, surely they haven't lived enough to know about such matters; it has to be a phase. But if a child doesn't know, then how come every message coming from my young brain was saying, 'This isn't right, why am I like this, this isn't right'? It wasn't an informed message, it was an intuitive message and it was there day and night, rain and shine. This was my brain, this was my childhood, but there was something amiss. Those were my questions, and they wouldn't leave me alone.

PART ONE

INTO THE BLUE

1959–1992

1

THE GREEN DRESS

1959–1973

My father was a soldier in the Royal Artillery. He joined the British Army as a boy soldier in 1946, at the age of thirteen. He was a big man in many ways: six foot topped with regulation-cut black hair that grew curly when too long, crowning a strong, square jaw, brown eyes, a big nose and sticky-out ears. He had a heavyweight boxer's body, well-built with large muscular limbs and huge hands. His arms displayed tattoos: a sword and a python on one, and a Bengal tiger and unit crest on the other, badges of loyalty to his unit, 132 Battery (Bengal Rocket Troop). As a child, he lost part of a lung as a result of pneumonia, but it didn't stop him from becoming a tremendously fit and active soldier, who had represented his troop and regiment in rugby, boxing or throwing the hammer. He was a resilient character who seemed to enjoy brawling in his early Army years, usually as harmless inter-unit rivalry, though it did sometimes result in demotion for a while. He admitted he wasn't a well-educated man, but he had an annoying trait of having an answer for everything, and it always had to be right. He liked nothing more than a good argument – as long as he won – and, although his heart was big when it came to family and friends, his young Army years influenced an outspoken bigoted streak, the only negative trait in his wonderful character.

Mum was an averagely attractive woman around five foot four, with blue-grey eyes and short, curly brunette hair. She worked part-time in various factories whenever she could get the work. It clashed with the old-fashioned principles my parents had, but the extra money was handy. When Dad arrived home from work, he sat down in his favourite chair and was waited on hand and foot. Mum's place was in the kitchen; she was solely responsible for the cooking, cleaning and looking after the children. Mum was born in Douglas on the Isle of Man and Dad was born in Birkenhead, but they had grown up in the same road as each other in Liscard, on the Wirral Peninsula in Cheshire. She always agreed with Dad, never visibly taking our side when we made mistakes or behaved in a manner that met with disapproval.

Within four years of my arrival, I had two younger brothers and a baby sister. I was gangly with pale, freckled skin, ginger hair topping blue eyes above prominent cheekbones, hints of Viking ancestry. I was shy, and happiest reading books or drawing. My younger brother Stanley, usually shortened to Stan, was another gingerhead. He was seemingly the brightest child, but if there was trouble, he was usually involved from the start, an often annoying character who would wind the others up, forcing me to intervene as the eldest. My youngest brother was Richard, known as Rich. He was blond, a stocky, quiet but strong character. He wouldn't cause trouble but he would invariably end up involved, though usually on the right side. He was easily drawn by Stan, but otherwise he usually went with the flow; anything else seemed like too much trouble. Sandra was the youngest and she was my favourite sibling. I enjoyed her company but, although we got on well, I longed for a closer friendship, one that only sisters could share.

Most of my youth was spent moving wherever my father's duty took him, from British military bases in the UK and Germany to western Malaysia (or Malaya, as we then knew it). Contact with extended family was therefore infrequent but always a highlight of any journey home. Life abroad was usually lived in family housing provided on small estates within the confines of a military garrison.

Doubts about my gender were already confusing me as I began infant school, but I had also become aware of how unacceptable it was to question it. Boys were boys and girls were girls: there were clear boundaries. It wasn't acceptable for a boy to be feminine let alone be one of the girls.

How could I possibly think I was a girl when I was constantly controlled and identified as a boy by my parents and teachers? Surely they knew everything? It would be some time yet before medical research would determine that mind and body, gender and genitalia, could conflict within the same person, but I already knew that. I was sensitive to how people reacted to anyone considered 'different', and I quickly understood the consequences: it was shameful, abnormal and 'queer' to feel the way I felt. Queer was a word used offensively. I knew I was one of those people my parents would call queer; the outside world had too much diversity for their liking, and that wasn't good.

I was hurting. I knew I couldn't reach out; I was scared to reach out, especially to my parents. Instead, I turned inwards, living in hopes and dreams of change, of acceptance.

Early school reports described me as introverted though imaginative. In Malaya, my playground was a dusty yard bordered by tall wire fencing and the building where my father worked, when he wasn't out with the guns. He would occasionally see me through the white shuttered windows, sat on my own, cross-legged at the edge of the school playground, seemingly in quiet reflection, in a different world.

For me, it was a world of confusion and worry, but he would never question what he saw, never challenge the idea that I just wasn't fitting in. Many years later that realisation would come to trouble him.

Life in Malaya was otherwise amazing; it was a fabulous place to live as a child. Home was a house within Terendak Camp, a British Army base with a substantial beachfront just north of the town of Malacca. Blue skies and hot, humid, sunny days were occasionally disturbed by stormy clouds bearing warm and heavy rain, especially when the monsoon came. The countryside offered ordered plantations bordered by wild jungle, contrasting beautiful white beaches with crystal-clear blue water, in some places so shallow you could wade out for what seemed like miles and still feel the sand between exposed toes. I learned to swim here. After school we were expected to go out to play, only to return for teatime. I would wander down to the beach alone, looking for the prettiest coral I could find, washed ashore in recent storms. On the way to the beach, I would pass an old wooden house surrounded by trees, sagging on its stilts, hidden by dense foliage. A drooping veranda surrounded the front half of the single-storey structure, and wide, shuttered windows either side of the central door formed a face with a sad look. An old lady was rumoured to live here with a pet python as her only company; she was supposedly a witch. I watched but never saw her. At weekends we would go as a family to the beach or the pool, sometimes into the jungle, following rocky streams, catching large butterflies and moths fated to join Dad's growing collection, ordered displays of dead beauty.

It wasn't until my sister became a toddler that my troubles became more recognisable. I gained visual confirmation that all that was wrong lay in the differences that gender enforced. The traits expected for boys didn't fit my own sense of being; hers did. Yet identifying with girls remained totally unacceptable. One day I was sheltering in the cool shade of the house when I noticed a small dress in my parents' bedroom, laid out on a bed framed by softly draped mosquito nets. I knew I just had to wear it, so I did. It felt so comfortable, so natural, so right. My brain was working overtime, hiding the heavy footsteps rapidly approaching. Almost too late I realised my imminent dilemma. I found the dress too tight to remove and my only escape was to dive beneath the bed, watching as familiar sandal-clad feet entered the room, and then I saw bent knees, and then a face, right in front of me. It wasn't a happy face.

'Get out here... Now!' Dad bellowed. 'Get that off!' The dress seemed to come off easier now. I knew that wasn't the end of it. I didn't hear the words so much as feel the sound waves. There was a lot of anger and my ears were ringing. His final words followed me as I was dismissed to my room; they were the only words that I heard clearly.

'... if I ever catch you dressed like that again, I'll send you to school in a dress, with ribbons in your hair, so all your friends will see... Do you understand?!' I would have delightedly accepted that offer if it had been a genuine question, but I knew it would make matters worse to answer back.

The dress was never mentioned again. The angry warning was apparently sufficient. Actually, it wasn't. My feelings ran too deep to be changed by a loud reprimand, though now those feelings were suffused with hate for being me. How could I do this to my parents, wanting to change? I must be weird and I knew how much they despised 'weirdos'. 'People like that should be taken out and shot.' I didn't want to be thrown out. I definitely didn't want to be shot. I was weird and that was worse than being bad. Nobody else must know. I had to make sure I didn't get caught again. I made myself a promise: one day I would be a girl, a real girl. I didn't worry about how, I just would. In the only guaranteed secret place I had, I dreamt of a better future, and my life became a masquerade.

Something else happened in Malaya that would influence my life for ever. Our house was on the boundary of a large, rectangular field often used by military helicopters. I watched as they brought troops in or took them away. Sometimes a heavy-looking stretcher would be unloaded, met by a green Army ambulance waiting patiently in the corner of the field. I became fascinated by aircraft for the first time, particularly helicopters.

Malaya became a place of memories that would be significant parts of my life for ever. We eventually returned to Germany, where Dad was based with 27 Regiment at Lippstadt. By now I was dressing secretly whenever I got the opportunity, though this was rarer than I wished. The houses we lived in were small and I had to share a bedroom with my brothers. I resorted to sneaking a dress from my sister's room and locking myself in the bathroom whenever the occasion presented itself. I would sit on the closed toilet seat reading a book, or on the cold linoleum floor and draw a picture or write short stories, happy I wasn't being treated like a boy. Goodness knows why no one challenged why I was spending so long in the bathroom. It was remarked upon occasionally, casually, jokingly, but I was never pushed for an answer. If someone interrupted me I would place the dress in the linen basket then pretend I was using the bathroom for genuine reasons.

I was constantly living in the shadow of getting caught but I tried to wear an item of girl's dress underneath my boy clothes whenever I could, close to my skin, a way to stay attached to who I was. I made mistakes, suddenly realising I had bared my flower-patterned knickers or partially revealed a pretty top hidden beneath my boy clothes, but amazingly I seemed to get away with them. Nobody knew that, once the light had gone off and my brothers were sleeping, I often slipped into a nightie under my bedclothes, happily trying to help my dreams along, risking discovery if I overslept. I wanted to confide in Sandra, but I feared she wouldn't be able to keep my secret, and I couldn't take that risk.

A highlight of school was the fortnightly after-school dance class. When I missed the bus once, my parents didn't understand why I became so upset, blaming them. Domestic Science classes also brought little wins, arriving home with cakes I had made myself, activities 'not really for boys', though the cakes always went down well. I was delighted when my Auntie Val came to visit and taught me 'how to make a good cup of tea' – a domestic chore I was allowed to practise as often as I liked. But even better was when I overheard Auntie Val and my parents discussing choosing children's names. Apparently, had I been born a girl – little did they know – my name would have been Karen. It would have been fantastic to have a girl's name given to me by my parents, and I liked Karen, but I had been considering girls' names for a while now, and one in particular kept coming back to me. It just felt right for some reason, and it was pretty, so I had already decided my name: it was Caroline. A few years later, we moved back to England, to Woolwich, though not for long.

I began writing my stories sat in front of my family, the words hidden from their gaze. 'It's just homework,' I would innocently claim. It was handy having parents who never got involved with homework. One story was inspired by memories from Malaya. A boy who ventures deep into a forest discovers a sad, old, seemingly abandoned house. It is inhabited by a wicked witch who despises little boys and turns them into little girls. He deliberately enters the house and lives happily ever after, and the witch doesn't know it was a reward, not a punishment. One day the book went missing and I waited for the inevitable questions to come, but they never did. I would find it again over twenty years later in a cupboard at home. On the last page of the story someone had scrawled 'The End'. To this day, I don't know who.

Christmas and birthdays were difficult. I was always grateful for any present I received, but I desired the lovely things my sister got. I was happy with books or drawing pads, though I invariably got Meccano sets, trains and Action Man toys. Action Man was really just a doll, though, and there was comfort in knowing I would eventually get to enjoy some of the gifts Sandra received, even if not openly.

As I entered my teenage years, Dad retired from the Army and we were provided with a council house on an estate in Moreton, on the Wirral Peninsula in Cheshire; both my parents had extensive family living in the area. I was coming to realise that my wish wasn't going to happen, but it didn't stop me hoping or dreaming. I tried tempting fate: if I 'accidentally' stepped on a crack in the pavement, or I walked past a marker, such as a lamp-post, before the car I could hear approaching from behind got there, I would change. Of course, my steps found a crack and I beat the car to the lamp-post, and nothing changed, but it was a way of keeping my hope alive. If I let go of hope, I would fall.

School wasn't going particularly well. I was always dreaming of what could be, of magic and fantasy where I got to live my life as I wished. Some subjects held my interest more than others, such as history, geography, art and languages, but I couldn't get my head around mathematics and that meant sciences became weak options. Stan was frequently acclaimed by my parents as their cleverest child; he passed his 11-Plus exam, making him eligible to attend a grammar school, though he ended up going to the same school as me.

At home came even more distractions, now I was tall enough to fit Mum's clothes and was delighted to discover she owned a wig,

high-heeled shoes and bras. Dad insisted boys had short, mili-
tary-style haircuts even though they weren't the fashion, so the first
day I wore that wig was a day of joy indeed. I found bras awkward to
do up at first, but I took to high heels like I was born with them fitted.
The bathroom had also gained a large wall-mounted mirror. Dad had
been guarding a posh house in Heswall as it was being repossessed by
a bank. When the former owner visited, with a legal access permit, he
gave away some of the house contents, including the mirror. I could
see my whole height now, perfect. Though I always made sure my
back was to the mirror if naked.

I loved it whenever my parents decided to visit local family. 'Sorry,
I have loads of homework today, can I stop here and go next time?'
I would watch excitedly from Sandra's bedroom as the car disappeared down the road, anticipating my freedom. At the top of our
stairs stood a beautifully carved camphor wood storage chest, with
Chinese figures, elephants, houses and trees carved in amazing detail
on the lid, presenting a 3-D picture of Chinese drama that continued on the sides. My parents had shipped it back from Malaya, along
with the black wood bookshelf units and the water buffalo, tiger and
elephant carvings, all bringing the Far East to a 1950s mid-terrace
three-bedroom house otherwise displaying various items of militaria.
Inside, I discovered something wrapped carefully in paper, sealed in a
clear plastic bag. Unwrapping it revealed the most exquisite peach silk
cloth. Carefully, I unfolded it and my heart began to race. Standing
up, I watched as surely the most beautiful dress in the world unfolded
from my outstretched arms. I pulled it to my shoulders and ran to
the bathroom, where I gazed at a '60s-style dress, knee-length with a
full-circle petticoat, capped short sleeves and a V-shape neckline. The
back zipped down to the waist, a long sash draped off one shoulder
and a pretty black lace rose adorned the waist. The silk came to life

with body heat. I felt its cool touch, the embrace as the zip pulled it to my body, the skirt falling around my knees; the feeling was fantastic. My reflected image was the most wonderful I had ever seen. I felt pretty for the first time ever. I sat in the lounge, I made a cup of tea. I even went on the swing in the back garden, I was so happy.

I had grown confident moving around the house, always keeping a wary ear open for the sound of a car arriving home or a key turning in the front door. A change of clothes, placed in an attached toilet shed at the back of the house, provided a safety cache, used on more than one occasion. In winter months, I watched for house lights coming on as a warning signal. I was careful not to use the lights myself, should neighbours call when I didn't want them to. I longed to venture away from the house, though, to see the world outside from a new perspective.

Perhaps I was subconsciously hoping to get caught, even though I knew that would end in disaster. Years of gauging reactions from my family had resigned me to continued secrecy; I was too frightened to tell them. Now we had a television, and I heard words that only confirmed my worst fears. Anyone even assumed to be gay wasn't spared; a 'man dressed as a woman' was even worse. Les Dawson or Kenny Everett comedy sketches were OK, 'he's just being funny', and curiously Danny La Rue was acceptable, as an obvious drag entertainer, but any other man in a dress was a 'weirdo' and therefore totally intolerable. Entertainers revealed to be gay were no longer watched. When they came on television, it was immediately switched to either of the other two available channels; anything was preferable. Dad's long-time best friend stopped visiting with no explanation. Years later, I was told he had 'confessed to being homosexual'. Anything they read in the newspapers 'must be true' and the papers weren't kind to difference, always mocking, hurtful and insensitive. The media was a huge influence on my family's values, fuelling their intolerance to difference. It had a major impact on all our futures. I wasn't gay, I knew I wasn't gay: my dilemma wasn't about sexuality, it was about gender. I had never had or wanted a girlfriend, but I didn't want a boyfriend either. I was so confused about my gender, I never even thought about such things.

I was happiest alone, and I spent hours sat on the sofa in my dress, reading a book, my legs curled beneath me, until one day a bright flash crossed my eyes and triggered alarm. I raced to the window, worried my dad had returned early. The bay window of the lounge provided a good vantage point, hidden by net curtains. There was no one there; perhaps a car had passed by, reflecting light. It looked so bright and warm outside, it seemed a shame to sit indoors. Without much thought, I opened the front door and walked happily to the far end of the garden path. I could see all the way down the road. There were no fences, the mix of terraced and semi-detached houses all quiet with their net curtains and darkened rooms, no one in sight. Our house looked so far away, though it was only thirty feet. My dress seemed to float in the gentle breeze, my arms showing goose pimples of excitement. I felt fabulous. Then my error hit me in the face like a brick. Net curtains and darkened rooms! How could I be so foolish? Had I not moments before been stood behind my own cloak, watching for people outside? I turned and ran back to the house, seemingly even further away now. The open door flashed by, I was safe again. Back behind my own net curtain, my heart raced as I scanned the road for signs of observation from neighbours. Nothing. Panic over. What I couldn't get over, though, was how wonderful I had felt in the moments before the realisation of exposure had dawned, how free of constraint I had been. I had to go out again – but not today, it had to be away from the house next time. I planned what I was going to wear, where I was going to go, and then waited for that day to present itself, the thrill of anticipation quickly passing the time away.

Opening the front door, I peeped around it one final time and sprang outside, too late now to turn back. It was April, it was another beautiful sunny day, I was fourteen, I was a girl, and I was outside, joy! I was off school with flu but that wasn't going to stop me making the best of this day. Mum and Dad were at work until 5.30 and the others were at school. At 12.15 p.m., as Mum had left the house, I was already choosing my clothes. I felt great in my sister's green flower-print summer dress, a padded bra defining the extra curves I longed for. For unknown reasons I chose a pair of Sandra's red knee-length socks to go with my low heels, a foolish choice. I had only walked about 500 yards down the road when a young couple emerged from a house, observed me and began following just behind. I could hear them talking but I couldn't make out the details. I began to panic: they surely knew? How could I be more feminine? I began to walk like I'd seen catwalk models do; it must have looked ridiculous. Quickening my pace, I practically ran around the block back to the house. I was so disappointed with myself, I had to try again. I would need to get even further away from the local area, though, somewhere quiet, where I could relax. The seashore was a good place: it was less than a mile away and had a mix of open space and grass-tufted sand dunes, tall enough to hide behind if necessary, but I would have to be quick to cover such distance in the time available.

Proudly wheeling Sandra's bicycle down the shady, cold entryway we shared with our neighbours, I emerged into the bright sunlight glowing like an incandescent green butterfly fluttering its wings in the sun for the first time. My happiness was short-lived. On the opposite side of the road, two women stood chatting. One I recognised as my next-door neighbour. They turned, we were face to face. What should I do? Should I go back? No, too obvious. What, then? Just carry on? Maybe they wouldn't recognise me? I decided to bluff them and carry

on, before they had time to challenge me. Flashing a nervous smile, I
got on the bike and pedalled away, as fast as I could go. I was aware
of their stares following me all the way up the road until I turned
out of sight, into a side road. I stopped there for a while to collect
my thoughts. What should I do? I cycled off for a while, trying to
make my mind up. I was enjoying cycling around the houses: I felt
free, liberated. I knew I wasn't whole, but for now everything was forgotten, the clothes adding to the aura. It wasn't just that they were
pretty and feminine; it was as though they were a tonic, a medicine. I
wasn't hiding, I was liberated, the truth totally forgotten. I didn't want
to see it; I couldn't see it; the only way to spoil this was if I removed
the clothes. Until I had to do that, I could be me, no question. I was
hoping that other people seeing me now saw a girl out on her bike. It
meant I was accepted. It didn't cross my mind that even as a girl I was
out of place, a schoolgirl cycling aimlessly on a school day.

I worried the neighbours would phone Dad, reporting a stranger
at the house stealing Sandra's bicycle. He worked locally as a cash-in-
transit security guard for Securicor; he could be home within minutes.
I had to go back. Feeling great disappointment, I slowly cycled down
our road until I could see the house. It sat inside the crown of a bend,
so I had to be close to see. There appeared to be nobody in the road
adjacent, so I cycled as fast as I could now to the entry, then moved
through it as carefully and as quietly as possible. Gently, I opened
the garden gate, secured the bike and entered the house, free from
challenge. Back in my bed I waited a nervous eternity. What should I
say? What explanation could I give? Fortunately, the night remained
calm and the following day I was deemed healthy enough for school.
I was on a high all day. I had forgotten my worries as I returned to the
house, but there it was, a family inquisition waiting in the front living
room. I sensed danger.

'Did you see a girl riding Sandra's bike yesterday?' Dad began. I grimaced nervously. 'The girl was rather boyish,' he added. 'Mrs Comber saw her wearing a green dress and red socks.'

I didn't know what to do, admit or deny. Each had value but one would rain down fury. The whole family was there, surrounding me, staring, stretching from their chairs in anticipation of my explanation. I had been home all day, I must have seen something. Shrugging my shoulders wasn't going to work for long. I felt overwhelmed, alone, troubled about what would come. I turned, looking for escape, hating the idea that 'she had looked rather boyish'. Then I heard a word that gave me something to think about. Stan added his tuppence worth, as always.

'I think it was you. Sandra has red socks, you're a transvestite!' Clearly they had discussed this already. I sensed revulsion now. I walked away and hid in the bathroom, the locked door shielding a very lost child.

What was discussed after my exit I'll never know; nothing else was said to my face. Their job was done, the hostile interrogation had scared me, and I wouldn't venture further than the safety of our enclosed back garden for several years, not in a dress that was visible. My life had reached a disastrous stalemate. So much for joy.

The next day, in school, I looked up 'transvestite' in a dictionary. *Transvestite: one who practices transvestism. Transvestism: the practice of dressing in the clothes of the opposite sex.* I didn't consider I was dressing in clothes of the opposite sex: girls' clothes were wholly appropriate. They were an essential part of my true identity. But I had heard a word that described what people would think of me. It sounded like a troubled word, an aggressive word, mocking while implying antisocial behaviour. At this point in my life, I didn't realise this word didn't apply to me at all. There was another word people would use for me, but I hadn't heard it yet.

2

BLUE SKIES

1973–1979

Life wasn't going well. My body was changing and my voice was becoming rusty. I knew where that was heading. It was an awful time of resentment and fear, and there was nothing I could do but feel more and more alone. I couldn't see a happy ending. Then, in school, I noticed a poster for an after-school activity that drew me in: 'Venture – Adventure, Join the Air Training Corps'. It promised the experience of flight and adventure and there was a unit based at Hoylake, a short train journey away or a four-mile bicycle ride, No. 472 Squadron, with twice-weekly meetings and occasional weekends. I got permission from my parents to visit for an introduction night. I wasn't keen on the uniform, harsh grey woollen trousers with a matching bomber-style jacket, covering a blue shirt with black tie and all capped with a matching grey beret, but the promise of flight was very appealing. I decided I would give it a try, and my brothers decided to join too, prompted by my parents.

I was part of a group now, a group with similar interests, learning more about aeroplanes, and there was an annual visit to a Royal Air Force station for a week, where we could see aircraft up close, and sometimes even get a chance to fly in one. I did well in my exams, which tested aviation subjects such as principles of flight and air-craft recognition. I was even rewarded with promotion, and after proving proficient at rifle shooting I was placed on the squadron team, shooting a rather heavy .303 Lee Enfield. I was proud when I won my Wing Colours after representing the team in inter-regional cadet competitions. I was beginning to see the satisfaction of achievement, but it was the attraction of flight that was going to keep me safe. I desperately needed a clear focus and this was it. Another dream was also forming, but this one was different: it was coming true.

In 1976, aged sixteen, I was accepted for a gliding course with No. 631 Glider School at RAF Sealand, on the England–Wales border, a few miles north-west of Chester. It was a twenty-mile cycle to get there each Saturday, so I would usually get buses or hitchhike; drivers would offer a lift if I was in uniform. The gliders were Sedberghs, a curious-looking, old-fashioned aircraft whose front looked like it belonged on a small motorboat. The two-seat side-by-side open-air cockpit had two small semi-circular windscreens providing a hint of face protection for each occupant. The wing was fifty feet long and braced each side by a strut from the fuselage. It looked like some kind of prehistoric bird, with a red-and-white body flying on red-tipped silver wings, but it was fabulous fun to fly. The sides of the cockpit were below shoulder height when seated; a harness held me tight but it felt like I could put my hand down and touch the ground. The view when airborne was amazing, with no glass to distort it. I got on really well with the aircraft and found it easy to fly; it had to be to let youngsters fly it.

Gliding was a team event: everyone was expected to help with moving the aircraft to and from the hangar, and pushing or pulling them back to the winch point from where they finished their landing roll, everyone eagerly anticipating their own turn to go flying. On a bright, sunny, blue-sky day, there wasn't anything better.

As the pilot sat in the aircraft, someone would connect a cable to the front. A flashing light from the control caravan signalled the winch driver, way across the grass airfield, to accelerate an engine, pulling the cable tight, winding it in. A shout of 'All out!' and another light signalled for full speed on the winch. The glider was dragged along the ground into the wind, wing handlers briefly running alongside, letting go as it quickly gained enough speed to stay wings level; once airborne and above a safety height, the climb was steepened, feeling almost vertical, tremendously exciting. At the release point, the pilot lowered the aircraft nose to slacken the cable and there was a reassuring clunk as the release knob was pulled to disconnect the winch cable. After that was beautiful silence, a soft swirl of air. The view was amazing: the Clwydian mountains to the north-west, Snowdonia in the far distance, the River Dee winding its way from the south, becoming unnaturally straight after serving Chester, a man-made diversion guiding it to its wide, silted estuary to the north-west. On its west bank, Shotton Power Station was a good source of rising air. Thermals were a glider pilot's best friend, permitting extended flight, circling to gain height like vultures, everything below getting smaller and quieter, houses, vehicles, trees, people, farm animals all looking like sets in a child's toy world.

In the air, all my worries were forgotten. This was meant to be, this is what would keep me alive. Saturdays couldn't come around quick enough. I did well on the course and eagerly awaited my chance to go solo, to fly on my own, to be totally free. First I had to prove I could react correctly to various emergencies, mostly involving simulated cable breakages at various heights, and my landing rolls were stopping in the perfect place, enabling the briefest reposition to connect and go again. 'Land there once more and you can go solo this afternoon,' my instructor said. It was a challenge, but when I managed it, he was true to his word. 'Enjoy this next one… I'm getting out here.'

Only those who have sat in a cockpit knowing they are about to take an aircraft into the sky, on their own, for the first time, could know what I was feeling. It's a feeling that reaches deep into your heart, and mine was pounding away now in pure excitement. I truly felt alive, the excitement of achievement, of trust, of flight. I can't ever recall thinking how I was going to get down; I was going up, the rest would just happen. The sky was calling and I was feeling its call.

'All out!' I shouted. I was only to do a circuit – take-off, turn downwind then turn to land – an orbit, but an orbit that climbed and descended over a thousand feet. I was talking out loud to myself all the way around.

'…hundred feet … good … pull back … climb … climb … good … don't forget to push forward if the cable breaks … a thousand feet … push forward … check airspeed … release … watch the speed … height is good … turn now … gooood … landing area? … there! … nice glider, nice glider … there's the road … keep it on the left … relax … height good … turn now … relax … this is amaaaaziiiiing! … height is good … speed is good … nice glider … landing point … goooood … line up … nice … clear of other gliders … and people … speed … height … speed … height … rate of descent … good … wings level … feel for the ground … feel, feel, gently, there it is … and … touchdown! … wings level … keep them up … keep them up … almost stationary … rest the wing … and … done … huge smile!'

The flight only took two to three minutes, but it lasted for ever. I had even managed to relax a little and enjoy it, I think. I had just turned sixteen and I had been on my own 1,000 feet above the ground with a grin so big it was surely seen from Liverpool. Three times I flew on my own that day, but it was with some sadness that I made my final landing. It meant the course was complete and there would be no gliding for me again. I already knew my next target, though: to win a flying scholarship for a powered aircraft course.

I had to wait until I was seventeen for that, but as soon as I was eligible, I applied and was invited to the Royal Air Force Officer and Aircrew Selection Centre (OASC) at RAF Biggin Hill for medical and aptitude tests and an interview. The four-week flying course was sponsored by the RAF, and successful applicants were assessed at the same place as candidates seeking to join as an officer or aircrew. After two days of assessment, I returned home to wait for news. Months later, I had almost resigned myself to being unsuccessful when a light-blue envelope arrived for me. I didn't finish reading the letter: I saw the words 'successful', 'flying scholarship' and 'Cambridge Aero Club' and jumped up in joy.

Having the course to focus on was important to me: if my other dream was allowed to take centre stage, it triggered realisations of despair. It was still important to be the real me whenever I got the opportunity – that dream was still very much alive, even though it had no voice – but flying was dragging me out of my shell. I was gaining confidence in me, in my own abilities.

Dad's advice regarding my ambition or ability was rarely inspiring – I believe he thought it kept me safe to stay 'within realistic expectations' – but I was reaching outside of those now. I had already said I wanted to join the Royal Air Force and be a pilot, but when I did, he would reply, 'You can't join the military', 'None of you will join the military ... unless you're an officer ... and you'll never be an officer, because your father was a sergeant.' He was implying that I had a place, and no one would let me rise above it because of my humble family background. But I had already risen above that place. We didn't have wealth, we lived on a council estate and I went to a secondary comprehensive school, yet I had been solo in a glider, and now I had been offered the opportunity to learn to fly a powered aircraft, and it would all be paid for by a scholarship. Having such a positive thing to hold onto was a massive counterbalance in my life.

The school careers liaison officer didn't seem so keen, though. 'You have to be physically fit and clever to be a pilot. And a military life isn't an easy one. Are there any other careers you would like to follow?' I only had one career in mind, and I wasn't worried about my fitness.

As I emerged from my shell, I made a couple of good friends at my all-boys' school, Henry Meoles Senior Comprehensive. In the summer, Roy and Bob and I would set off for week-long cycling trips into Wales, stopping overnight at youth hostels, riding hundreds of miles around, up and down mountains. We'd never heard of mountain bikes, but we had bikes that did mountains.

I was also an active member of the school rowing team. It provided a great excuse to get out of playing rugby or football during sports afternoons; they were too boyish for my liking, and I was uncomfortable baring my body in company. Girls didn't seem to participate much in rowing, but at least it wasn't a contact sport. My school borrowed boats from Liverpool University, at their clubhouse on West Float, Birkenhead Docks. I had to make my own way there for weekend commitments. It was a three-mile cycle each way, and traffic wasn't the only danger. As I neared the dockyards I had to run the gauntlet of local youths, who took delight in throwing lumps of brick at me. I found a route that had a downhill gradient as I approached the danger area, committing myself to a fast-straight-line approach, through to the safety of the dockyard gates; surprise and speed was usually the best tactic. I enjoyed rowing the Fours. If we didn't have another crew to race, we would wait at the Duke Street swing bridge for a tug to come through, then race it down the docks, scurrying behind corners in the dock wall at the last moment, the turbulent bow wave mostly absorbed by the dockside; the rocking of our boat dampened by oar blades held flat on the dirty grey water, with its swirls of oil occasionally casting rainbows amongst the congregation of flotsam and jetsam. At least when we entered regional school competitions they were held on quieter, cleaner rivers and reservoirs.

In the summer of 1978, I arrived at Cambridge Airport, sharing a detached house opposite the main entrance for four weeks with two other students. All we had between us was a tape player and a cassette, with an endless loop of Santana songs eventually wearing me down, making me wish I'd brought my ABBA tapes.

I was in awe of my instructor when I learned he had flown Spitfires. He worked for Cambridge Aero Club and as a test pilot for Marshalls of Cambridge. I got time at the controls of a twin engine, and in a Cessna Citation business jet, in a cabin covered in deep-pile carpet with lacquered mahogany-veneer trims, a matching cocktail cabinet, and leather loungers for cosseting half a dozen passengers. I'd never seen such luxury before. It even had colour-radar in the cockpit, far different to my little Cessna 150 two-seat trainer. The 150 was a forgiving aircraft to fly; its high braced wing reminded me of my Sedbergh glider, though this time I was confined in a rather cramped, all-enclosed side-by-side cockpit.

My first solo came after eight hours of airborne instruction, and once again I was talking to myself as I flew solo around the circuit, my instructor listening to my radio calls from the air traffic control tower, watching my progress. On a solo cross-country navigation sortie I had to land at Ipswich and Norwich Airports to get a signature from Air Traffic Control, proving I had been there. Midway between the airports, I was rocked in turbulence as two American F-111 bombers suddenly appeared, passing very close from behind, disappearing from sight as quickly as they had surprised me. It was motivating, seeing military jets moving so quickly past me.

I enjoyed the navigation elements as much as the flying. Flying the aircraft was actually quite easy, once I'd levelled it at my intended cruising altitude; as long as the controls were trimmed out properly, the aircraft was flying in balance and the power was set properly, it 'flew itself'. The hard work was everything else that was needed, everything wrapped in a parcel called 'airmanship': the navigation, communications, situational awareness, instrument monitoring, flight instruments, engine instruments, fuel contents, flow and balance, and lookout. Lookout wasn't just about admiring the view, which was always amazing: it was seeing potential problems far enough away to avoid them, such as bad weather or other aircraft that had a habit of blending into the sky around them. Keen eyes and knowing where and how to look were essential.

No sooner had I begun my course than my final flight test loomed. Then, disaster: I learned the scholarship only covered thirty hours' flying, but a pilot's licence required a minimum of thirty-five. There was no way my parents could afford to pay for an extra five hours, nearly £100. From the confines of a red metal and glass phone box at the side of the road, I asked anyway. The following day, as I walked back to the phone, I expected the worst. Thankfully, Mr Peabody, my Air Cadet Squadron Commander, had approached the RAF Association in West Kirby and they had agreed to fund the difference from what my parents could contribute, which couldn't be very much at all. I was incredibly grateful: had I not gained my licence from the scholarship my future would have been grounded. Flying was the only thing I seemed capable of doing. I enjoyed it; it was keeping me focused, energised. It was the only thing motivating my future.

I rewarded their faith in me with a successful final flight test, and I had my pilot's licence before I had learned to drive. My career in aviation was one step closer. Ironically, none of this would have been achievable if I was identifiable as a girl. I couldn't have joined the Air Cadets, and I wouldn't have received the scholarship. There were undoubtedly some advantages to being considered a boy – but given the choice there is no question which life I would have chosen.

The confidence gained during my flying adventures now showed in my schoolwork. I even won a book prize for Humanities, presented to me personally by Tony Davis from the Spinners folk group. But meeting the entrance requirements to join the RAF was hard work: the RAF required its pilots to be officers. I had already decided the military offered the only option for me to fly. Commercial aviation required me to pay my own way and I didn't have pennies to my name, let alone thousands of pounds. Not focusing earlier in my schooling had presented a huge hurdle, especially in those subjects I now needed as mandatory entry requirements. After failing my first attempt at Maths O-Level, I enrolled in extra classes and five months later was rewarded with a cherished Grade C. A pass was still a pass, but now I had ten of them, far better than I had ever anticipated, taking me to the top of my family class. The loveliest fallout from doing exams was the free time that was generated between them. Of course, it was intended for study, but there were no rules to say how you were dressed when you did that study, and the house was always empty in the afternoons.

Once I was eighteen, I made my application to join the Air Force. I knew the military wouldn't let me join if I was known to be gay, or suspected of being gay; Dad embodied what the Armed Forces thought of gay people. I knew I wasn't a gay man, but I hadn't yet found my place in society. I still didn't understand any of this myself. Why had I been cruelly tricked by nature? Why me – why wasn't anyone else like this? Surely there would be books on it if other people were like me.

It's not the body that makes the person; it's the mind that is our very existence, our soul, our identity. A body is nothing without a mind, and as much as it bestows character, and allows procreation, the overwhelming evidence was that my body didn't match who I knew myself to be. But no one can see a mind, and people only believe what they can see. I wasn't a boy who liked wearing dresses; I was a girl, who liked wearing dresses, with a body that convinced nobody, and which gave even me doubts. How could this even be possible? My doubts made me more vulnerable: if it was just me, then could I be wrong? But if I was wrong, why had I struggled with this for thirteen years or more now? It wasn't a 'phase', it was trapped in my heart. I knew my gender before I understood the differences. When I was scared into hiding my feelings as a five-year-old, I survived through magical dreams and hopes, but now I knew there was no magic, now I knew my dreams were just dreams. I could see no way out of this, but neither could I switch it off. This was me, a girl, without any way to prove it. I saw no evidence that anyone would accept me for who or what I was. If my own parents couldn't, then surely nobody would.

People assumed that a man who wished to be a woman was a gay man; the word transgender didn't exist as it is known today. It was im- agined that he only wanted to be a woman to have a relationship with another man, and surely that could only be a gay intention. The idea that there could be a difference between sex and gender, that someone could look like a man on the outside but be a woman on the inside, wasn't considered. Being gay wasn't illegal in civil law, but military law still declared otherwise, arguing it wasn't in the best interests of the morale of an organisation responsible for the defence of the nation, and would be a security risk. Gay men and women who joined without revealing their sexuality risked harassment and humiliation if discovered, followed by immediate dismissal, regardless of how successful their career had been until then. There would be no qualms in 'outing' someone, regardless of what devastation that might bring. So when I was asked the question 'Are you gay?' at the RAF Careers Information Office in Liverpool, with all honesty I was able to answer 'No.' But now I was trapped: if I told anyone my secret there would be no going back. The truth would be out and I would be at their mercy. Friend or not, if they found this too much to believe and turned against me, mocked me or even spread gossip, then my career and effectively my life would be over. I couldn't take that risk.

Outside the military too, my family and society in general would only accept me as they saw me now, not as I saw me. Whichever career path I chose, my life was in the hands of others. With everything to lose, I decided only my passion for flying offered a focus for my life.

And so I found myself back at RAF Biggin Hill for OASC. All went well until the final stage, when we entered the practical exercise phase in a small hangar-style building, laid out like a sports hall. All candidates wore blue boiler suits, with a bib showing a large letter and number designating the team we were in, making the individual nameless. There were several groups rotating through a variety of pre-organised obstacles. On arrival at each scenario, one of the group would be nominated as the task leader, then we were briefed on the aim and the rules. Invariably, the challenge involved using a rope, a pine-pole and one or two large oil drums, with a time limit. Assessment was for teamwork as much as it was for leadership. It had been going very well and my own turn as leader had passed without much worry; now I was trying to be a good team-worker. The final exercise involved crossing an imaginary ravine that stretched to infinity either side of the required crossing point, marked by two parallel tapes on the ground, just wider apart than the pine-pole was long. 'Anyone touching the floor between the lines means you have fallen to certain death into the ravine.' We knew the drill by now; he didn't need to add that the task would be restarted but the clock would remain ticking, but he did anyway. We had managed to bridge the gap, using the props available, and were all shuffling across the balanced pine-pole to reach the other side. I was at the front and I had three guys shuffling along behind me. The one at the back lost his balance and grabbed hold of the person in front of him, who grabbed hold of the person in front of him, who grabbed hold of me, and slowly we all inverted on the pole and fell 'to a certain death'. Sprawled on the wooden floor I could not stop laughing: a Looney Tunes Roadrunner cartoon scene flashed into mind, our eyes popping out wide as, one by one, we realised our doom, hanging upside down before falling as an ever-decreasing dot, a small puff of smoke marking impact far below. It seemed so silly, so funny. I noticed our ever-watchful assessor, making Queen Victoria proud with his 'We are not amused!' face, but I still couldn't stop laughing. It was one of those moments when you lose control of your laughter: it was impossible to stop, as much as I wanted to. The exercise was reset and completed, the rest of the assessment process proceeded uneventfully and we all went our separate ways.

Several months later, I received another blue envelope. 'Thank you for your attendance at OASC, you scored well in the aptitude tests and did well at interview, but we feel that you would benefit from experience outside of school. We look forward to hearing from you next year.' In other words, I wasn't mature enough yet; I guessed where that came from. I was devastated, but this was important to me and I was keen to reapply. I didn't want to get a job that was going to bind me for over a year, but I had to be seen to be mature, self-sufficient. I noticed an advert calling for lifeguards at a local leisure centre swimming pool. At school, I had gained several qualifications in life-saving skills in the water, earning a Distinction Award from the Royal Life Saving Society and becoming an instructor. I felt suitably qualified, but my interview was halted after just a few minutes: 'You are too qualified to be a lifeguard… This isn't for you… Have you seen this?' The interviewer presented a job being advertised in a Wirral Borough Council newsletter which sought a trainee manager to work in the municipal leisure centres, ranging from Seacombe's Guinea Gap Baths, a fabulous Edwardian building containing a salt-water swimming pool, to The Oval in Bebington, a sport complex complete with pool, sports hall, football and hockey pitches and an athletics track with stadium. I thought such a job would look good to the RAF, and if they didn't accept me it would leave a different career option open, to help gain my independence. I needed my own life: opportunities to relax at home were still far too few, and each instance risked discovery. I was expected now to get a job and contribute to the household income, but what I needed was my own sanctuary, and money to buy my own things.

'I'm interested, but am I able to apply for an internal job?'

'Leave it to me,' he said. 'I'll be in touch.' That evening, I received a phone call asking me if I could start on Monday.

It was an incredible job and I met some lovely people, though my heart was still in flying. I was hiring a four-seat Cessna 172 from Cheshire Air Training Services at Liverpool Speke Airport whenever I could save enough money, flying friends and family. It was wonderful when I got to fly Dad. We only flew together once; the cockpit was uncomfortably cramped for a man of his size, but he still smiled all the time we were airborne. He never verbalised pride, but he soon had me taking his friends flying. I wasn't a commercial pilot, so they couldn't pay me, but they contributed towards my 'travel costs'. Otherwise I wasn't earning enough to fly more than once every month or so. Living at home still meant sharing a small bedroom with my two brothers; finding my own accommodation offered privacy, and somewhere safe to create my own wardrobe. I worked at several sports and leisure centres, learning different jobs, one week working with a pool engineer, another working on reception, a day as a lifeguard, one day a week at college, working to gain a professional qualification, and the rest of the time learning on the job as a shift manager.

Out of the blue, I received a familiar envelope: the RAF was inviting me back for selection, before a year had passed. Once more, I found myself at RAF Biggin Hill. I messed up the interview slightly: having read up on current affairs in the newspapers, I got mixed up discussing events in Northern Ireland, laughing as I realised I'd said 'the Romans were in conflict with the Catholics'. Fortunately the interview board also laughed. Then a doctor challenged that I had cheated in my medical. Apparently on my first visit I had had perfect colour vision, yet on this visit my colour perception was degraded. Colour perception is permanent, so the conclusion was that I had cheated first time around, memorising the pages of different coloured dots that blended hidden numbers. In fact, the tester was moving the pages so fast I never had time to focus on the page, let alone discern any differences and camouflaged numbers. After a further test, involving identifying small pinpoints of white, blue, red and green lights, I waited in an empty reception area before eventually being summoned to learn my fate.

'You passed the eye test, but your colour perception means you can't be a photographic interpreter.' Well, I had never asked to be a photographic interpreter, but I didn't want to show disrespect.

'But I can still be a pilot?'

'Yes. That's it, thank you for coming.' I was happy with that.

Several weeks later, I received another blue envelope inviting me to start No. 42 Initial Officer Training Course at the Royal Air Force College Cranwell on 20 January 1980. I didn't need anything else for Christmas. I felt tremendously guilty when I asked to see my manager at work and told him that I was resigning, to join the Air Force as a pilot. I had taken a few days 'off ill' to do the selection, just in case it didn't work out. The team manager and my colleagues couldn't have been happier for me. They were amazed that I was going to do such a job and we all went to a local pub to celebrate.

I hadn't forgotten who I was. My success in joining the RAF was only disguising the turmoil inside, not replacing it. My childhood hopes and dreams were seemingly unreachable. There was no magic, no dream come true. For some reason I was born like this, and I would somehow have to live with that. Even if there was a way, my parents didn't deserve me ruining their lives for them. Although they wouldn't express their excitement to me directly, I knew they would be making sure the whole family, as well as work colleagues and friends, were aware I was going to be an officer. They would enjoy breaking that news. It was such a big achievement for us all. How could I possibly let them down? Now, more than ever, I had to try and live to their expectations. I still naively assumed that if I focused on a flying career, my life would be bearable, and I could keep my innermost conflict secret for ever.

3

NO GIRLS ALLOWED

1980–1982

On a cold, crisp, bright-sky January day, I arrived by train in the quiet market town of Sleaford and caught a bus to RAF Cranwell. I was handed my arrival paperwork at the guardroom and given directions to my allocated accommodation, located further along the road and through a different gate. As I walked, hauling all my worldly possessions in one brown plastic suitcase, I caught glimpses of an impressive old building through gaps in the hedges and trees lining the road. It was College Hall Officers' Mess, known as CHOM, a majestic-looking neo-classical building inspired by the architectural design of Christopher Wren's Royal Hospital at Chelsea, though opened only forty-six years before I now stood in front of it. An 800-foot-long frontage, with an impressive entranceway capped by a tall, domed clock tower, boasted the furthest inland lighthouse in the UK; evidence of its brief heritage as a Royal Navy base struggling to identify with such an inland location.

But I wasn't going to be living here; I wasn't yet worthy enough. I turned my gaze to three white, two-storey barrack blocks framing three sides of the main parade square: this was to be my home, at least for the next five months. My room was on the ground floor of the block occupying the west side of the square. I had a bed, a wardrobe and a chest of drawers. A communal bathroom and a laundry room were located at the end of the corridor linking the bedrooms. The bed wasn't exactly comfortable, clearly built in days when people didn't stretch towards six feet, the sheets stiff and barely big enough to tuck under the wilting mattress, and the scratchy black woolly blanket did little to keep the cold at bay, but I wasn't expecting any comfort here. From now on my daily routine would begin with an early morning parade and roll-call, followed by a pedantic room inspection in which white-gloved hands wiped over door frames, light fittings and wardrobe tops, seeking evidence of dust, swiping places I hadn't yet thought of. Uniforms and gym clothes carefully pressed and laid out, in an exact order, shoes, belt buckles and boots highly polished, everything had to be immaculate and ordered. Errors would earn a black mark. I was used to sharing a small room with two brothers; at least here there were just two of us, and I had my own wardrobe. My first room-mate quit on day two: he had already decided military life wasn't for him.

After room inspection, we would all be marched off, in two columns abreast, to the first classes of the day. Lessons and briefings on air power and doctrine, history, organisation, office and management skills were interrupted frequently with periods of physical fitness, leadership exercises, military skills or drill. There were no computer aids – they didn't exist yet. Instead, tutors used overhead projectors, slide projectors, boards and books. Study work and essays had to be handwritten on lined paper; typewritten reference books and handwritten notes were vital for pre-exam study.

The most dreaded part of physical fitness became the twice-weekly LAT (Leadership Agility Training) run, a cross-country run against the clock, wearing running gear but with heavy-duty steel-toe-capped work boots and an olive-drab canvas webbing vest, with four ammunition and storage pouches attached around the waist belt. A pre-run inspection

ensured the pouches contained the mandatory bags of sand and that the
water bottle was full – water only, no juice. Lincolnshire wasn't as flat
as we'd all assumed; a long uphill slope dominated the last part of the
run. My pouches brimmed with permanently damp sand, the compacted
contents possibly the result of wicked humour from whoever filled them.
The further I ran, the more I noticed them. These tests were psychological battles of will, the will to finish even when worn out, run into the
ground; determination was the key to success. I did well on the fitness
tests, dominated by long-distance runs carrying increasingly heavy loads:
pine-poles, oil drums, laden stretchers and military equipment. As finish
times improved, the burdens we had to carry became heavier, or bulkier.

I did well in the classroom too, but unbeknown to me I was being
marked down on personality, assessed as a quiet, inconspicuous individual, an introvert, not really one of the boys. A fair assessment, but
not for any reasons my Flight Commander would realise. I had also
become a number: after swearing an oath to Queen and country, and
signing the Official Secrets Act, I was allocated a seven-digit service
number. It would stay with me for the rest of my life; I still carried
Dad's in my head. But it wasn't just a number: it also identified my
month of birth, the fact that I wasn't a graduate, and my sex.

Halfway through training, we were allowed to go home for a weekend. It was a short weekend by the time I had caught a series of trains
there; on the way back, I hitchhiked from Liverpool via the M62 and A1.
A relay of trucks and cars eventually got me back to Cranwell, though
it still worked out quicker and cheaper than by train and bus. The only
people on the course with cars were those who came from wealthier
backgrounds, or the few senior NCOs who had been in the RAF for a
while before successfully applying for officer training. I would soon discover that the RAF tended to build its bases in the middle of nowhere.

After two months of learning the basics, we were moved into the

College Hall Officers' Mess. It was just as grand on the inside as it was outside. Corridors lined with tall paintings of famous graduates from the College, of senior officers and recipients of medals for courage in action. There was a bar now; socialising was an important skill for an officer, and this was also quietly assessed. After my weekend break, I went there to join my colleagues. Entering with a high-spirited jovial greeting, I noticed my Flight Commander sitting in the corner, chatting to other students. I wasn't aware he had taken note. He hadn't seen me be so loud before – and neither had I! His opinion changed dramatically, and my assessments rose from 'not sure' to 'strong'. One moment of spirit had revealed a happier self somewhere inside of me. Funny how such a moment could be so important. If I didn't graduate as an officer, my flying career was doomed. I had to work hard to achieve my goal: nothing was easy; nothing was taken for granted.

Then, out of the blue, something threatened to halt my career in its tracks. Following a routine physical, I was summoned to the medical centre.

'We have some concerns regarding your EEG [electroencephalogram] results.'

'What is the problem, sir?' I asked nervously. The doctors wore rank; this one was a Squadron Leader.

'We aren't able to say. You'll be further advised by specialists in London. An appointment has been made for you at the Central Medical Establishment [CME] there next Tuesday. I will authorise a rail warrant for your journey.'

All aircrew had to have an EEG, a scan of brainwave activity. In the event of any future trauma to the head, an EEG trace would enable medical teams to identify any possible brain injury. After several days of worry, a black cab collected me from CHOM. As we drove away, I looked back, thinking that perhaps my flying career was over.

CME was in a multi-storey office block near the Post Office Tower in London. An Air Commodore medical officer explained that my first EEG had shown abnormalities, requiring the second one to be performed. This too had caused some concern, so I was to undergo further tests and analysis. No one could explain what the issue was, just that the scan result was different to what would normally be expected, but my mind had its own ideas. What if this was the cause of my gender identity issues? Could they be related? I hoped that my brain hadn't given me away, or that whatever the concern was it wouldn't stop me from flying. Further tests didn't clarify the issue, but I was permitted to return to my course, with a medical note requiring annual tests and reassessments.

Back at CHOM, it was soon 'Black Monday', the day when we learned one by one if we had passed the course. I was astonished to learn I had done very well, and that I had just missed out to someone else on winning the top honour! In reward, I was offered first choice of holding postings available to graduating officers. A holding post was temporary employment while waiting for professional training to begin. It was generally used to develop service experience, during the often long gaps between courses, though sometimes it was also used for adventure training, such as sailing or skiing expeditions. Top of the list for my graduation course was two months in Gibraltar, so I took it.

There was to be a parade for our graduation day. Rehearsals included foot and ceremonial sword drill, and we were measured up for our No. 1 uniform. No. 1 was best uniform, worn for parades, ceremonies, funerals and weddings. Blue-grey woollen trousers matched a single-breasted jacket, adorned with brass-coloured buttons featuring an embossed RAF eagle, over a long-sleeved blue shirt, worn with a black tie. Rank was worn in light-blue banded grey rings on the jacket sleeve. A very thin ring indicated my rank at graduation: the first level of officer rank, Pilot Officer, though for the first year I would be considered an Acting Pilot Officer, a probationary rank. No. 2 uniform was considered normal, working-day uniform, referred to as 'working dress': similar grey trousers, usually with a woolly jumper, though open-collared short-sleeve shirts were permitted during the summer months. The girls' uniform permitted trousers or a knee-length skirt, worn with an authorised brand of 'barely black' tights and black court shoes. If only. Approximately three in 100 graduating officers were female.

Family were a big part of the graduation ceremony, but Dad didn't want to come.

'Sorry, but I don't have a suit, and I can't afford to get one made.'

I knew it was an excuse: he was embarrassed about his size, after putting a lot of weight on since leaving the Army. But I wanted him to see me graduating as an officer, to see that I could 'rise above my station'. Wages during training weren't exactly generous, but I insisted, and paid for a tailor-made suit.

On graduation day, Mum and Dad arrived with Sandra and Stan. To the sound of an RAF band, eighty-four of us marched onto the parade square with the magnificent backdrop that was CHOM – how could anyone not be impressed? After a formal inspection by the reviewing officer, General Wijting, Chief of the Netherlands Defence Staff, we marched off and up through the front door of CHOM, throwing our hats in the air in traditional celebration, then removing the white hat-bands, as proof that we were now the newest officers in the RAF. My family were being hosted by my Flight Commander. Sandra looked lovely and openly expressed her delight. Stan was smart in his Merchant Navy uniform; he told me Dad was proud of me. Dad had been told I'd done extremely well and had the ability to attain senior rank in the RAF, but when I spoke with him, he wouldn't express his pride openly. After the traditional church service, they bade farewell and left for home.

• • •

I had to get a passport for Gibraltar; I'd never had one of my own before. It was a great place to visit: I worked in Air Traffic Control, the Station Operations Centre, the Admin Headquarters, 1102 Squadron Marine Craft Unit, and with the RAF Police Counter-Drugs team. I was also well hosted socially, in the town as well as the officers' mess. One night, after I'd enjoyed a few drinks in the bar, my bed began shaking from side to side, and I fell out. I was relieved to learn there had been a strong earthquake around the same time, and thankful that there had been no serious injuries reported. My role was to observe and learn, mostly through hands-on experience. As an Acting Pilot Officer, I was considered like a mature teenager, with no responsibility other than to learn and enjoy. I managed to get some jump-seat flights on Yogi Bear to explore Tangiers, in Morocco. Yogi Bear was a Vickers Viscount, a four-engine propeller-driven airliner belonging to Gibraltar Air, known as Gib Air. The legend was that one night someone had stealthily painted 'Yo' in front of the 'Gib Air' lettering on the aircraft fuselage, sealing its popular nickname.

On one of my trips to Tangiers, I joined two young female officers, and it was so nice to have their company. It was possible to hire a taxi for the day for a carton of 200 duty-free cigarettes, and the taxi driver provided a guide for our visit to the colourful and bustling Grand Souk. I was convinced we were only directed into his uncles' shops, but the guide was useful at shooing away the army of persistent market traders keen for our business. We also got to ride on one of his uncle's camels. I bought, amongst many other goods, a Moroccan carpet and some traditional hand-cut leather shoulder bags for Sandra and Mum. When I got to present them, I was hoping they would appreciate my choices being 'in touch with my feminine side'. Back at Gibraltar I was invited on flights in RAF Nimrod anti-submarine patrol aircraft and an airborne early warning Avro Shackleton, an aircraft whose ancestry could be traced back to the Lancaster bomber. It was important to experience a variety of aircraft roles, in case I needed to make career decisions regarding where I went after my flying training.

My next destination was RAF Linton-on-Ouse, a pilot training base ten miles north-west of York. As I arrived at the officers' mess, I was greeted by two characters, one of whom introduced himself as Paul Bishop and kindly showed me the way to my room. He was on the pilots' course ahead of mine, the senior course. I didn't know anyone here yet, so I appreciated the friendly gesture, especially when his course was busy enjoying a fancy-dress party in the mess bar. I couldn't help but smile: the last time I had been here was 1974, when I was an air cadet, staying in a barrack block called Thunderbird Block. I had watched the aircraft here, not daring to believe that I would be back one day to fly them, and live in the officers' mess.

I was joining No. 47 Basic Flying Training Course straight from officer training, whereas my fellow students had come from an RAF flying training selection course, or they had been members of one of the RAF-operated university air squadrons. I was part of a trial in which people who already held a pilot's licence went straight onto the Jet Provost. Known as a JP, it was a small red and white single-engine jet aircraft with side-by-side cockpit and ejection seats. My instructor was a foreign air-force air-tanker pilot on an exchange programme with the RAF, and I was one of his two allocated students. I started well, but after a while I began to see a fall in my assessments; I knew I wasn't meeting his expectations but I didn't feel I was being supported to learn. He seemed to have a far better relationship with my colleague, and I began to feel as though he had lost interest in me. There was both an expected attitude and an expected progression for students. We were expected to want to be single-seat fast-jet pilots; desiring to fly helicopters or air transport aircraft demonstrated poor motivation. Experiencing the RAF's instructional style and standards, in the way my fellow students had, might have prepared me better, but it was too late.

I never got to be a two-seat military pilot, let alone single-seat. I had qualified to fly the aircraft on my own, but one day, after a dual sortie, I was summoned to the Squadron Commander's office, which wasn't usually a good sign.

'Your instructor tells me your last trip didn't go as well as he'd have liked... I'm going to put you on the flying programme tomorrow with the deputy chief flying instructor. You'll have the chance to do it again... OK?'

I was so disappointed. Maybe Dad had been right, maybe I wasn't as good as I thought I could be. I had one day to prepare, and it was a day of worry, of mounting pressure. My confidence was broken; if I failed this sortie, I was finished. Eventually, late into the night, I decided I could only do my best.

I thought the second trip went well, though I wasn't expecting to be asked to do an aerobatic sequence, especially as I hadn't done much in the way of aerobatics yet. I did a loop, some steep turns, then another loop – I didn't know much more. My examiner demonstrated how to fly a barrel-roll manoeuvre that I did my best to replicate, a kind of half-looping manoeuvre with a twist in it, like flying along inside an imaginary barrel lying on its side, running from one end to the other while sliding up and over the inside; mine was a long narrow barrel but I thought it was a good first attempt. Finally, I was asked to take us home.

When the examiner, my instructor and the boss all shut themselves behind an office door, I knew I was in trouble. The boss then invited me to his office.

'I'm sorry, if we had a few more hours I know you would get there, but we don't, so I'm afraid that's as far as you go on this course.' I was devastated. I didn't know what to say, what to do. I couldn't focus. My career was finished, my lifeline was gone. My only avenue into the world of aviation had collapsed – what would I do now? I returned to my room, where no one could see my tears. It was all over.

It was a very different place to today's training system, where students are given every chance to succeed, and a series of graded performance warnings trigger extra flying hours, more flexibility, the possibility to catch up. I had failed two trips back to back, so I was 'chopped' as they put it so nicely in the military: the axe came down on my neck. On the walls of the corridors, black-and-white photographs recorded all the course members who had passed through this training unit. An average of ten young faces for each course, all male, with five seated and five standing behind, faces of keen anticipation. Black felt-tip pens scrawled drawings of axes over those who never finished the course, graveyard crosses marked those who had perished before the end of their careers. I wouldn't be the only one to wear an axe sign. A couple of weeks later, a student on my senior course would also be marked with a cross. I was saddened to learn it was Paul Bishop, the student who had helped me find my room on my first night. He died in a crash shortly after take-off at RAF Leuchars in Scotland. After entering cloud, at 1,000 feet off the ground, he was seen coming straight back out in a steep dive, then he was gone.

● ● ●

The process of deciding my fate was set in motion. I felt somewhat disadvantaged by being part of a trial that had not worked, not for me anyway, and I was sure a different instructor would have helped, but there was no option for appeal. My choices were presented during an interview with my Flight Commander, 'I could see if navigator is available if you wish?' I hadn't considered that until now. The alternatives were to switch to a ground branch such as Air Traffic Control or Admin, or leave the RAF, resign my commission and seek a career outside as a pilot, though I knew I didn't have the money to do that.

I gave it a lot of thought. My passion was for flying and navigator would still get me there. I could always continue my private piloting, and a navigator job would help finance that. I did get one bit of good news: my test results from OASC permitted me to switch to navigator training; not all pilots had met these requirements. So I agreed, and the paperwork was rushed through to get me on the next course at No. 6 Flying Training School, at RAF Finningley, near Doncaster, South Yorkshire.

The course was set to last fourteen months – hopefully. Initial training was flown on an aircraft called the Dominie, a silver, red and white, twin-engine, small business jet conversion, with a weather radar in its nose. This phase taught basic navigation techniques, and it was very different from pilot training. Here I had to succeed with high-altitude airways flying techniques first, flying from navigation beacon to beacon, like airliners do, the realm of the large air-transport aircraft; if I failed, I wouldn't get as far as the fast-jet skills phase – the exact opposite to pilot training roles.

It was flying, but not what I had hoped for. In the Dominie, two trainee navigators sat side-by-side facing backwards, at the rear of the aircraft cabin. We each had our own tasks, though only one of us was charged with the primary role of navigating the aircraft. A staff instructor peered over our nervous shoulders, sitting back down to scribble away his observations, evidence for the debrief. Some people liked it, but I didn't want to be tucked away in the fuselage. My sorties in Gibraltar had provided a brief insight into the 'office space' for navigators on such aircraft: they were respected jobs, but not in a cockpit. I passed, though I didn't star; however, the next phase introduced low-level navigation skills and this was more encouraging.

It was a great feeling to be back in the Jet Provost, back in the cockpit of a two-seat jet; this time flying a Mk5, a little faster than the old JP I had flown before. This was now low-level visual navigation: a map, a clock and a widescreen view of a world moving towards me at a planned 240 knots (kts), just 250 feet below. After a few sorties, the speed was bumped up to 300 kts – a bigger challenge than expected, as the navigation features seemed to come and go far more quickly than the extra 60 kts hinted.

All chart distances were measured in nautical miles, so speed was reported in knots; 300 kts was 345 mph, approximately. It was no coincidence these speeds were a factor of sixty: it made navigation time and distance calculations so much simpler. Two hundred forty miles per hour is an even four miles a minute, much easier to multiply than 260 mph, four and a third miles a minute. One of the golden rules of military life is the 'KISS' principle: 'Keep It Simple, Stupid'.

Even the maps were more interesting now: they included more detail, with terrain, towns, rivers, roads and more colour, not the plain white and blue of upper airways maps. The aim of these sorties was to navigate a route using map, compass and time, building up to hit three simulated targets, with a planned time-on-target accuracy mark to achieve.

Each route had been carefully planned and rehearsed so many times in my head before take-off, visualising each target and key navigation features so I could – hopefully – find my way if my map fell out of reach, or the instructor pilot snatched it away from me! Of course, it was never a simple matter of flying the planned route. Calculating time, speed, distance and direction sums was so much easier when sitting at a desk than it was when wearing an oxygen mask and helmet, strapped into an ejection seat, in an aircraft that was usually bumping about in mountain turbulence with the weather not quite as forecast, forcing quick mental gymnastics while trying to route around the worst of it, striving to keep to planned timings overhead the targets as briefed. Then there was the additional pressure of someone sat right next to me, expecting information and assessing every decision made, or not made, in a constantly changing scenario. I loved this stage of my training: it was incredibly hard work but so much fun too. I got on very well with my instructor pilots and that made a huge difference to my confidence. Having just two seats meant no nav instructor peering over my shoulder, the secretive scribbles in his notebook creating worries that I must surely have done something wrong, again. The JP pilots I crewed with seemed to have an amazing capacity to remember everything I did for the debrief. Next, it was back to the Dominie, though this time for low-level flying and navigating using the aircraft's radar – the skills needed for flying aircraft such as the Vulcan bomber.

The key to low-level radar navigation was recognising the shadows or shapes the ground created in the radar picture. High ground blocked the radar from seeing what was behind it, and the lower we flew, the more the ground behind it fell into shadow, hidden from the radar line-of-sight, a dark space on the radar display, like the sunlight being shaded in valleys. Some surfaces reflected radar energy, some absorbed them: metal shone bright, wood didn't. Bright or dark returns on the small monochrome display created shapes and features that had to be recognised for what they were. Cities and industrial complexes produced the brightest returns; water showed as a dark shadow, making coastlines good features to aid navigation. Understanding how to use these skills was the key that would get me through this part of the course.

Pre-flight preparation meant mentally flying the route, in a room with a map and a pen, visualising the terrain from the approach aspect, picturing what shape it would make on the radar – radar prediction. I could plot the bearing and distance of identified features back onto my map, to calculate accurately where we were, and where we were going. One known feature created two adjacent circles of shadow and was known by all navigators as Mickey Mouse's Ears. It always made me smile saying, 'Mickey Mouse's Ears are twenty degrees right of the nose.'

The Dominie was flown single-pilot, with two student navigators and one instructor. While one student was assessed for radar navigation, the other sat in the co-pilot seat, providing visual safety back-up and assisting the pilot with cockpit tasks, such as radios, fuel management and lookout – a vital role, particularly when flying at low level. For me, the bonus of this role was that I received some training to be able to get the aircraft safely on the ground, should the pilot become incapacitated. I could do this, I knew I could: I was current with my civilian pilot's licence, and the Dominie was a gentle aircraft to fly. I enjoyed this low-level work and it showed in my results. As much fun as the radar was, I still longed to be in the cockpit with a view on the world. The best way to combine both was to be a fast-jet navigator. To do that, I had to do well in the final stage of my training, and for that I was back in the Jet Provost, but this time it was in an air defence role; now I would fly basic elements of the visual skills and techniques used by fighters, such as the F4 Phantom.

My instructor for this phase was Jim Squelch, a big man who made the cockpit seem very small as we sat shoulder to almost touching shoulder. I don't think I could have been placed with a better instructor. Air combat and attacking other aircraft at low level was where I soon knew I was meant to be. Rat and Terrier, it was called, ambushing aircraft doing ground attack sorties (the Rats), attacking them randomly around their route, simulating shooting them down – a form of attack known as bouncing. If we weren't flying bounce missions, we were high up in the bright blue spring skies above Lincolnshire doing air combat, fighting one against one, trying to maintain spatial awareness in a high 3-D arena, talking the pilot through manoeuvres that would enable us to turn in behind our adversary and shoot them down, before they did the same to us. One minute we would be racing along at low level, down in the valleys, trying not to be seen, and the next we were hanging against our seat straps, upside down 10,000 feet above the ground, surely the most fun that could be had in an aeroplane.

In April 1982, my course finished, and I was proud to learn I had done well enough to be recommended for a fast-jet posting. However, nothing was guaranteed until the Role Disposal Board decided. A team of instructors, posting officers from personnel management headquarters and Squadron Commanders, or their representatives, from the aircraft roles requiring 'new blood', would all decide our fates. The role representatives weren't just interested in how good we were; we had to 'fit in' too. Squadrons were families, close families: they didn't want someone who wouldn't fit in, socially as much as professionally. Fortunately, enjoying the advanced stages of training meant not only had I done well but I had come further out of my shell, no longer an introvert escaping into dreams. I joined in with my colleagues on the course, dining with them, socialising with them. It was an important part of the qualities I had to demonstrate as an officer, but I was also enjoying the social company, and for the first time, without the pressure of failure, I was able to do that with confidence. Perhaps I didn't fully fit in, and I certainly wasn't the extrovert leading the pack, but there was 'potential'.

At no stage in the fourteen months I was at Finningley was there any opportunity to be me. That didn't mean my thoughts had gone away.

I always imagined a future where I was happily female, I always imagined wonderfully feminine images. In life, girl clothes hid what was
beneath, they presented the correct image, but for now they had to
remain a remote need, a tormenting but essential loss. Domestic staff
in the accommodation blocks had full access to my room and, therefore, wardrobe. A locked door would only cause suspicion, and master
keys were a realistic threat. I couldn't risk being caught with anything
that might give away my secret. My few visits home allowed rare but
wonderful opportunities to once again borrow Sandra's clothes. The
turn of the lock, the safety of a bathroom door – these were my only
escapes. I still couldn't see any way of discussing this with anyone: the
world remained hostile to difference, there were no help groups, no
support teams, no information or guidance documents, that I knew of.
There was nothing, just me on my own, with a media that still hated
or mocked what I allegedly represented, 'a gay man who liked wearing
dresses'. Revealing my identity concerns – or having them exposed –
was still a path that would not end well.

But now I was part of a team that was exclusively male, a team full
of masculine bravado and life, and this was a growing dilemma. There
was an image the world expected to see, but how could I possibly
ignore something so strong and deep inside of me? It still wasn't easy
for me to understand why I was like this, why would anyone want to
be like this? There was no gain, only distress and loss. If I could only
accept the body I had, life would be so much simpler. But my identity
was at the heart of my consciousness, and it yearned to be female, it
always had. It wasn't a lifestyle choice, a fashion choice, a choice based
on sexuality; it wasn't any kind of choice. I could only imagine that
every other person knew who they were with equal conviction, but
they never had reason to question their identity. Fortunately for them,
they had instincts supported by visual assurance: the very fabric of

their being was male or female, and the body they had reinforced that. But how would they cope had their body become one of the opposite sex, against their will – what then? Would their self-identity change? Would the person they were be switched off, and a new person created? Or would their mind be in turmoil and desperately seek to regain the body to match, to function as they wanted, to be accepted? That was how I felt: my body didn't match my very soul. It was my sex that was wrong, not my gender. Because I knew of no way to resolve that, my life was being driven by societal expectations. The life I had always dreamt of was getting further and further away. The life I was living was someone else's ideal now, not mine.

Our end-of-course celebrations included an individually allocated pint of beer that had a picture on the bottom of the glass, depicting the aircraft type the drinker was posted to. The picture wouldn't be visible to the drinker until the beer was gone and that could only be drunk in one go. The more I drank, the more the shape took form, finally I could make out what it was: a Phantom! I looked at my Flight Commander expecting the inevitable second glass, the first just being a tease, but everyone was cheering, it was true. That night, my head was too busy for sleep to bring it any rest; I had a great job to do, and I was going to do it in a supersonic fighter. It was a fantastic feeling of achievement.

My next course would be on No. 228 Operational Conversion Unit (OCU) at RAF Coningsby in Lincolnshire. The role of the OCU was to train pilots and navigators how to fly and operate the Phantom as an air defence fighter-interceptor. I had already been warned that my hard work had only just begun: it was considered a course with a demanding reputation, and I already knew the hand of failure. The date for my course was several months into the future, so I got to choose and organise my own holding post. I wanted to hold with a

Phantom squadron, to learn more before I began my training in earnest. I learned that the Phantoms went to Cyprus every year for currency training in air-to-air shooting, so I made enquiries and No. 19 (F) Squadron based at RAF Wildenrath was my best bet – even better that it was a base in West Germany. I liked the idea of revisiting a country I had lived in as a child. A quick phone call secured my visit. They were due to begin their APC in three weeks' time, but I was invited to join them straight away – perfect.

APC (Armament Practice Camp) was an annual visit rostered for each air defence squadron to RAF Akrotiri on the central south coast of Cyprus. The visit allowed each crew to work up and qualify, or re-qualify, for air-to-air shooting, an essential skill for any fighter crew. The climate allowed good weather continuity so the whole squadron could qualify in a four- to six-week period. It also provided an air defence presence in the eastern Mediterranean and protection of the UK sovereign base areas, without deploying a valuable resource out of the UK more permanently.

Within the week, I was with the squadron and on a rapidly steepening learning curve. I soon learned that life on a fighter squadron was one of 'work hard and play hard'. Opportunities for socialising were always taken up, and I saw the kind of 'family' I could be joining. It couldn't have been more different from my life so far. My quiet, reserved, secretive habits would not fit here; I would have to become louder, more extroverted, and live at a faster pace. I had a choice: reject this lifestyle or embrace it. There could be no half-hearted acceptance – that wouldn't convince anyone. Rejection meant an unsure future: it would mean I didn't fit in, and that would be the end of any fast-jet flying career, especially in Phantoms. Embracing it meant adopting a completely new lifestyle, and doing it convincingly. This was life on a fighter squadron, it couldn't get more macho than that – no girls allowed. Could I cope with that? Perhaps this would provide enough restraint to live the life everyone expected me to live. On the other hand, if I was discovered now, I would have a much harder fall: there would be no mercy. Humiliation, ridicule and a complete loss of dignity would top the list, followed by an open door to civvy street. Shame and rejection from my family would seal my fate. Flying had given me a life-saving focus in my school years, but it had led me down a path where a trap of love, pride and expectation could kill my dream for ever. My family had placed me on a pedestal for becoming an officer in the RAF, flying fast-jets, and now they expected me to progress as they hoped. But revealing my secret would bring this all crashing down. In particular, it would destroy Dad. He wouldn't be able to face his friends, his wider family, the world – and I couldn't do that to him. I loved him, I wasn't ready to hurt him so badly, for something that I had managed to live with for so long. I was trapped by my love for my family, and my need to protect them from the disgrace I would surely bring. Then, one day, I came across an article that threw another spanner into the works.

I was in the ante-room of the officers' mess, a large lounge furnished with comfortable leather armchairs and sofas, pictures of heroes in action bathed in light entering through the tall windows, large paintings of biplanes dogfighting above the trenches of World War One, Spitfires climbing to meet distant black crosses of fuselage and wing, a blue summer sky contrasting with the dark grey water far below. In my hands I gazed open-mouthed at a different kind of battle, a surprisingly recognisable one. A *News of the World* headline read 'James Bond's Girl Was a Boy'. I turned to hide what I was reading, thinking my confusion might somehow give me away. A glamorous female model called Tula, Caroline Cossey her real name, had been exposed as having been 'born a boy'. I was electrified, completely amazed, not only because she looked so good but because it was the first time I had ever seen evidence that this could happen. I certainly couldn't look as glamorous as Tula, but here was an option for change I knew nothing about – a new outlook on hope.

My mind racing, I hid the newspaper behind a chair to collect later. Removing it from the mess was not acceptable practice, but I needed to read this slowly, again and again. It was truly amazing. How could I do this? I couldn't – my family, I had to think of them, how it would crush them. And my own life too, that would certainly be at risk. Losing my job meant losing my income; losing my family and friends meant losing shelter and support; becoming the subject of derision and hate would destroy my self-respect. Where would I go? What would I do? Could I live with such consequences? It was a dream again, my impossible dream – but there was a possibility now. If Tula could do this then maybe I could.

I watched as someone turned the same pages, stood with a copy opened flat on a table, others sat in comfortable armchairs, reading papers, sipping coffee. Now came the shock, the laughter, the mocking, the papers held wide open.

'Seriously!'

'Looks like the one you had the other day, mate, did you know it was a man?'

There were no positive reactions: all I saw was shock, deceit, aversion, mocking banter and derogatory names. Later that evening, I entered an empty ante-room and retrieved my hidden copy. It had caused much thought throughout the day. One day, my circumstances might change, maybe, but for now life had just become more difficult again.

4

A PHANTOM LIFE

1982–1989

Cyprus was a great introduction to Phantom squadron life. Friend-ly characters made me feel welcome and included me in all social activities. The 'play hard' ethos was very much alive, any excuse for a social event was taken full on, and given a piano and a bar, the singing wouldn't be far behind. There was a song about anyone not part of the group, there were special songs about erring aircrew from other squadrons or aircraft types. Everyone knew the songs and everyone joined in, the louder the better. Popular songs gained lyrics that would have made the original composers blush.

In the South Atlantic, the UK was at war with Argentina over sover-eignty of the Falkland Islands, and we were losing people and ships to aircraft that shouldn't have been able to get close to them. Bar room chat was full of military people itching to get involved, F4 crews lamenting the loss of HMS *Ark Royal*, a recently decommissioned aircraft carri-er that had previously carried Phantom fighters and Buccaneer strike attack aircraft. A force that would have been formidable. But I also sensed a feeling of respect for the Argentinian pilots, for achieving their missions with remarkable determination and courage. It dawned on me that going into combat was more likely than I had anticipated.

The 19 (F) Squadron routine on APC began early in the morning, because the base tended to close mid-afternoon due to the high average daily temperatures. The sight of cockpit canopies open, aircraft being prepared for flight, armourers with long belts of paint-tipped bullets loading the guns, all ready for the day's air-to-air shooting, was inspiring. An early finish meant enjoying an afternoon swim at Submarine Point, a favoured swimming place at the foot of some cliffs with a small beach surrounded by igneous rocks. At the weekends came the opportunity to tour Cyprus in its unspoilt pre-tourist factory days. I managed to get to the north side, in Turkish-held territory, to visit Kyrenia. I remembered a photograph from a short deployment Dad did to Cyprus with his regiment. He was standing beside an arrow-slot window in Kyrenia Castle, with the town's small, picturesque harbour in the background, and I was able to get a photograph of myself in that very same spot. It could have been taken the same year, so little seemed to have changed.

Flying Phantoms promised to bring me here annually – well, as long as I passed my course first, and that had just jumped forward. I was recalled to the UK for a brief introduction to fast-jet operations on a Hawk aircraft lead-in course, at RAF Chivenor in Devon. It was designed to familiarise me with flying in a tandem cockpit jet, and at a higher speed than the JP I had been used to in my training so far. Four weeks later I was beginning my Phantom course with No. 228 OCU, at RAF Coningsby.

My fellow students were a mix of 'ab initio' students, fresh out of the RAF training system like me, and experienced aviators who had flown different aircraft types before. The Phantom was a two-seat fighter: the navigator was responsible for controlling and interpreting the aircraft's powerful radar to find 'target aircraft' and then direct the pilot with height, speed, direction and manoeuvre instructions to a position where the target could be visually identified, escorted or engaged, as ordered. As much as the aircraft was a handful for a pilot to learn, the most testing part of the course was the radar intercept work, a 3-D high-speed battle of geometry. This was where most failures came. It was incredibly hard work, but I was coping. After essential ground school, learning the aircraft's technical systems and capabilities and much more, we got ready for first flights. Drills for every possible major aircraft emergency, from hydraulics failures to engine fires, had to be perfect before we could go anywhere near the sky. My first flight in the aircraft was a local area familiarisation with an instructor pilot, then I flew my second sortie with Dave, a student pilot I was crewed with, where we went off and did the same. With less than eight hours between us on the Phantom, there was an incredible feeling of mutual trust.

The Phantom F4 was an extraordinary aeroplane with an international pedigree. The British version had a few more curves than any other F4, having been adapted to take the more powerful Rolls-Royce Spey engines and the radar that gave it a trailblazing 'look-down shoot-down capability'. It outclassed other fighters of its generation in this regard; I had a lot to live up to. Some of the aircraft still wore the grey-green camouflage pattern from their low-level ground-attack days, but most were now wearing the air-defence light grey that distinguished its fighter role. It was a large aircraft, fifty-eight feet long with a wing span of thirty-eight feet, weighing up to twenty-five tons. The cockpits stood about eight feet off the ground and there was something about climbing up the outside of the aircraft, stepping down onto the ejection seat and then strapping in to it, that made it an exhilarating way to start any flight. It was quick, too: Mach 1.5 was the average top speed, Mach 2 at a real hard push. Mach 1, the speed of sound, is roughly 760 mph in the air at sea level, on an average day, so Mach 1.5 (1,140 mph) was covering a mile roughly every three seconds. Weapons included eight air-to-air missiles, four guided by radar and four infra-red heat-seeking versions, plus a 20mm Gatling gun firing 6,000 rounds a minute. It was the most capable all-round fighter-interceptor the UK had in the Cold War period.

As well as carrying extra fuel tanks, the aircraft could refuel in the air from various tanker aircraft if necessary, to extend its range and time on patrol. The UK's air defence in the 1980s was a layered system focused primarily on the threat from the Soviet Union and Warsaw Pact. The Cold War was still in full swing and the Phantom was the first line of defence. Early warning ground-based radar sites formed part of the UKADGE, the United Kingdom Air Defence Ground Environment, the ever-watching eyes of the defence network, manned by teams of fighter controllers 24/7.

It is impractical and too expensive to have fighter aircraft continuously on patrol, unless in heightened periods of tension or war, or acting on intelligence. Because of the early warning capability and the speed of the aircraft, however, it was safe to have aircraft waiting ready on the ground, able to scramble airborne fully armed at very short notice, to intercept any incoming threat. This was known as Quick Reaction Alert (Intercept) or QRA(I), a 24/7, 365 days a year responsibility, shared between the air defence fighter squadrons and bases. At the end of my course, I was posted to 111 (F) Squadron, part of Northern QRA(I), at RAF Leuchars, a coastal station just north of St Andrews, on Scotland's eastern coastline.

My home at Leuchars, for the foreseeable future, would be a first-floor room in the west wing of the officers' mess. Regardless of the orientation of an officers' mess, the west wing was always to the left when entering through the main door, the east wing to the right. The room was a basic box with white painted walls, tall ceilings and two tall, eight-pane sash windows letting in plenty of light. A double wardrobe was fixed against one wall; a single bed made up with sheets, a woollen blanket and a blue bedspread was placed with its head between the windows, with a bedside table and lamp at one side; a writing desk with a wooden chair was placed against the opposite wall. The communal bathroom was about forty feet down the corridor from my room. My possessions added little to the décor: I had only a few clothes and a portable television/radio unit, showing a black-and-white picture.

No. 111 (F) Squadron – '(F)' for Fighter – was known as 'Treble One', or 'Tremblers'. To begin with, it was based out of a hangar fronted by a defunct 1930s air traffic control tower building, housing the squadron offices and crew room, a large room on the first floor with a wall of windows that provided unrestricted views across the runway, towards the Eden Estuary.

My first six-month stint of flying was called Convex, short for Conversion Exercises. I had learned the basics of fighting a Phantom; now I had to learn the squadron-specific role and build up my skills, to be accepted as 'Combat-Ready'. Leuchars was a well-kept secret for flying opportunities: to the west and north were the Scottish Highlands, to the east was the North Sea and to the south were the 'hunting grounds' of Northumberland and the Scottish Borders, perfect places to find and practise attacking low-flying bombers, routing between their English bases and the weapons ranges and training areas of Scotland. Exercising our skills in varied environments, in all weathers, day and night, meant we were ready to face any opposition should war come. Low-level supersonic flight overland was not permitted in peacetime, to protect the population from noise disturbance and from possible damage to property caused by triggering a 'sonic boom'. (A sonic boom is a pressure wave that is caused by the aircraft when it transitions to supersonic speed.) Supersonic flight out over the sea was permitted at all heights.

Intercept profiles could be aggressive or covert, to sneak up behind an aircraft and see what it was without it seeing us. Further orders would be passed over the radio. Our objective could be to intercept a military threat, or to escort a lost civilian aircraft. Any threat could be on its own, a pair, or part of a much bigger formation; it might be over the sea or land, it might be in cloud or flying at night, possibly with its lights off not wanting to be seen. Matching the speed of a target doing Mach 1.5 meant we were closing at one mile every one and a half seconds; decisions had to be quick, and right. Our foe didn't tell us where they were, where they were going, what their intentions were. Everything was a challenge, a puzzle that had to be unravelled, with serious consequences for getting it wrong. It sounds aggressive, and it was, but I felt comfortable knowing that my role was to help protect the UK, its people and its assets from potential enemy forces focused on destruction.

Very few people got the opportunity to do this, flying at nearly 600 mph at low level through the breath-taking landscape of Scotland, then climbing up high to do air combat against other fighters, hanging upside-down in my seat straps, looking 'up' at the west coast islands over 56,500 feet below me, or somewhere else equally beautiful. The sun was always shining too – sometimes we had to climb high to find it, but it was always there, shining above the clouds. How could I not enjoy life when the sun was always shining?

But it wasn't proving easy by any means: I'd had to work hard to be here, and now I was in a new fight to stay. I was taken aside after one sortie and told that I wasn't doing as well as they expected, that maybe I 'should look for another job'. When I was crewed with Neil, one of the squadron's most experienced pilots, I knew I had been given the chance to prove my worth, but it meant he was in a position to decide my fate for the worse too. Everything I did, everything I was, seemed to be a challenge; why could life not have some simple facets? But each challenge made me stronger. If I was expected to give in, that wasn't going to happen. I worked harder, and Neil always matched that, and as my confidence grew stronger, my ability did too. His laid-back attitude and encouraging manner helped. Soon I was out of danger and ready for a 'Phase 3 check', intercepting and then closing in on an unlit target at night, with no night-vision aids. This was one of the hardest sorties I would ever fly, mainly because I knew my career rested on that result.

It wasn't any easier personally. Being a female aviator on a front-line fighter squadron still wasn't allowed; being transgender was unthinkable. People didn't understand, they wouldn't understand, not unless they learned the truth, and all the evidence being presented was wrong. How could isolated and mocked individuals possibly challenge that? I had to maintain my double life, I had to fit in and make sure no one knew what was going on in my head. Living in one room in the mess was the hardest scenario for me. It allowed some great social mixing, the bar was only a two-minute walk away, and there was never an excuse needed to spend an evening there. But my only privacy was my small bedroom; everywhere else, the ablutions, dining room, relaxing in the lounge, was all communal. Even my bedroom wasn't a secure enough sanctuary: other people had access to spare keys, mess staff entered the room daily, to clean it, make the bed or change its linen, or even just to empty the bin. Occasionally, when I was sleeping off night-flying duty, I would hear my room door unlocking, someone trying to enter assuming I was out of the room, never hearing my 'Not today, thank you!' calls. It was far too risky to store women's clothes, let alone wear them.

The time became right to buy my own house. My job was at least secure now, and I had been saving hard. St Andrews was a local university town, famous for being the ancestral home of golf, and that meant raised property prices. In Scotland, sealed bids 'above the asking price' were usually tendered, but a good friend from work, who originated from the local area, advised me to bid low, against my solicitor's advice, and I won. It was a great place, but the best part of having my own home was having a far more secure freedom. I might have to be one of the boys at work, but in my own time I could be me. I quickly explored the benefits and had soon expanded my own wardrobe, with the clothes that enhanced my life. I was too scared to venture into womenswear shops and buy clothes; I always felt I would give myself away. I had tried, but when a till assistant once said 'Are these for you? ... Only joking!' I never went back. When I did feel brave enough to go shopping, I would favour department stores rather than dedicated womenswear shops; it seemed less embarrassing. I was an officer; dressing in women's clothing would be considered 'conduct unbecoming an officer', and lead to dismissal from the military. The likely impact on my family justified the extremes I took not to get caught. I still had to be very careful even around my own house, not to leave any clues that visitors could pick up on. Anything remotely feminine had to be hidden away when it wasn't being worn or used. I used the large brown plastic suitcase my parents had bought for me when I joined the RAF, locked and stored out of sight. Having to hide its contents was demoralising, but the anticipation of a weekend or an evening when I wasn't expecting visitors was a wonderful reward. Each time I unlocked it was like a childhood Christmas had returned. But in the relaxation of my own home, my demons preyed on a mind now quiet enough to reflect on life. I moved around the house with curtains drawn, flinching at any noise outside and staying as quiet as I could, hiding behind a sofa in case it was an unexpected visitor and they saw a shadow through the curtains and called out, 'We know you're home, what are you playing at, open the door!' I was haunted by the thought that I was a pathetic being. But I could never let people see that. They saw the opposite: the brave face of masquerade, a smokescreen perfect, from every aspect, a smokescreen honed from having to share close spaces with two brothers, to shield myself from parental eyes and instincts designed to see everything and know everything.

It became a very distressing part of my life, swinging between periods of highs, finally enjoying a private home life, and lonely lows. I still wasn't sure why I was like this, what it was that made me believe so passionately that my life was all wrong. Something that was so clearly at odds with the rest of the world. But it wouldn't leave me alone. I still wasn't able to just switch it off, even though I knew it was close to destroying me. Maybe the easiest way to resolve it was to end it all. I considered destroying any evidence of my secret and ending my life in such a way that no one would be any the wiser, so my family would mourn the person they always knew. I lost count of how many times these thoughts crossed my mind, but, regardless of how low I got, I never found the nerve to follow it through.

I actually loved the amazing thing that life was; I feared the darkness on the other side was permanent. While I was alive, there was hope; when I was gone, I was gone. Why should I end my life because of what other people thought? Allowing them to laugh at my loss. Yet still, I could not shake the idea that it was the best thing to do. I worried it would hurt, or I would do something that left me in a paralysed world, trapped with no way to be the real me at all. I had recently lost a good school friend and some of the evidence pointed towards suicide. It hurt that if it was suicide, no one knew why, no one had seen signs of distress. It preyed on my mind. I reasoned that if I killed myself, without any known motive, then people I loved would be left in a similar situation, and I wouldn't want them to feel that.

But none of this took away the idea that I couldn't go on living like this, and it was always worse when I was alone. When my mind was preoccupied, I rarely felt that way. Occasionally I did consider that ejecting, while flying over the North Sea on a dark stormy night, might be an option. Unless the ejection seat was found, it would likely be recorded as an undetermined cause. Regardless of how much I contemplated ending my torment once and for all, I didn't want to put anyone else in danger because of my failings, and ejecting on a stormy night would have done just that. It was one option amongst many that I discounted. It was difficult because I had everything to live for, but too much to live with. Talking about it would have helped, but who could I talk to? There were no support groups that I was aware of, and I worried that confidential 'suicide dissuasion' telephone helplines might be recorded or overheard and the military informed. Neither could I place the burden of such news on military friends. Even if the friendship remained intact, I would have placed them in an awkward situation: should they protect the identity of someone with a 'character flaw' that wasn't permitted in the armed forces, or should I be encouraged to own up to something that clearly transgressed military law?

The fact that I was living this way was crazy: at one end of the spectrum was my visible life as 'top gun' aircrew, flying an amazing aircraft in as macho an environment as there could possibly be; at the other, my invisible life, where I needed everything to be reassuringly feminine. Remarkably, the scale of the opposites did afford me some protection: nobody could comprehend that someone with my lifestyle had such a secret, or would even be able to keep it. The one thing that my friends did notice, however, was that I didn't have, nor ever had, a girlfriend, and that was drawing attention. On numerous occasions I was set up on a date, but I always found an excuse or treated it as going out to dinner, or lunch, with one of the girls, before making an excuse not to have a second date; though that was a shame as I did enjoy the social company of another female. I wasn't enjoying being alone. I didn't want a relationship with another woman, but neither did I want one with a man. I didn't have a female body but I didn't have a male mind. How could I possibly form a relationship? Surely no one would want that in a partner anyway. My personal life was a disaster, and that only added to the gloom growing stronger inside me.

At work, I was now doing very well, and in March 1986 we had moved out of the hangar site into new accommodation on the far side of the airfield, a wartime setting in an idyllic location up against the Eden Estuary and overlooking St Andrews Bay. NATO had funded Hardened Aircraft Shelters (HASs), small reinforced-concrete shelters, that protected aircraft and personnel from any possible Warsaw Pact pre-emptive attack. I had also passed my 'Phase 3' and 'Combat-Ready' checks, which meant I could be on QRA(I), and that I could go to the Falkland Islands as part of the Islands' air defence capability, deterring further aggression from Argentina. The Falklands was an amazing place, for the flying, the social activities, the people, and for being surrounded by so much natural beauty and so many spectacular creatures in their natural habitat. I did three tours in this wonderful setting, but that must be a different tome. QRA(I), usually shortened to 'Q', was a national commitment that the Soviet Union regularly tested with long-range bombers, exploring our defensive responses and exploiting any weaknesses. It was a 24-hour duty period for aircrew, and a week-long duty for the ground-crew. We all ate, slept and worked in a small detached building beside the end of the western runway-threshold, next to a small corrugated-metal hangar that was just big enough to contain two Phantoms and their necessary equipment; this was known as 'The Q Shed'. The aircraft were fully fuelled and live-armed with eight air-to-air missiles (though this was later reduced to seven, for weight reasons). The commitment was to get at least one of these fighters airborne within ten minutes of a scramble, at any time of the day or night, in any weather, unless it was too dangerous to launch. Even then, if the risk was identified but the Air Defence Commander, sat in his underground bunker in Kent, said 'Go', then we had to go, without further question.

I felt strongly that QRA was what my job was all about, protecting the UK, so I always enjoyed the responsibility. I had more than my fair share of QRA launches and intercepted a final total of thirty-four Bears, Soviet bomber aircraft. The Bear was a giant four-engine contra-rotating propeller-driven bomber, used for many different roles, including nuclear strike.

Night added an extra challenge because some Soviet aircraft tended to fly with their lights off. I had a hand-held night-vision tube, attached to a short wooden handle, which worked by amplifying any available light, to form a low-resolution green video-image in its viewfinder, but it was an early first-generation device and there was rarely enough light for it to magnify. On one pitch-black night I got us as close as we could possibly get using radar to what we believed to be a Bear bomber, but the only way we could know was to carefully edge closer and illuminate it by using our engine afterburner. It was a Bear Foxtrot, the shyest of all the Bears, an anti-submarine aircraft. A diplomatic complaint was later lodged against us for 'getting too close', but Bear Foxtrots played hard; they had to expect hard back.

We would take photographs of any intercepted aircraft; if I saw anything unusual, I could load a colour film, if I could justify it afterwards. I couldn't believe how much it must have cost to launch and support such a mission, but the fact that I had to explain why I had used a colour film always amused me. It was apparently because colour film took longer to process. We were always met by an RAF photographer on landing, who would hurry the film away for intelligence analysts to inspect. I always hoped I had taken pictures they approved of. Some Soviet crews showed non-aggressive forms of greeting, holding up cans of fizzy drink, or happily showing off copies of *Playboy* magazine. On one intercept, a small olive tree branch was waved at us, from within the bubble window at the rear of the aircraft. On one Q launch we were scrambled and vectored to the west Welsh coast, to fire a missile. It was a test of our capability to shoot down a target if need be – this time a target being towed by a drone, but a rare opportunity to fire a missile, and thankfully a successful one, even though it had been complicated by 'unexpected external factors'. Failure would have meant questions in Parliament.

It was around this time that I was taken aback by an advert I came across in *Exchange and Mart*, a weekly retail magazine, for a shop that specialised in female clothing and feminisation products 'for men'. It was in Manchester, which was too far to go in a day, so I waited until I was visiting my parents then made an excuse 'to visit a friend'. The shop was open late, so I used the protection of darkness, arriving at 6 p.m. on a winter's evening. I drove past first, twice, assessing the area, looking for people watching, not liking the fact the pavement outside was floodlit and the shop brazenly advertised its business. I didn't want to be seen here, to be recognised, but I had come too far not to visit now. My car was an identification risk so I parked half a mile away, in a pre-selected multi-access residential area, after studying an A–Z road map at a local motorway service station. I walked quickly, raising my hood as I approached the shop, my senses alert to trouble. Quickening my pace, I rushed inside, only then lowering my hood. The chances of someone seeing me, and recognising me, were tiny, but tiny was still too risky. A lady at a till welcomed me and offered coffee, but I declined; I felt embarrassed even being here. The shop sold clothes, shoes, makeup and magazines. I quickly purchased a magazine and a catalogue, raised my hood and stepped back out into the floodlit night, taking a longer, different route back to the car. As I drove away, I was still looking for evidence I was being watched. It felt risky and my heart was racing. In the magazines I found articles that helped me to realise I wasn't alone with my feelings. I wanted more. I would have to visit again.

Each time I visited my parents I now took time to 'visit my friend in Manchester'. But each visit brought the exaggerated worry of exposure, and a fear that military police were waiting, tipped off, watching, ready to pounce. I always parked a good distance away, then walked in, following my secretive routine, a different route each time, looking for signs of surveillance, making sudden stops, random turns, checking the shadows, using them myself. Could there be someone hiding there? Is someone following me? It was nerve-racking, but I was gaining from it. I had makeup, hair, shoes, and, more importantly, someone to talk to: the ladies who worked there were good listeners, always respectful, never judgemental.

But my privacy at home had taken a step backwards. Colleagues at work had realised I owned a three-bedroom house, and before long I had two male friends lodging with me. It was difficult to say no; I could hardly say I had a secret life that required privacy. Fortuitously, they both had girlfriends in England, so my weekends could still be spent alone. On the positive side, it added to my camouflage. How could I possibly be who I was? Surely someone would notice? By now I'd had over twenty years' experience of hiding who I was, and the fact that I lived this way for so long without discovery, in a close and non-permissive environment, was testament to just how hard I worked at not being discovered, not making mistakes.

It was frightening, though, especially on those moments when I did get caught out. Like the day I foolishly undressed hastily, donning just shorts to answer a knock at the door. It was a friend from my squadron passing on a message. He looked distracted, looking at my shoulders as he spoke. As soon as he had gone, I raced to the bathroom mirror, horrified to see reddened lines in my skin, evidence that my bra straps had been too tight. He never mentioned anything, to me at least; I never knew why. But I wasn't always hidden away in my own home. I drove to an out-of-the-way valley one day, wearing an outer layer of male clothing over a skirt and blouse until I reached my destination, where I took off the top layer and added hair, makeup and accessories. After a short walk along forest tracks, I was back beside my car when a Land Rover drove past. I hadn't heard its approach, lost in the joy of being outside. I watched in horror as it braked to a halt and then reversed back to me. I ducked down behind the car – it was instinctive, but stupid. How could I hide now, they had already seen me! I stood up, facing them, not knowing what to do, or what they would do. Seconds seemed to stretch to minutes, then they drove away. I drove off in the opposite direction until I found a place to change my clothes. I worried irrationally, for a long time, that they had recorded my car's details and somehow the military police would be notified. For a while afterwards, my garden became outside enough, though occasionally I would step beyond that, using the quiet of dawn, setting an early alarm to walk outside, while my neighbours were still sleeping. The moments I got to be me were invaluable, they were literal life savers, but I wondered how much longer I could bear this lifestyle.

• • •

This extraordinary pressure wasn't exclusive to my personal life: flying Phantoms was a challenging and dangerous occupation. We trained for war in realistic and extremely demanding scenarios, and I already knew several colleagues who had been killed in tragic accidents doing so, but there were many more to come. On 20 April 1988, four Phantoms raced airborne to intercept a large raid of inbound bombers during Exercise Elder Forest, an annual NATO exercise testing the UK's air defences. The weather was poor at low level, but that was where the targets were showing on my radar. We descended to greet the threat, as low as we dared. Grey cloud veiled the grey sea; there was no horizon. It was an uncomfortably dangerous place to descend any further. My pilot Geoff and I decided to pull up and 'shoot' them through the cloud, but only three aircraft could do that; one had no serviceable radar. Her crew, Phil 'Nobby' Clarke and Kev 'KP' Poysden, were very close friends I had enjoyed my first tour with. They had recently moved to 43 (F) Squadron while I remained on Treble One. Their crash was unwitnessed, undetected for several hours – they 'went missing'. For a long time, I believed they would turn up, having diverted somewhere else, but eventually that became impossible; they had clearly diverted for the final time. Their loss was incredibly hard-hitting, and for the first time I truly appreciated how short life could be, how much it had to be lived. Dreams had to be captured while they were still possible.

For every crew lost, there were many close escapes, where luck played a significant part. It was the nature of military flying in the 1980s: it was the 'work hard' side of the coin, and the reason there was a 'play hard' balance. It was challenging flying: learning essential skills for war against a formidable threat pushed us into environments where the smallest misjudgement or mishap could kill. I had many heart-racing incidents: a crash-landing at RAF Akrotiri closed the runway for many hours and our aircraft was damaged beyond economic repair, ending her days as a gate-guard at RAF Leuchars. Another accident saw us crash 800 feet across a Kent field, while landing at Biggin Hill, after a brake-failure at 110 mph, and there were several more, but I was enjoying the flying! On occasion, I got to pilot the Phantom myself. We had a couple of 'two-stick' aircraft for pilot training and, if the controls were left in the rear cockpit, the opportunity was always gladly taken. I was also hiring light aircraft to fly in my spare time, from Tayside Flying Club in Dundee, and for a while I had a one-third share in my own aircraft, a 1950s-design two-seater Jodel D115, a tail-dragger, with a cranked wing like the Phantom.

I had many adventures at RAF Leuchars and I enjoyed seven and a half years of demanding flying, but my time there was coming to an end. The F4 Phantom was nearing its end-of-service date and there was a new pretender on the block, the F3 Tornado, but I was off somewhere different. It would be impossible to cover all my airborne experiences and exploits in this amazing period of military history without them dominating this book, so I shall tell them another day, but within this arena of masculine bravado was a female voice that couldn't be heard, that was too scared of the consequences. Alone in a secretive and necessarily overly cautious world, with fear, confusion and self-loathing balanced with a love for life, but no life for love. Love could only come if I learned to respect myself, and I couldn't see how I could do that without understanding, without being understood, without being allowed to be open.

From my early days of struggle on the squadron, through to the responsibility of leading multiple-aircraft fighter formations into attacks against multiple-aircraft raids, in demanding environmental as well as wartime exercise conditions, I had proudly developed professionally. It had made me strong, and I would need that strength more than I could have ever guessed. For now, I had been selected for a posting flying the Hawk in a tactical training role at RAF Chivenor, in north Devon. It was a great posting, but it was sad to be leaving an aircraft, a place and people that had all grown to mean so much to me. My future was uncertain, but now I was facing it with pride in myself and my skills.

5

THE WALL COMES TUMBLING DOWN

1990–1992

RAF Chivenor was on England's south-west coastline, just west of Barnstaple, in north Devon. It was open to the full force of the Atlantic weather, with cool, wet winters and mild, wet summers, but when the sun shone, it lived up to its name of 'Heaven in Devon'. I couldn't sell my house in St Andrews quickly enough to buy a new home straight away, so I moved into the officers' mess, moving all my possessions in a self-hire transit van.

I would be flying the Hawk TMk1A here, a single-engine tandem-seat jet trainer, able to carry weapons, including small bombs, a gun and two air-to-air missiles. Student pilots were already very familiar with the aircraft, fresh from their advanced training at RAF Valley, on Anglesey, but there was a big difference between flying an aircraft and operating it. Here they would learn fighting skills, tactics and weapons, before they went to operational aircraft such as Phantom, Tornado, Harrier, Jaguar and Buccaneer. My posting was to No. 63 Squadron, on No. 2 Tactical Weapons Unit (TWU), to be the squadron's sole staff navigator, with responsibility for ensuring the navigator students received appropriate training and development opportunities, and to introduce student pilots to flying aircraft as a crew.

When I wasn't doing that, I was getting as much flying of my own as I could possibly want. I had the privileged freedom to choose the best and most interesting sorties on the daily flying programme, from air defence and air combat sorties, my bread and butter in the Phantom, to ground attack and recce sorties, or weapons training. Standard training missions consisted of a pair of aircraft flying in tactical formation at 250 feet and 420 knots, around a route that had two or three targets to attack, at a pre-briefed time: these were known as Simulated Attack Profiles, or SAPs. On more advanced sorties, a third aircraft would get airborne before them to set up an ambush, hoping to prosecute an unseen attack, to simulate shooting them down before they got to the first target, and then again at various places around the pre-briefed route.

The Hawk was a small aircraft, especially head-on, perfect for honing the eyes, lookout techniques and tactics of those crews it was attacking in training. It was a tactical strength, as many of the big jets had discovered to their cost. If you can't see it, you can't fight it; if you can't fight it, you'll get shot down.

But being difficult to see also created a safety problem: unlike civilian aircraft, military aircraft deliberately operate close to each other, whether for attack or protection, or even for penetrating bad weather. Even when they didn't want to operate close together, they invariably got squeezed into the same airspace, and that meant an increased risk of mid-air collisions, something I had already witnessed and would gain more experience on later. Behavioural experts and risk analysts had been working on this for a long time, and it was at Chivenor that I got involved in the latest research. Flying in a Hawk, with a light-meter and a stopwatch, we set ourselves up on various 'pre-determined collision profiles', where I timed from when we saw the other aircraft to when we passed it, sampling light levels at the same time, and with the other aircraft in various trial paint schemes. Clearly there was a lot more science to this than me with a stopwatch, but I was on the front line of proving the research, and this was the beginnings of my involvement in aircraft trials. Strangely enough, black was the safest colour during the daytime, and Hawks soon began to be seen in a gloss-black paint scheme, still used today. The squadron also had a war role called Mixed Fighter Force, where the Hawk was used for short-range defence of the United Kingdom, joining with the larger air-defence fighters or protecting allocated sites, from airfields to cities, and we did get to practise it in Germany too. When I arrived in Chivenor, the Cold War was still very much the operational focus, but times were changing and there was revolution happening within countries bordering the Warsaw Pact side of the Iron Curtain.

• • •

I needed to get out of the officers' mess, it was too restrictive. I was recommended a landlord with an upper floor flat within his country house, set in an enchanting secluded rolling valley in the low hills just north of Chivenor. The flat was above the landlord's kitchen, with open-plan stairs leading up to a stable type door, meaning my girl's wardrobe had to be safely hidden and locked away. The landlord and his wife were friendly enough, but creaky wooden floors meant they would know I was home, and high-heeled footsteps made an obvious noise. The bathroom was the only place I could consider private, with a bolt on the door. It wasn't a very comfortable place to relax, but I was committed, until I had gained my local bearings. I wondered if I had made the right decision.

I had been at Chivenor just four months when I was unexpectedly introduced to a girl, as a date, totally against my better judgement. A married colleague had 'realised his error' when a woman he had been chatting to in a bar had asked for a date; he pleaded for me to meet her instead. So, once again, I was put in a situation that was uneasy for me. I was annoyed with myself that I couldn't simply refuse. I knew people muttered things about my single status; it wasn't 'usual' for a thirty-year-old male to not be seen with a girl. But even the slightest untrue gossip getting to the wrong office would mean an interview with the Special Investigations Branch (SIB), a branch of the military police that conducted investigations into cases that breached military law, and being 'gay' was considered a serious breach.

Besides, I didn't want to continue enduring life alone. I still needed to find myself. All my friends either had marriages and families or were well along that pathway, and life as a 'singly' was becoming lonelier. And so I met Sheelagh. She was a lovely Irish lady, a blue-eyed, blonde nurse approximately five foot five tall. I enjoyed her company and we would meet up for a drink and just talk, but that was all. One night when I drove her back to her accommodation, she went to kiss me and suddenly her tongue was 'exploring my mouth'. I was completely shocked and jumped back. She looked back at me strangely, taken aback at my reaction. I didn't have a clue why she would do that: why would you put your tongue in someone else's mouth? We never kissed again.

Twice, after a long evening of talking, she asked to stay overnight in my flat and twice we slept on the only bed. On both occasions, it was her that asked 'not to be touched', which was great for me: it meant I didn't have to explain my uneasy reluctance. I didn't want to go to bed with her, I was scared to death she was going to want sex. I'd never had sex: just the idea of intimacy, or copulating, using the body

I had held no appeal whatsoever. Whether she secretly wanted me to take the initiative or whether she was exercising a Catholic principle, I never found out. Sheelagh slept under the sheets and I slept on top of the bed, the other side of a line of pillows. On a few occasions I came close to telling her about me, but I could never pick up the courage. If she found me repulsive and informed anyone in the military I would be in deep trouble.

After a few months, she said our relationship wasn't going any-where and we parted company. I was so relieved. On a positive note, Sheelagh had met my friends, and she had met Sandra and her family when they booked a holiday cottage in north Devon and we drove across to see them. Sheelagh got on well with Sandra and her family, but I felt guilty that they believed I was happy. I never intended to use our friendship to ward off assumptions about my sexuality, but it did have that effect. My family and colleagues were happier now. I also knew Sheelagh felt her time was 'passing by', so I was so pleased when I received a letter saying she had met someone else and was pregnant. We never stayed in touch.

• • •

At 7.45 p.m., on 1990's May bank holiday Monday, the phone rang. I was sat at home with my parents, enjoying a spot of leave, eating dinner. Mum answered it, then poked her head around the lounge door, looking at me, the phone held in her hand, stretched on its cable. 'It's for you!' she said.

'Hi, it's the Station Duty Officer [SDO] at RAF Chivenor... Can I ask what you are up to at the moment?' It was an odd question to be asked. I wondered if I had missed a duty responsibility or something.

'I'm at home on leave... Why?'

'You need to get back here as quickly as possible… You are being deployed, but I can't tell you where yet. How long will it take you to get back?'

'It's about a five-hour drive, so if I leave now it will be just after 1 a.m.'

'OK, I will call you back on this number shortly.'

We had been watching the news, we knew Saddam Hussein's forces had rolled into Kuwait and the world was angry, so I had an idea I would be heading east. I waited by the phone in our hallway, pacing up and down, curious, energised, but for what? My parents sat silently in the adjacent lounge, watching through the open door.

At 8 p.m. the phone rang again. 'Hi, it's the Duty Officer at Headquarters Personnel Management. I understand the SDO at Chivenor has been in touch. You are required to return to your unit immediately for deployment overseas.'

'May I ask to where?'

'We're not currently sure, but it will likely be Saudi Arabia, probably Riyadh.'

'For how long?'

'That's unknown at this moment.'

After some brief family goodbyes, I set off south. As I drove, a bag was already being packed for me at my base by the SDO. On arrival, a medic gave me a couple of injections in each arm and I was given a few hours to pack any essential personal kit, before being driven to RAF Lyneham, via RAF Innsworth. At Innsworth, I received some ground-force clothing, a 9mm Browning pistol and more injections, this time in my bum as my arms had too many holes already.

Within twelve hours of the phone call I was on an RAF C-130 Hercules flight heading to a possible war, routing via Akrotiri and Oman. The possibility of being in a war didn't worry me. If the worst happened, my lifetime worries would be over. I'd always imagined if I went to war, though, it would be in a fighter, a role I was trained for, but for this one they wanted me in a specialist role on the ground. I felt honoured I had been selected, but I didn't yet know what job I was destined to be doing, and I worried whether I would meet its expectations. I wasn't alone, though: a friend from F4s had received similar news and shared my journey. Chris Weightman, known as 'CJ', was a navigator in the same training role as me, but located with a Hawk squadron at RAF Brawdy in Pembrokeshire. It was great to have his company: he was an easy man to get on with, and was very well thought of by all who met him. Sixteen hours after leaving Lyneham, we reached an airbase called Dhahran, in Saudi Arabia's Eastern Province, where I was met by a Squadron Leader with a signal message in his hand, authorising me to get off the aircraft here. Apparently this was my ultimate destination. It was CJ's stop too. We were so glad to be getting off: it was no fun being a passenger sat on a canvas-webbed bench for that long in a loud, rattling, windowless cargo space that smelled of oil and machinery, pitching, rolling and bouncing without visual reference.

Dhahran was a huge airbase with two-mile-long runways, and it looked like the whole of the US 101st Division was arriving here with us. I had never seen so many combat aircraft in my life, far more it seemed than we had in the whole RAF inventory. We learned we were part of Operation Granby – or Desert Shield, as the US called their contribution. US operations always had punchy and meaningful names; operations for British forces came from a random word generator and held no link to region or role.

Our domestic accommodation was off-base, in a BAE Systems-owned gated compound of apartments. I had a small single room with a bunkbed, but at least the complex had a small pool to escape the heat when off duty. Work became a twelve-hour shift in

the Tactical Air Operations Centre, covering the management of UK
fast-jet operations in Saudi Arabia. CJ was on the opposite twelve-
hour shift to me. We were always armed, due to the risk of kidnap or
terrorist action.

The daily intelligence briefs were fascinating as negotiations with
Saddam continued. There was an expectation that he was going to
continue the momentum he had built with his invasion of Kuwait
and carry on into Saudi Arabia. We were here as reinforcement: to
demonstrate support, deterrent and intent. Dhahran was in a hot
desert climate and by 9 a.m. the temperature was already rising above
36°C. I had to take precautions against extreme sunburn, one of the
troubles of fair skin. But the sun wasn't the only threat. Soon we were
helping to construct air-attack shelters around our workspace. Sand-
bag walls and camouflage nets rose around our Portakabin, then came
chemical and biological warfare drills, with full protective clothing
and respirators. Saudi civilians walking past seemed bemused, but I
wondered what would happen to them when we took shelter in a real
chemical attack. Scud missile attacks were also a real danger and we
got used to the sound of attack alarms and practice drills. Everyone
became focused. These were the same drills we had practised over
and over in the UK; Nuclear, Biological and Chemical (NBC) training was always a part of our transition-to-war exercises, part of the
expected threat from the Soviet Union and Warsaw Pact weapons
arsenal. But now we all paid that extra attention to detail; now the
threat was next-door, and an attack was possible without warning.
Amongst all this came signs of normality: photographs of families,
partners and children took up desk spaces or were pinned to walls. All
of a sudden I felt very lonely.

Then I received a letter from my landlord stating that I had missed
September's rent and he was going to throw my belongings out. He

was aware I had been sent away with insufficient notice to plan far ahead, and he knew the military looked unfavourably on officers who ran up debts. Unresolved debt would lead to a formal warning and, in the worst cases, dismissal from service. But my biggest worry was that interference with my possessions might reveal my hidden wardrobe, and I had no way to contact him other than by letter. I sent a cheque and made plans to move out as soon as I returned. It wasn't a great place to be Caroline anyway.

We still had no word on how long we would be here, but towards the end of September, CJ was posted back to the UK for a Phantom refresher course. Phantoms still protected the Falkland Islands, and some were providing air defence of the main resupply base at RAF Akrotiri in Cyprus. I was quite envious of CJ's posting, though it would end in tragedy for him within the year. By now it was obvious that a war was imminent; the forces available to defeat Saddam were unprecedented.

Terrorist activities in Saudi Arabia had increased by October, with two drive-by shootings, a sail-by beach shooting and a bomb attack on an armoured fighting vehicle in the first three days. One morning, I was driving the lead vehicle in a two-car convoy when my passenger took a photograph of a camel by the roadside. At the next roadside check-point we were reported and informally arrested, spending the rest of the day and night being moved between a damp, bare prison cell and a Saudi police station for questioning. Phone calls 'dialled for us' were always 'engaged'. Just before midnight, we were handed to Saudi military police for further questioning, before being released, with all camera film confiscated. All for a camel! I was never threatened, but it was disturbing being held so long, without being able to tell anyone, in a country on the verge of war.

As December approached, my replacement arrived. A ground war was still looking imminent. I would likely miss that, but that wasn't a bad thing. I had played my part, dashing off to help protect a country I'd never been to before, with just fifteen minutes' notice. Back in the UK I was placed on twenty-four hours' notice to move (NTM) to return if need be, which seemed generous by comparison.

When I got home, the first thing I did was to remove my belongings from the apartment and move into the officers' mess. Then a good friend arrived and invited me to rent a room in his house. We had shared a house in St Andrews for a short while and we had been crewed together on Phantoms. Once again I wanted to say no, but I didn't have any excuse, other than a demanding private life that it was best he didn't see. The good news was that he was spending a lot of time away: his marriage had broken down and he was on the hunt for company. The bad news was that he persistently tried to arrange a date for me too. I didn't want to be alone for ever, but I just couldn't see a way around that; it really was soul-destroying.

Flying was still my saviour: just as in my school days, it gave me focus and I threw everything into it, flying on as many sorties as I could. When a visiting film crew needed air-to-air action shots for use in an RAF recruitment advert, I was given a hand-held movie camera to film on their behalf, as civilians weren't often permitted to fly in ejection seat aircraft. The final film was shown in UK cinemas and, although I didn't receive any credits, I was included as one of the crews walking in from a mission at the end. It was a short story about two boys on a cliff-top who wish themselves into the cockpits of two passing Hawks. It was such a shame it wasn't a boy and a girl, but girls weren't allowed to fly in combat aircraft at this stage. That, however, was beginning to change.

In 1991, the first female pilot arrived on a TWU course, Sally. Some of the instructors seemed tormented by this, opining 'Not on my watch!', 'It's political correctness gone mad!', 'Don't worry she won't get far' and 'She won't cope with the G-forces anyway.' Reassuringly, most willed her to do well and pave the way, though they weren't necessarily outspoken with such opinions. 'Why shouldn't women be able to fly combat aircraft?' I wondered. The skills involved had nothing to do with gender.

For me, the arrival of the first female pilot was amazing, but I couldn't tell her why. For years, I had known that even if I could become somehow female, I wouldn't be allowed to do the job I loved – now, here was the opportunity. We eventually got to fly together, but there was an agenda hidden in the scheduling. She had been marked down on a couple of sorties, and the chief instructor wanted her gone. To 'appear fair', they put her on a sortie with me in the back seat; flying with a second pilot usually put extra stress on someone already under pressure. Navigators were there to help, to off-load pressure, to take on the responsibilities that didn't involve 'hands on sticks', controlling the aircraft. We flew a standard low-level route together, as a pair of Hawks, with Sally leading. She flew the sortie without major fault, hitting her targets as briefed. There were a few minor debrief points, but nothing to get worked up about. As we taxied in, I told her so.

She untoggled her oxygen mask and sighed. 'Can I ask you a question? Off the record?'

I didn't keep records. 'Yes, of course… What is it?' I replied.

'Should I quit?'

'Why?!' I wasn't expecting that question.

'It's pretty hard, but I get the impression people want me to go.'

'Why on earth would you quit?' I said. 'If you quit you will never know if you gave it your best shot… You will never know that you could have succeeded… and you may regret that later in your life. If, however, they do chop you, then at least you know that you will have done your best, and it's something that is incredibly difficult to do. Don't go because a small group of old-school idiots don't want you here. Not many people will ever do this, and you will have been one of them... No... Don't quit!' I was speaking from experience.

Back in the ops room, I was greeted by the chief instructor.

'Well, how did it go?'

'Fine, sir.'

'What do you mean, fine?' He guided me by the arm into an adjacent empty briefing room.

'There were a few debrief points, but nothing of concern, the same kind of learning points anyone has.'

'No... If you pass this sortie, we have to start the suspension process all over again!'

'Well, I have already told her she passed, and I'm not going to change that!'

'But you must!'

'No, sorry, sir, I'm not going to change it for no reason.'

He walked off in a huff, and I suspected any possibility of a good annual assessment for me went with him. Annual assessments were concealed from subjects in this age. I would have made the same decision for any student – I wasn't going to discriminate – but I was proud I had stood my ground so resolutely.

The Hawk was a great aircraft to fly, and some instructor pilots were happy for me to fly from take-off to landing, 'brakes off to brakes on', though I did overstress it once, pulling too much G during an air combat fight against another Hawk. It was Bastille Day and the French exchange pilot I was flying with happily provided a traditional slab of beer for the engineers. My final sortie before I was posted included a low-level mission and releasing a couple of practice bombs on a range at Pembrey in south Wales. I flew the whole sortie, and actually hit the target too! I realised I could log Hawk flying hours, as a single-engine aircraft weighing less than 4,700kg, on a private pilot's licence (PPL). I couldn't be 'Pilot in Command', as I hadn't completed a certified course or check-ride, but I sent off logbook evidence of recent hours flown with an instructor pilot to the Civil Aviation Authority, and they signed my hours off as dual. I would love to have flown the Hawk solo! But I gained thirty hours' Hawk flying time in my civilian logbook, which would be a unique record to look back on. Few military pilots sought private licences so I was often asked to take their partners or family members flying, to give them some basic air experience; and some of my passengers were inspired enough to pursue their own careers as civilian pilots!

In the past few years the Berlin Wall had come tumbling down and the Cold War was technically over. 'Options for Change' had already decimated the post-Cold War military, and several RAF squadrons, including some returning from service in the Gulf War, had disbanded. On 1 April 1992, No. 2 TWU rebadged and became No. 7 Flying Training School, the squadrons became No. 19 and No. 92, after they had disbanded with Phantom F4s, now shamefully being scrapped on landing; Tornado F3 was the new air defender. Competition for flying tours was high, and aircrew found themselves moving to ground roles or leaving the Air Force; 75,000 jobs had already been cut in the RAF alone. It was time to find a new aircraft to fly, and a very interesting offer was put on the table.

PART TWO

THE EDGE
OF PINK

1992–2004

6

DOWN AMONGST THE TREES

1992–1993

If the Phantom had still been in service, my next choice of posting would have been easy. The Tornado F3 wasn't getting a smooth ride into service – very few aircraft do. However, my draw to the RAF in the first place had been helicopters, and I had heard a rumour. For a long time, helicopters had been considered as 'support assets', operating mainly behind friendly forces, to move troops or resupply. The RAF was gradually understanding the wider potential of helicopters; it had long looked upon fast-jets and 'V' bombers as its fighting forces. But UK military helicopters were already contributing to the fight against terrorism in Northern Ireland, and had proven their value in the Suez Crisis, Borneo, Malaysia, the Falklands War and more. American lessons from Vietnam were slowly being realised and helicopters were gaining complex systems to enable their survivability on the modern battlefield. In 1992, the RAF decided that the practice of single-pilot operations, aided by a squadron navigator or crewman when need be, was no longer appropriate and helicopters were to be flown with a two crew cockpit, with a pilot/navigator, or a pilot/pilot combination. The aim was to free one pilot to focus on flying the aircraft, while the other pilot/navigator managed the mission and aircraft systems. It was decided that navigators experienced on two-seat fast-jet aircraft provided the necessary skills to fulfil this role. When my posting officer mentioned he was seeking volunteers with air defence or 'mud-moving' experience, I stepped up.

In November 1992, I arrived at RAF Shawbury, in Shropshire, and moved back into an officers' mess. Being in the training environment and learning new skills wasn't a major worry for me, but storing all my female possessions was. Hiding them in the mess was dangerous; privacy was impossible. Permission to live off-base was rarely granted while on a major course, but I successfully reasoned I was a mature student, and I had too many possessions for living in a single room. The extra £300 a month it cost me in rent for a small bungalow in the local village was worth every penny.

The course began with the usual academic phase, learning about much of what I already knew: navigation, airmanship, rules and regulations, meteorology and so on. However, the technical aspects and principles of flight theory were a whole new kind of magic. After a while, we began our flight phase on the Aerospatiale Gazelle HT1. I was crewed with a pilot student, Ben, and when I didn't have my own sortie in the left-hand seat of the aircraft, I would fly in the back, watching, learning and looking out for the fleet of other red-and-white helicopters that darted around the skies above Shropshire and north Wales. My course was a mix of students, some straight from the training system, through to experienced aviators like me, with over 2,000 hours in the air. Also on my course was Ian Wright, another ex-Phantom navigator, a knowledgeable and likeable character who would become a very important part of my story.

Flying at helicopter speeds made for a vulnerable target, and the best defence was not to be seen or heard in the first place. The best way to do that was to fly low and use the terrain. But the UK was criss-crossed with power and communications cables, and a wire-strike was usually catastrophic. Wires marked on navigation charts still had to be seen to be avoided, so flight up at fifty feet was safer, unless tactical reasons demanded otherwise. So, although helicopters flew slower, flying down amongst the trees challenged my fast-jet navigation skills.

• • •

I discovered my rented home was close enough to the base for no-notice visitors, but it would take time to de-feminise the house before opening the front door, so I still hid behind closed curtains. I made a mental note: next time I would rent a two-storey house. I took to telling the guys I was 'away for the upcoming weekend', then I'd conceal my car in the garage. Most weekends would be spent confined to the house, occasionally with nervous ventures into the garden, always wary of the risk of unplanned visitors. I would invariably have new clothes to try, and I was still experimenting with hair and makeup styles, but mostly I would just read, write in my diary, watch television, cook and relax. It was just so nice to relax properly.

After a while, one of our young student pilots, Stu, confided in a female student from another course that he was gay, and he couldn't hide it any more. She had tried to persuade him otherwise, but he'd made his decision. As soon as he informed the chain of command, his fate was sealed: he was removed from the course and within weeks he was out of the RAF. He was a very well-liked, cheerful soul, a good pilot and a loss to the fabric of the course; it didn't matter to us that he was gay. It was such a shame to lose someone with the gifts that he had, purely because of his sexuality. It reinforced my need to hide my gender identity: as long as society regarded it as an extreme version of being gay, I stood to lose everything I had achieved. Military opinions reflected those of society, but 'exemptions' existed for laws argued to be inappropriate for the armed forces, such as health and safety conflicting with operational and training risk; equality, age and disability being contrary to 'suitability to be in a fighting force'. Being gay wasn't against the law in the civilian world, but in the military it still was. Seeing my colleagues show their support for Stu, I knew it didn't mean they understood what it meant to be transgender. The risk remained substantial, and the final consequence was glaringly inevitable.

Relaxing in privacy gave me time to think, but also time to get depressed. I considered counselling, but it carried a risk of diagnosis that endangered my flying category. My parents still believed what they read in the press. One day Dad had argued with me that I couldn't have been involved in a particular aircraft crash, because the news report had said it was a Jaguar aircraft, not the Phantom I was in at the time! They watched far too much television, and the most familiar 'man in a dress' figures they saw were drag queens, or stereotypical feminine gay men with pink feather boas. Slapstick presented men dressed as women with beards and deep voices, and these images were sustained in the press, especially in the tabloids. The papers seemed to enjoy referring to a transgender woman as 'he' and 'him' as often as possible, or referring to someone who had 'changed sex' in their old name: 'Dave is now a woman!' I could hear the reporters sniggering as they wrote the stories and dreamt up their crude, mocking headlines, like 'She's a he!' It was only transgender women who were reported on, reinforcing it as a male-to-female problem. In fact, transgender men did exist, they just weren't as visible. 'Wanting to become a man' was considered logical, 'wanting to become a woman' wasn't; being male was supreme. To my family, the way the press used the terms 'sex change' and 'transsexual' reinforced the sexuality aspect, that it was all about gay men finding novel ways to have sex with other men – and I saw how much they loathed gay men, people they deemed degenerate.

I still wasn't strong enough to lose everything. I was at odds with the picture I presented at work; there, I was strong and outwardly happy. Underneath all of that I was fragile and lonely. It was a striking contrast, the outer military strength versus the vulnerable inner being, If it wasn't for the confidence my job was giving me, I would have been struggling more with my personal life. I feared people laughing at me, rejecting me. This was the side that nobody saw, these were the thoughts that troubled me, the thoughts that gave me dark days. If my conflict was a liability in my job, it was only because it had to be hidden; it wouldn't matter if I could serve openly. Hidden, it was dragging me down. Maybe I had a professional responsibility to tell people this, but without any possibility of proving my worth before compulsory dismissal, it wasn't an option. I would just be losing even more than I had already lost. My need to resolve my sex was becoming stronger and stronger all the time, driven by a need to live my life true to myself. I considered finally giving up on my battle, by revealing to family, friends and my employer that I was transgender and that I wanted to transition, and just accepting the consequences, as hard as they would be to live with; they surely couldn't be as hard as the growing stresses of containing this conflict.

• • •

The course bonded well and we enjoyed a great social life, especially when Ian Wright and I introduced them to TACEVAL, a no-notice social call on someone's home address, based on the NATO no-notice TACtical EVALuations of a unit's capabilities to fight, which we were used to on Phantom stations. Our targets were the instructor pilots living in on-base housing, and the visits were usually reserved for a Friday night. We allowed targets the grace of twenty-four hours' notice, by having a 'traffic light' alerting system: green for 'safe', amber for 'twenty-four hours' notice', and red for 'imminent'. Once the notice went 'red', many potential victims hid behind closed curtains, but one instructor and his wife enjoyed the socialising so much they put all their lights on, and left the front door ajar. They were John and Agnes Coxen, and they were wonderfully sociable people. When their music system broke, due to constant high-volume demand, they proudly announced they had bought another one so they were good for further TACEVAL. They were the only couple to get multiple visits.

After eighty-eight hours flying the Gazelle, we moved to the Wessex. The Gazelle had been an easy aircraft to fly, and whenever I flew in the left-hand seat I was often given control, hands-on. My first instructor was impressed with my piloting skills, apart from when I bounced the aircraft on its landing-skids on the concrete landing spot right outside the squadron, after being a little too keen on lowering the collective lever, to land the aircraft vertically. He had been impressed I was able to hover the aircraft on my first sortie; few students could, and he was keener than me to show that off back at base! There was no harm done to the aircraft, and the small knock to my confidence was soon ironed out. I would have loved to have done a pilot crossover course. I had recently learned that my instructor on my basic pilot course had been 'chopped' not long after my own demise. A different instructor may have seen me through, but then I would have missed my subsequent career on Phantoms. My private pilot's licence would have to suffice.

The Wessex was also an easy aircraft to fly. She was a gentle old girl with a tough record – a bit like me, really, but a little younger! Wessex had flown on operations around the world, including in the 1982

Falklands War. They were still in operational use in the RAF and provided a vital capability in Northern Ireland, but they also made good trainers. It was a step up for the students, two engines instead of one, and three crew instead of two, because now we were joined by the air crewmen students, the guys and girls who would manage the troops, aircraft loads, refuels and basic post-flight maintenance in the field. They would also assist with navigation and radios when the cockpit workload became excessive. The aircraft now had a two-colour green camouflage too, not a red-and-white one. The cockpit was mounted up higher than the troop cabin: access was a climb up the outside, using the undercarriage struts and inbuilt foot and hand holds. It was just like the Phantom: it felt right to me, climbing up into an aircraft rather than stepping into it. She could carry up to sixteen soldiers, though the more equipment they carried or wore, the fewer she could carry.

I flew nearly forty hours on the Wessex, doing emergency training, handling exercises, navigation, mountain flying, under-slung loads (cargo carried in nets or straps hooked by a sling and carried below the aircraft), leading a pair of aircraft on a mission, and a three-ship. My end-of-course check combined all these skills in one mission. It went well, but, although we had technically passed the course, we still had the search and rescue (SAR) phase to do. This was flown at SARTU (Search and Rescue Training Unit) at RAF Valley, on the Isle of Anglesey, off north Wales. Troop helicopters have a secondary role of search and rescue, so all crews undergo the basic training. I enjoyed the SAR phase, but I knew I was destined for the tactical role: that was the whole reason I had been posted to helicopters, and that was where I saw myself. SAR was a peacetime function; it wasn't the kind of flying I preferred, though it did offer stability, and the attraction of not living in a field while working with the Army.

On my final sortie, after conducting a simulated search and rescue mission management exercise in the mountains of Snowdonia, I flew the aircraft back to RAF Valley. It was an enjoyable trip and I was happy when I was complimented on my flying, particularly my approach, hovering and landing at Valley. I gave the aircraft, XR524, an appreciative pat; my helicopter course was complete. I couldn't have known that she was about to enter the history books, for all the wrong reasons. The next day, 12 August, was a final sortie for Dan, one of our ab initio navigators on the course. During a simulated emergency over Llyn Padarn, a two-mile-long lake near Llanberis, they had a real emergency and crashed, in XR524. When the pilot flying Dan's sortie applied power following their simulated emergency, a drive shaft to the tail rotor failed, rendering the aircraft uncontrollable. Four young air cadets were in the back of the aircraft for an air-experience flight. I had chatted with them in the crew room that morning; they were excited to be going flying. Only one cadet and the crew escaped the aircraft as she sank. All Wessex flights were grounded until the cause of the accident was investigated, and rectified. As aviators, we knew the risks of flight, but it was incredibly sad to lose youngsters so tragically.

I was posted to No. 60 Squadron at RAF Benson from 31 August 1993, continuing with the Wessex HC Mk2, and Ian was posted to Pumas on No. 33 Squadron, at RAF Odiham. The Puma was a faster and better-equipped helicopter, and it would have been nice to fly something different, but I enjoyed flying the Wessex and looked forward to joining my new squadron. But I was also looking forward to settling in a new area, and once more having the freedoms gained by having my own home.

7

THE CONSEQUENCES OF CHANGE

1993–1995

RAF Benson sits in a lovely part of rural middle England, beside the River Thames and close to the historic town of Wallingford in south Oxfordshire, fifty miles west of central London. I was determined to live in the mess for the shortest time possible, but I hadn't appreciated how costly it was to buy or rent property in this part of Oxfordshire. An apartment was too public for me to venture outside dressed how I wished, but I eventually found a small detached house to rent in a village called Chalgrove, five miles north of Benson. Its £550 per month rental fee would have left me short of money to do other things, but on the squadron I had become good friends with a pilot called Donald Frost, 'Frosty', who'd asked if he could share the property and rent. It wasn't ideal by any means, but I agreed. I'd just have to be careful; I had got away with sharing before, and the need to get away from the restrictions of the mess outweighed the restrictions of sharing.

The squadron's role was to support the Army. The training role was the same as it would be in times of conflict: inserting troops to attack an enemy, extracting them when need be, moving them between main, remote or forward operating bases, or resupplying them there, casualty evacuation (casevac), escorting road convoys through higher-risk areas, and mutually supporting other helicopters against threats when flying as a formation. The Wessex was armed with one 7.62mm general purpose machine gun (GPMG) for self-defence. It wasn't an attack helicopter; if the landing site was under attack, an Army Lynx helicopter would provide an armed escort, to help keep the enemy focus away from the troop-carrying helicopter. The GPMG was accurate enough with reach against enemy forces armed with smaller-calibre weapons, such as rifles and light machine guns, to persuade them to keep their heads down, buying time for the task to be completed or to evade the threat. It was operated by the crewman, from the cabin door on the right-hand side of the troop compartment. Arming troop helicopters came from the Vietnam War, where the US military had lost nearly 2,600 helicopters to enemy action, mostly due to small-arms fire and heavy machine guns (HMG). A helicopter will always be slow and easier to track than a fast-jet: it can't fly above the range of many weapons, so it remains vulnerable at all times. But flown correctly, tactically, with accurate intelligence information, and provided with a good defensive system to detect guided missiles, warn the crew and release countermeasures, its chance of survival was significantly enhanced.

Less than two weeks after completing my Operational Conversion Unit, I was flying operational missions in Northern Ireland. Crews from 60 Squadron would be detached to Northern Ireland to reinforce the Wessex crews on 72 Squadron, a unit that was permanently based at RAF Aldergrove, four miles south of Antrim. It gave the 72 Squadron crews the opportunity for leave, stand-down or just rest, and it gave 60 Squadron crews the opportunity to work in a demanding environment, hone operational skills and gain the local experience to be called on at short notice.

The procedures just to get to Northern Ireland on a scheduled airliner gave an indication of the additional risk that being in the military carried, a threat I wouldn't have expected from any UK citizens. I had been briefed not to mention my 'military connections' to anyone I met on the flight to Aldergrove. But of course people in the next seat are likely to innocently ask questions about your business, it's just harmless chat. Nevertheless the security brief was clear. I decided, if necessary, I would say I was collecting a light aircraft and flying it back to England on someone else's behalf; I could bluff my way through such a story. RAF Aldergrove shared an airfield with Belfast International Airport and I had to look for a specific 'private entry' door out of the arrivals hall that would take me away from the public eye, and through to a discreet office area, where transport would be arranged to take me across to the military side of the airfield. I was already getting the idea that there were people here who would not think twice about killing me, no doubt after some violent abuse first.

I had been used to the threat of personal attack for a while now; long gone were the days when servicemen and women could travel between home and work in 'observable uniform'. The military had lost its image as an invaluable resource, a means of connection with local populations. Now, it was out of the public eye, nobody knew much about what it did any more. The IRA was a terrorist group who were happy reaching into anywhere in Britain, and even British military units based abroad, as much as in Northern Ireland. I was ingrained with the need to search my car for IEDs (improvised explosive devices) before I got into it, especially if it had been left unattended anywhere in public. Additional car searches, on entry to any military base, reminded me of the very real threat that existed because of the

uniform I wore. The role of the British military in Northern Ireland was counterterrorism; it was given the formal name 'Operation
Banner', ordained to 'support the police and government, in allowing the population to live and work without the fear of violence and
extremism'.

The threat became more evident when we were issued personal
weapons on our arrival day, a Heckler and Koch 53 (HK 53) semi-
automatic rifle, and a 9mm Browning pistol. There wasn't room in the
cockpit for full-size rifles, but the HK had a stock that folded, so they
could be stowed close at hand. After an intelligence update briefing
and a 'ground cat' (test) with an Aldergrove-based instructor pilot, we
were ready for our first scheduled tasking, to be airborne at 6 a.m. the
next day, with a 4.15 a.m. alarm call.

I worked hard and enjoyed the flying, operating out of Omagh,
Dungannon and Enniskillen. We worked with the troops day and
night, sometimes staying at the forward operating base (FOB) overnight. At some locations I felt quite vulnerable. With the Wessex
cockpit so high above the ground, it gave a great view when landed,
but sometimes I could see over the security fencing and that meant
people could see me from a distance – and that meant a sniper attack
was a possibility. Aircrew flight vests contained the usual survival aids,
but also a zipped-in ceramic-armour breastplate that covered the
chest area, and particularly the heart. It was reportedly good for stopping bullets up to 7.62mm, but it didn't protect the head, the arms, the
lower body or the back, or from damage from explosions.

Roadside bombs alone had claimed many lives over the years,
and heavy machine guns, mortars and MANPADS (man-portable
air-defence systems) infra-red 'heat-seeking' missiles had been used
to attack helicopters too, with eleven damaged or lost as a result of
hostile action in an eighteen-year period. Navigating at night, using

night-vision goggles, was a demanding environment in which I only had five hours of experience. There was no GPS yet; navigation was still down to visual lookout, a map, a compass and a stopwatch, though local crews quickly became familiar with the area. I was here for a short deployment during part of the parade season. 'The Troubles' in Northern Ireland varied in intensity by season, and the marching season was a particular trigger for violence.

Our task was moving troops and supplies in and out of FOBs, and also inserting troops for intelligence missions, arrest operations, vehicle stop and search patrols, or 'foot patrols'. This could be by day or night, and in all weathers. I quickly learned that putting soldiers into a field required a lot more thought than just dropping them off at the grid reference. The last thing they needed was to be trudging around in a bounded field looking for a way out in the dark, with the risk of being funnelled through a gateway or access point which could be booby-trapped if the same field had been used before. The IRA watched and adapted: if a landing point was used frequently it would be used as an ambush for the next visit. On 27 August 1979, near a place called Warrenpoint, beside the border with Eire on the east coast of Northern Ireland, the IRA ambushed a convoy of British Army trucks by detonating a large roadside bomb as they passed by. A second bomb was detonated as a Wessex helicopter, sent to the scene to recover casualties, was taking off. The IRA had been studying British Army tactics and correctly predicted where the reaction force would set up its control point, killing many more soldiers who had arrived to rescue and treat or retrieve the victims. Eighteen soldiers met violent deaths and many were seriously injured. The Wessex was damaged but managed to fly away. On the same day, Lord Louis Mountbatten, the Queen's cousin, was blown up on the west coast of Ireland. The incidents refocused the need to be unpredictable against an enemy that could strike anytime and anywhere. It was the use of ways to counter such threats that hooked me into the world of helicopter tactics.

I discussed my aspirations with my Squadron Commander and he offered to sponsor my application to the Helicopter Tactics Instructor Course (HTIC), run annually for RAF helicopter crews, though Army Air Corps pilots were beginning to join it too. In September 1994, I joined the course at RAF Odiham for three weeks of ground school lessons and three weeks of flying exercises. First I was taught the tactics, then I had to prove I could teach it back and had the necessary knowledge to back that up. We covered tactical low-level flying in formations, mutual support in threat areas, surviving against fighter aircraft attacks, ground-based weapons and radar units, and much more. It was hard work, but tremendous fun, and I wanted more. I enrolled on other courses, the Electronic Warfare Officer's Course, and a Weapons and Tactics Course sponsored by the RAF's Central Tactics and Trials Organisation. I wanted to expand my knowledge as much as I could, and began to specialise as the lead aircrew expert for Wessex trials, looking at countermeasures against heat-seeking missiles. It was all fitting to my role on the squadron, because the original idea of navigators going from fast-jets onto rotary-wing was exactly this: to use experience to enhance the tactical expertise of the helicopter squadrons.

I did well on my own course and the following year I was invited back to instruct, something that became a regular part of my career from then onwards. The more I instructed, the more I practised and the more I learned; anyone who climbs into a military aircraft thinking they know it all has a death wish. The boss decided it was time he did a Combat-Ready check on me. We were tasked to support Army units on a training area in Shropshire and in North Yorkshire – it was going to be a long day. Flying helicopters for long periods of time is fatiguing on the spine: the position of the controls fosters a hunched forward posture for the cockpit crew, the seat back becomes unused, and for the crewman their knees are constantly punished, especially in aircraft not tall enough to stand up in. After a couple of hours flying, the boss asked if I would like to take the controls for a short while. The big smile was all the answer he needed. 'I'll take it for the tasking, but you can fly the transit legs in between at 2,000 feet,' he added.

He quickly became happy with my transit flying. After flying several approaches and landings to his satisfaction, he barely touched the controls again. The real confidence winner was when he allowed me to fly the aircraft to RAF Stafford's Tactical Supply Wing (TSW) refuelling site, land next to the refuel point, take the fuel with our rotors still turning, and then depart onto our next task. I was delighted he had displayed that amount of trust, and that I hadn't let that trust down. Back on the ground at Benson, we debriefed the mission, its flight safety points, flight domestics, mission planning, mission management, navigation, communications, fuel management, departure, arrival, then the tasking, as a crew. Then the boss asked the crewman to leave and turned to me for an individual debrief.

'I don't really have anything to add, a very good sortie... Would you like LCR [Limited Combat-Ready] pilot or CR [Combat-Ready] nav?'

I laughed out loud, but he was looking at me, waiting for an answer. 'LCR pilot?' There, I wasn't hearing things, he'd said it again, more obviously this time.

He had just offered me the option to transfer to pilot.

'Is that possible?' I asked incredulously.

'Leave it with me. Good sortie, well done!' And he walked out the room.

My brain was whirring, I had tried for pilot crossover opportunities before, but the RAF system always turned me down because of age.

The ridiculously low age rules for beginning pilot training were based on 'a return of service', for the military to get value out of the expensive training costs involved before the prospective pilot possibly left for higher-paying civilian opportunities. They deemed that if I left at my standard retirement point, aged thirty-eight, by the time I finished a couple of years of training I would only be on the front line for another couple of years, and that wouldn't justify the costs. I was happy to sign on for as many years as they thought it would take to repay the investment; unfortunately, the people who make the rules and count the money didn't see it that way. As much as the boss pushed for a crossover course for me, the answer was 'no'. And I did hear from third parties that he tried very hard. It wasn't meant to be. However, as a navigator on helicopters, I was guaranteed the left-hand seat in the cockpit of an aircraft with full dual-controls. I would still get to fly – in fact, it was essential to have that ability. The very real risk of being shot at brought the danger that the handling pilot might get hit. It would be an awful scenario if the aircraft crashed because I wasn't able to take control and get everyone back on the ground as safely as I could, given the possibility the aircraft might also be damaged. It was another reason I accepted as much hands-on flying as was offered, and, during annual flight checks with a qualified helicopter instructor (QHI), my basic piloting ability was usually reported on positively.

In contrast to all this military expertise and 'masculine image' was the person I wanted to be, and my life struggles were still getting worse, not easier. I was fed up of hiding in darkened rooms behind closed curtains, bumping into things in the dark because I was too scared to put the lights on, lest my timing was wrong. I needed to be true to myself, but my family remained foremost in my mind. I spoke with my parents each Sunday night by phone. They rarely ventured out, so it was up to me to visit them, and that was what I always did with my leave, with the occasional surprise weekend visit too. I would catch up with my brothers and sister during these visits too; Sandra and Rich lived locally, with their own families, and Stan wasn't far away. I felt close to my family, and hurting them was not something I wanted to do.

Frosty had become a good friend, we frequently flew together, and enjoyed a positive social life. It was difficult getting time alone, but whenever he went away for a short while, I was dressing almost as he left the house. On one occasion he was meant to be out at a rugby club weekend meet, but in the early hours of the morning I heard scrambling around outside the house. My name was being called out, with the sound of a door being pushed against the restraint of a security chain – thank goodness I had secured it. It took me a good ten minutes to be sure I had removed every trace of makeup and hidden away every item of female attire and accessory, without making it obvious I was awake. In the darkness of the back garden I found a prone figure, snoozing on the grass. I gave his shoulder a shake and he muttered something about deciding to walk home. Apparently, the evening of drink and celebration had come to an earlier than planned end. I could see why. We had a good laugh about it afterwards, but I never told him the real reason it took me so long to respond to the noise.

I enjoyed sharing a house, but the stress was becoming too much, and I couldn't be far from a revealing slip-up. I began to look for options to sell my house in St Andrews, to fund something in Oxfordshire. Coincidentally, I came across a newspaper article that provided a far more tempting reason to sell my house. 'Nigel spends £30,000 to become Nicole', it stated. Nicole was just twenty-eight and looked great. She had the support of her mum and other family members, which was a vital means of support. It was a lot of money, but if I sold my house I might clear enough funds for my own needs. Maybe I would even have enough left to buy a small property in the right place. But how could I keep it from my family? Perhaps I could emigrate, somewhere they wouldn't want to visit.

I wasn't getting any younger, and I wanted so much to be a young girl and grow older gracefully. I didn't want to grow to be an old 'man', regretting my past decisions. If I was going to follow my dream, I wanted to enjoy a lifetime. I wanted to be able to wear young fashions, share makeup and fashion tips, have girls' nights out, laugh about boys, fuss over hair, the simple things in life that I imagined most girls would take for granted – but most of all, I just wanted to be me. But there was more to this article: apparently some 200–300 patients a year went to Charing Cross Hospital, the only National Health Service gender identity clinic in the UK, for sex-change surgery. Of the 150 surgical procedures carried out per year, two-thirds were funded by individuals privately. The NHS waiting list was demoralisingly long, and the process of assessment was even longer. If I did this, I wouldn't want to be held in limbo-land for years. I would follow the private care route.

Ironically, when I did sell my house, Frosty wanted to get on the property ladder too, and, with house prices remaining barely affordable, we ended up buying equal shares in a large three-bedroom detached house, in the quiet Thames-side village of Moulsford. He was an honest, trustworthy and rational man, yet I couldn't bring myself to confide in him. It would have placed an unfair burden on him, and, as much as it pained me not to seek his understanding, I couldn't do that. I needed to find someone to talk to who didn't know me, but how could I do that? When Frosty was posted to Northern Ireland, his shift patterns there meant I had three weeks in every four alone in the house. The advantage of the new house was its large secluded garden, surrounded by trees and substantial hedges, a double garage for hiding my car away when need be, and a built-in wardrobe in my bedroom, to which I attached a lock. The downside was that it was in a cul-de-sac in a small village, with an active neighbourhood watch team. Privacy in the house still meant hiding behind drawn curtains; the garden was a welcome enjoyment, though always with nervous vigilance.

Then I was invited by Dan to be best man at his wedding to his fiancée Wendy. He had joined our squadron after recovering from injuries sustained in his tragic accident during our SAR course. I had hesitated, I felt uncertain, but I wasn't going to shun the honour of his request. We had only known each other nineteen months but had developed a good friendship from the first day. He was a tall, friendly man, with sticky-out ears, like my dad had. It was mostly Dan's unexpected visits to my bungalow in Shawbury that had me hiding behind closed lace-nets and curtains. I couldn't attend weddings without wondering if I would ever enjoy such a special day of my own, but it was always wonderful to see friends happy, and weddings were usually good military reunions too. And so, in August 1994, contradictory though it was, I became a 'best man', a role I had also performed for my brother-in-law, Stuart. Always the best man, never the bride!

As Christmas approached, depression set in again. I was seeing my life pass by, with short glimpses of joy and long periods of quiet reflection and loneliness. Every woman I saw I wanted to be. I was jealous of her hair, her shape, her clothes, her voice, her style, her life. I wanted hormones so badly, the right kind of hormones, and I knew now where to get some.

I checked the catalogue again, pleased I had picked it up during one of my recent visits to the shop in Manchester. 'Female Hormone

Precursors – to help effect a chemical change, a male to female trans-formation.' It was only £68 for a course, I could afford that. I didn't go on expensive holidays and my car was eight years old. All my free time was spent hiding any masculinity, or visiting my parents. I went shopping. I knew I was on dangerous ground now, but as 1995 dawned I finally did something for me.

'Oestrogen Breast Development Cream' – just the sound of it was wonderful, but I had to be careful. Opening the jar gave me unbeliev-able feelings of excitement. The opportunity to develop my boring flat chest was a dream come true – but if it developed too much I would be discovered, and then what? Was the reward worth the pain? I couldn't believe I was hesitating, but there was so much to risk. I weighed up the pros and the cons over a few days but, on 4 January 1995, my heart won over my brain. I rubbed the cold, pale pink cream into my chest. Here was the one thing that could bring me change, bring me true life. I went to bed like a child anticipating Father Christmas arriving, and I dreamt the most amazing dreams of change.

Over the next few days, I began to feel tightness in my breast area, and my nipples began to be more sensitive. I couldn't believe I had done this. It was clearly beginning to take effect, and worry set in for the briefest of moments, but I didn't want to stop now. Perhaps I was just blind to reality because of emotion, but, as much as it brought me hope, I knew I couldn't go to work with obvious breast tissue. The worry crept back: what if the development became too obvious? Would it de-crease if I stopped applying the cream? Would the oestrogen affect any decisions I made? Would my resolve to change become even stronger? This was an exciting and important part of my life. I was on a feminisa-tion programme without any medical supervision. Every now and then the stretching skin hurt just a little, but it was a welcome hurt, a sign that things were happening. I was overcome with a feeling of pride and anticipation. My chest was forming a soft, fatty feel. Reluctantly, I reduced the application to once a day. Then I began to notice shape, slight curves, they were too small for my liking, but certainly beginning to look over-developed for a 'male'. Perhaps I should stop now, until I was ready to accept the consequences of change.

I usually wore a flying suit to work and the zipped breast pockets were good deceptions, but the day I had to wear my blue uniform was the day I fully understood the potential ramifications of my actions. To me, it was obvious I had budding breasts. Pride turned to worry, worry turned to fear. What if someone else noticed? What about my annual aircrew medical! Surely a doctor would notice, tapping on my chest, listening to my lungs. It wasn't due for another ten months, perhaps the tissue would revert before then. But what if...? The product information suggested it could take three months for the first signs of development, and mine had been so much quicker than that. Maybe I already had hormones that just needed a trigger action. I read up about hormones: the advice was that the body returned to a male state if the hormones were stopped. I phoned the Albany Gender Identity Clinic in Manchester for advice. I had to be discreet, I worried my name might be linked to the clinic through phone records. It was a premium line number; it would stand out in any bills. I phoned from a call-box in the next village.

'If I stopped using the hormone cream for breast development, would my chest return to what it was?'

'Yes, the development is only as good as the creams... The breasts will regress if you stop using it,' the doctor reassured me.

'How quickly? Obviously they regress slower than they develop?'

'That's impossible to say.' She paused. 'It depends on the individual.'

'Thank you, that's all I wanted to know.' I wanted to know more, but I didn't want to stay on the phone any longer than necessary.

My dilemma was clear. I would have to refrain from using the product any further and be careful how I dressed at work. I envied young girls who knew none of these worries, just carefree development, anticipating the wonderful curves to come. The more I worried, the more I noticed. Even after stopping treatment, I thought I was still developing, I still felt occasional twinges. But I wasn't just imagining things: a tape measure revealed my chest size had gone up three inches already. In conversation, I stood with folded arms across my chest, my flying suit breast pockets 'padded' with items that wouldn't draw questioning eyes. I feared discovery.

I was programmed for my six-monthly dinghy survival drill, which meant getting into swimwear in front of my colleagues. I had never thought I'd be trying to hide breast growth from them, but the changing-room cubicles provided welcome privacy. I was grateful for once that the swimming test was done wearing a flying suit, and the dinghy drills wearing a life jacket. It didn't matter when I was in my own single-seat dinghy, but when it came to doing the multi-seat raft the life jacket gave protection from the squashed contact of nine bodies clambering over me in a confined space.

My annual fitness test in the gymnasium followed. I tried on five different tops to find one that worked. Patterns on the front gave curves away; a plain lilac T-shirt with a baggy blue sweatshirt on top was the best combination. I was doing the test on my own with an RAF physical training instructor; his focus would be on me. Usually there was a group being tested, but not today for some reason. A run of a mile and a half, followed by press-ups and sit-ups, all against the clock and factored for age and gender. During the run, I felt like I needed a bra to stop my chest moving about. But that would have shown up under my clothes. During the press-ups, the instructor placed a raised clenched fist beneath my chest to make sure I was doing them properly. It was an incentive not to go that low, but I was convinced he'd notice something 'not quite right'.

These were very worrying times. Had I been foolish? Although I never had any issues passing my fitness tests, I didn't relish doing excessive amounts of sport. I knew this was a contradiction and I had a responsibility to be fit to do my job, but the last thing I wanted was muscular arms and legs. It was fine for a girl to have upper body strength, but society still frowned if she had biceps that could lift a horse; macho beliefs would be offended. My school years of rowing and swimming hadn't done me any favours by adding to my shoulder muscle. For me, muscle was a sign of masculinity that I was desperate to avoid. I already carried too much of that burden – any more was unthinkable.

The beautiful thing about my budding breasts, however, was how they filled my bras. It was marvellous how so little tissue could form such obvious shape and cleavage. I wanted photos to capture my new shape; if I did 'revert', then at least I would have images of me as I wanted to be. I invested in a Polaroid camera with self-timer and auto focus; the film was quite expensive but it gave me essential security. I recalled the stunned faces on two female assistants in a SupaSnaps store in St Andrews, when I went to collect a processed film that had images of me in female attire. I had naively thought it was an automatic development process, without any direct human observation. Clearly not, though thankfully there was nothing on the film that betrayed my military connection. A Polaroid, on the other hand, saved the potential risk of blackmail. One of the reasons the military gave for barring LGBT service was the risk of blackmail, but if personnel were allowed to serve openly, then they couldn't be blackmailed just for being LGBT! Part of me was thinking that getting caught would open out my life, that I could get on with it – but then, I thought, I wouldn't have a life to get on with. My love for my family was unconditional, yet in return I had to accept unbearable conditions. I was slowly beginning to see the burden that put on me. Surely true family love should be unconditional, both ways?

8

IS THERE ANY REASON?

—

1995

From Benson, it was only thirty minutes' flight time via the heli-lanes into London City, and that made us popular for VIP tasks: flying visiting foreign dignitaries, or chiefs of defence, to various meetings in the south of the country. In October 1994, I had the honour of getting Boutros Boutros-Ghali, the UN Secretary-General, to a visit with HRH Prince Charles at his home in Highgrove House, near Tetbury in Gloucestershire. Russ Woodland was pilot for this mission, a good friend and my Flight Commander. We landed just beside the Highgrove gardens, where the VIP was collected to travel by car for the final hundred metres or so. Closing our aircraft down with Highgrove House and its gardens as the backdrop was amazing. We were hosted at a small security post nearby, with tea and sand-wiches sent out for us. The meeting only lasted an hour and a half, but when our passenger emerged he was accompanied by Prince Charles and Princes William and Harry. I was thrilled to see the young princ-es waving at us as we took off, so I waved back.

On a hot summer's day in 1995, while working with Army units on the Stanford Training Area (STANTA) near Thetford, in Nor-folk, I was reflecting on the picturesque scene of two camouflaged helicopters parked on a grass clearing, surrounded by trees, the crews relaxing alongside, lying or sitting in the grass, eating snack foods, swigging water from small plastic bottles, awaiting further tasking, when the peace and quiet was broken by the noise of new technology. The idea of having a mobile phone, albeit the size of a brick, was still new to us, but already we were thinking it was nicer not to be so easily contactable. Andy van Balaam answered the phone. I had been flying this task with him, and I wondered if we were off elsewhere. After a short conversation, he folded the phone's antenna in and set it down on the grass.

'It looks like someone's off at short notice to Bosnia… and it might be you or me, Phil.'

Phil was the captain of the other Wessex we were working with. He rested his smoking pipe and looked puzzled. 'Why us two?'

'They want a second-tourist pilot, someone with suitable helicopter experience, to be an adviser to a rapid-reaction force mobilising to go there.'

'Well, that's me out on both counts!' I chortled. I was still only in my first tour on helicopters.

I wondered if the reaction force was in response to the recent news of the genocide of over 8,000 men and boys in the town of Srebrenica, by units of the Bosnian Serb Army (BSA). Our training mission on STANTA was for UK forces deploying to Bosnia as part of the United Nations Protection Force (UNPROFOR). NATO was getting impatient; the war in the Former Republic of Yugoslavia had been going on for three years now. Its stalemate had recently begun a downward spiral, with increasing ethnic cleansing and instances of genocide that the UN-mandated forces were powerless to stop. Srebrenica had been a declared UN safe area. The Serbian-backed BSA was the most belligerent and was confronted by the Bosnia and Herzegovina (BiH) government army and Bosniak Muslims, now allied with the mostly Catholic Bosnian Croat (HVO) and Croatian Army (HV) forces.

After our tasking was complete, we returned to Benson and were told to report to the boss's office.

Wing Commander Dick Foster was a well-respected boss with a laugh that always made me smile. He was openly proud of his tenure as the Squadron Commander and passionate about keeping the squadron's distinguished history alive. Sat behind his desk, he motioned us to sit down.

'As you know,' he began, 'we've been asked to provide someone to support a reaction force unit heading to Bosnia. I've narrowed the list of those suitably qualified and able to go to you three. Is there any reason why any of you can't go?' I wondered how I now qualified as a second-tourist pilot, but accepted the compliment that I was as qualified as Phil and Andy.

We looked at each other. Nobody had a reason why they couldn't go.

'I'll give it a little more consideration and let you know in the morning,' he added.

A few days later I was sat in a departures lounge at RAF Brize Norton, waiting for my flight to Bosnia. I was worried about leaving my house in the hands of someone else. I had locked my secret away – my diaries, my clothes, newspaper articles and hormone supply – in the built-in wardrobe in my bedroom, and given a spare set of front-door keys to a neighbour, Tony, a trusted member of the local neighbourhood watch team. I joined a party of Royal Marines (RM) and their vehicles aboard a giant USAF C5-Galaxy transport aircraft to Split, in Croatia, from where we journeyed south by road to Ploče and boarded an RN Sea King to enter Bosnia. Ploče (pronounced Plochy) was to become the home of the UK and French rapid reaction force (RRF) 'green' helicopters. They weren't allowed into Bosnia yet, but the Sea King was supporting the UN; it was painted white with 'UN' in large black letters, identifying it as such.

After forty minutes' flying, I got my first glimpse of home for the foreseeable future: Kiseljak, a small town of red-roofed white houses and around 7,000 inhabitants, located at the junction of three river valleys and surrounded by wooded hills, about eighteen miles north-west of Sarajevo. It was a hot day with clear skies. As the Sea King departed, the place fell into a peaceful silence. I looked up at a large, white, alpine-style building on the slope above us. It was clearly a hotel that had enjoyed grander days, when it was built to host the press for the 1984 Winter Olympics. The local area bore the scars of war and the hotel hadn't escaped. From its entrance, I looked back towards the landing site, about four storeys below, a small field bordered by a river and a large black rubber fuel tank, for use by visiting helicopters. Hidden from sight by the building, the gentle hum of a diesel-powered generator could be heard. Plugged into the building mains-ring it provided an invaluable supply of electricity.

The hotel was a combined Anglo-French headquarters for the rapid reaction force operational staff (RRFOS) in the making, and it was where UN aid convoys formed up with their UNPROFOR armoured vehicle escorts before attempting to enter Sarajevo along one of the few roads into the city that could be used, though it still carried extreme risk of attack.

I was allocated an empty room, but it soon became cramped as more people arrived, firstly two of us, then four, and ultimately eight, all in metal-framed bunkbeds. The bathroom was communal and didn't have a lock on the door, so I had to be careful, especially when showering. It had been six months now, but there had been no visible reversion in my breast tissue, and I was still concerned people might notice. I always wore something covering my chest loosely, regardless of how hot the day became.

After shots were fired nearby, our readiness state was raised to 'red', with 'body armour and Kevlar helmets to be worn at all times'. Twenty-four hours later, it was relaxed to 'amber' and they just needed to be 'readily available'. That would have been nice if it were possible – it would be three days before I could be issued with mine. There hadn't been enough of this essential means of personal protection in the supply chain in the UK. 'You'll get them when you arrive in theatre,' I had been told matter-of-factly. I suspected a lot of what we needed was still in Croatia, where it wasn't needed at all. I had my weapons with me, but no bullets; they would apparently be issued with the body armour. I hoped we wouldn't be attacked in the meantime! My daily routine was established, beginning with an 8 a.m. brief and finishing 'when need be', and I was made responsible for creating and running a helicopter operations cell (Heli-Ops) from scratch.

My immediate boss was a Royal Marines Major, Mark, and initially I had help from two RAF Squadron Leaders, Mike and Dave, who were there to do the bigger-picture contingencies, such as a potential helicopter evacuation of British forces in the Gorazde enclave. A large empty room was identified for everyone to work in, and we divided it into cells, eventually separated by hard-board or cardboard stand-alone partitions. I was the most junior officer rank present; everyone seemed to have had 'field promotions' because they were deployed in an operational headquarters. The General's media ops officer wore 'Major' rank, but I recognised him from a task I had flown in the UK just three weeks previously, when he was a junior Lieutenant project officer, for a VIP pick-up I had flown from Battersea in London. The windows wouldn't open, so we created our own air-conditioning system by taking them all out; when the weather cooled, later in the month, they went back in.

I was given responsibility for the overall tasking, coordination and de-confliction of all UN helicopter assets in Bosnia by phone and fax. On a lower level in the building, a more permanent 'hardened' operations room was being built; we were set to become a TAOCC, a Tactical Air Operations and Control Centre. Then, a week after my arrival, a Squadron Leader Intelligence Officer visited from the Sarajevo headquarters to deliver an urgent briefing for me, Mike and Dave.

'Right, it's all going to hit the fan, and when it does, you are going to be in a whole host of trouble,' he began. It wasn't the kind of news we were expecting to hear.

'When the bombing starts, you're prime targets for the Bosnian Serb artillery in the hills around you. I would expect this headquarters to be overrun, along with ours in Sarajevo. In which case you need to just head west and make for the Croatian border.'

'But the countryside around here is littered with mines!' we pointed out. 'And we would have no idea if local populations are friendly or not!' The area was a mix of three different warring ethnic groups. Walking anywhere without a minefield map would be more dangerous than being overrun, perhaps. The mood certainly became a lot more sombre, and we wondered if we had been better off not knowing this information. If it came to it, then I was sure the best option was an extraction by Chinook or Puma, and I knew where to get one of those!

My first task was to draw up standard operating procedures (SOPs) and then design and promulgate 'safe routing' corridors, so that all crews operating within Bosnia worked from the same set of procedures and followed routes that could be used for de-confliction in poor weather and monitored by NATO airborne radars looking for hostile aircraft.

Meanwhile at Ploče, the UK Chinook and Puma aircraft and crews had arrived with a whole headquarters staff, equipped and manned to do the job I had, but they still weren't allowed into Bosnia.

We didn't know how long we were to be here for, but I had an idea in mind for keeping morale up. After persuading a French Colonel to 'obtain' some wine, I secretly made 3-D models of two helicopters out of plastic cups, cardboard and Sellotape, before 'silver-plating' them with silver tape I'd 'borrowed' from the RM vehicle mechanics. Then, one evening, I guided Air Cell team members to a dining table I had reserved, and where I had pre-placed the 'silverware', name plates and the red wine. We had an improvised 'dining-in night', and it went down extremely well. It was decided we would do the same again to celebrate any national days or upcoming birthdays.

At the back of the hotel, I found a large, unused balcony and in my off-duty time I would stand up there, or sometimes I would climb up onto the roof, through an access space that I suspected was full of bats, and just sit there, watching and thinking.

At 11 a.m. on 19 August I was on the phone to Heli-Ops in Split when a message came through for an urgent casualty evacuation (casevac). The on-call Sea King at Gornji Vakuf was scrambled to come to us for further instructions. Then matters got complicated. A military vehicle had plunged several hundred feet off a mountain road near Sarajevo, possibly into a minefield, leaving four injured, and another one very seriously injured. Because of the minefield risk, a helicopter couldn't just land anywhere, and it would have to traverse BiH and BSA territory, which needed their permission. BiH was easy and quick, but BSA authorisation took over three hours. Unless local commanders were briefed, they would fire on the aircraft, regardless of its colour – or, sometimes, its clearances.

Throughout the day, the injury reports grew worse and the casevac aircraft were put on hold as medics in Sarajevo fought to stabilise injuries. Soon it became two dead, then three, then four, 'including a US Ambassador'. In fact, the Ambassador was safe in a different vehicle, but the casualties included US diplomats. I sought out our two American Liaison Officers (LOs) and briefed them. It wasn't until 9.15 a.m. that Sarajevo was ready; the death toll was now five. I cleared the Sea King captain, an RAF pilot on exchange with the Navy, to collect the injured, but the French Puma crew, tasked to recover the dead, refused to go. They wouldn't take any 'orders' from me, Sarajevo, or our overall Air Commander, a French Colonel, eventually leaving only after he made an angry phone call to their boss in Split. No one was happy. It turned out to have been a tragic accident: the driver of their French armoured vehicle had pulled over, on a narrow mountain road, near Mount Igman, to let an oncoming convoy pass, but the ground beneath them collapsed. They were only there as part of the peace process, trying to save lives. I hoped the work they were doing would lead to peace, so they wouldn't have died in vain.

I had just set to work on making sure the orders for casevac launch were understood by all nations when I received a call from the Combined Air Operations Centre (CAOC) in Vicenza in Italy to say that a UK Lynx had crashed into the sea off Ploče. They offered an MH-53 CSAR helicopter, with a C-130 Hercules equipped for SAR. I phoned Ploče, who reported that rescue was in hand so they didn't need additional help. Sadly, of the five crew and passengers on the Lynx, only one had survived.

As our 'hardened' TAOCC became ready, I was joined by a Norwegian Arapaho pilot, Bent, and an Army Air Corps Lynx pilot, Mike, enabling us to operate 24/7. I was moved out of my sleeping quarters to make way for a Major, and rehoused in a leaky third-floor room that slept six in bunkbeds. I wondered if he was a real Major. A few days later, I found my belongings placed on another bed and a Czech officer in my top bunk. I preferred the top as I was fed up of my hair getting caught in the bedsprings above me. I couldn't be bothered arguing over a bed space, but my morale was at an all-time low. I hadn't been able to relax and be me for a long while now, and it was depressing me.

Then Bent offered me a morale boost. He needed to fly an Arapaho Bell 412 for currency flying, so he invited me along during one of my rare periods of down time. We flew to Split, where I got out for a can of Coke and a chocolate bar, before we flew back with some Turkish VIPs. When we landed, all hell had broken loose. Sarajevo Market had been mortared, with forty dead. The mortars hadn't been located but it pointed squarely at Bosnian Serb forces, and if that was proven, it was considered a trigger action for a punitive attack by NATO forces.

At 6.30 p.m. on 29 August, the General confirmed it had been 'declared a trigger action, and we should expect the situation in Bosnia to change for the worse'. I could already hear jet noise in the skies above us. I listened on our radio as a force of 137 aircraft gathered: an attack package and ninety support aircraft, including air defence fighters, tankers, early warning and intelligence gatherers. Their aim was to eliminate the threat of any further attacks on Sarajevo. History was taking place, so I produced a log book to record key events from our perspective.

At 2.40 a.m. we went 'State Red', requiring body armour and helmets to be worn. The French body armour appeared more protective than ours, especially when I was informed that mine was as much use as a paper bag. It was like a plastic waistcoat within a two-colour green camouflage outer jacket, with large, empty external pockets front and back. These were meant to contain 'ceramic armour' breast-plates. Without the plates, the jacket didn't afford the protection it was meant to, but I hadn't been issued the plates – they were 'out of stock'. There didn't seem much point wearing something that wasn't fit for purpose, but it helped keep me warm.

All the floors above Level Three had been evacuated; sleeping bodies cluttered the corridors on the lower levels. I smiled as I wondered which corridor the Major was now sleeping in. I visited my 'secret' balcony for a short break. UK, French and Dutch artillery were in action, their gun and mortar flashes hidden in the fog, but the distinctive dull 'crump' sound of big guns firing carried further on the otherwise still night. The ops room had tea and coffee urns and was full of people I had never seen before.

It was the start of a five-day campaign that wouldn't stop until the Serbs agreed to the terms put to them, until any threat to Sarajevo was removed, out of range of the city. The mood was of anticipation: we were still in range of their guns – would they dare launch their fighter-ground-attack aircraft? A building bristling with aerials was a good target. My new multi-national casevac plan got tested, for serious injuries on Mount Igman. I still had to challenge some decisions made by people not understanding the use of helicopters, but afterwards I was thanked by the senior French doctor.

On 2 September, an official 'quiet period' was extended to the Serbs: now was their chance to make the right decision. Admiral Smith appeared on CNN to say how successful the air raids had been. Then he told the world: 'It was all down to the success of the team at Kiseljak, who right now are under the noses of the BSA artillery.' We thanked him for reminding them! The world waited. People took advantage of the lull to move; bids for helicopter moves came at their fastest ever. Green Pumas also visited, but a BIH Commander threatened to shoot them down because he 'couldn't tell them from Bosnian Serb helicopters'. Finally, after the BSA briefly declared war on NATO, the Bosnian Serb military leader Ratko Mladić agreed to the NATO and UN demands.

In expectation of a ground war, a Norwegian MASH (Mobile Army Surgical Hospital) had joined us. A Swedish surgeon, explaining they were 'looking for trade', noticed I had a ganglion on my right wrist, a cyst that numerous doctors had tried to remove in the past, including by hitting it with a heavy book, evidently a much-tested medieval remedy! I politely declined her offer to remove it surgically. The next day, I was lying on my back on an operating table, with my hand resting on what looked like an ironing board beside me. After a local anaesthetic, she opened the back of my hand. 'Look... inside your hand, it is amazing, you must look!' This time 'no' meant 'no'. My hand was sore for a week, but the scar was barely noticeable.

Finally, peace was confirmed and people were going home. The General began interviews and asked if I was seeking a career. I told him I was leaving the military in a couple of years' time, but I didn't tell him why. I would never know if that revelation denied me a report that would have improved my promotion chances, but I wasn't expecting to stay in service. I had lived in a totally male environment for far too long, enforcing masculinity. I was looking forward to getting home. I needed to be me.

On a clear, bright Saturday in November, the French General presented UN medals to the British and the RM General presented medals to the French. The General's speech about peace was ironically interrupted by the sound of gunfire. As we moved into December, NATO assumed responsibility to enforce and reinforce the peace and to help rebuild the country, a mission now known as

IFOR (Implementation Force). The hotel was filling up with IFOR now, resulting in long queues for meals, but the food supplies couldn't cope. Food began to be rationed; by Christmas, a hundred personnel were ill with a stomach bug, but my stomach had clearly adjusted. Familiar faces became few and far between, and I was moved out of my room for the fourth time. I had to account for my 140 bullets and hand them in, along with my 'body armour'. Then I was re-issued the most useless item, my body armour; that said a lot. Nobody seemed to know what was going on. When the TAOCC was renamed Heli-Ops, things had come full circle. The UK Wing Commander taking over the Air Cell directed me stay as a 'Forward Adviser' so he could enjoy Christmas at home with his family, until the US General found out, ordering him 'to get his ass out here'. It was a white Christmas and New Year, with heavy snowfall, and then, finally, I received permission to go home. But no one knew who was responsible for clearances, and after being handed off to five different offices, and seven more the next day, I decided to just book myself on an aircraft directly, through Sarajevo Movements Control.

On 3 January, I accepted a lift in a US Special Operations Force Humvee that was going in to Sarajevo. The drive there was disheartening; so much destruction was powerfully poignant. But I was proud that I was part of the process that had brought about an end to all of this, even if it was only a little part. I had managed multi-national helicopter operations in a war zone, coordinating them, getting people to safety and care quickly, and it had been a good role.

As the SOF guys drove away, I was refused permission to board the flight. It was only ten minutes before the RAF C-130 departed, and I was at a loss now. It seemed no one wanted to let me go home. Amazingly, my Colonel at Kiseljak was located and confirmed my authorisation just in time.

It was dark as we departed Sarajevo. I heard a few sharp bangs against the fuselage: it seemed to be near the rear, and it was a sound that was vaguely familiar. The aircraft carried on as planned and we landed at Lyneham at 12.40 a.m. As I disembarked, the crew were looking up towards the tail. I followed their gazes and listened to the conversation. The aircraft had been hit by three bullets, on the tail and the tailplane, a Sarajevo farewell.

I phoned RAF Benson, for a duty driver to collect me, and two hours later I arrived home, in the final hours of night. I couldn't get in the front door. I pushed and pushed, but something was jamming it, I got my torch out, shining it through the gap, confused. Something was wrong. I pushed harder and got my arm in, to reach a light switch – nothing. The driver had already departed. I pushed even harder. Eventually the gap was wide enough. The house was cold and damp, in the light of my torch I saw furniture at odd angles. The wooden parquet floor was destroyed. I was too tired for this. I had been travelling all day; it had been a stressful day. I went upstairs and collapsed on my bed, fully clothed. I would try to unravel what was going on in the daylight.

Two faces were staring at me as I was gently shaken out of my sleep – Dick, my squadron boss, and Russ, my Flight Commander.

'Did you not get our message?' they enquired. 'Did you not get a brief off Tony, the neighbourhood watch man?'

'No… I've been travelling, what…?'

'Did you not see the message on the front door?'

We surveyed the house together. It was wrecked. Tony had been clearing mail when he heard running water. A mains water pipe had burst where it entered the main water tank, in the attic roof. Water had been running from the top of the house through every room, bar one, for at least three days. Stepping around the carnage, I was shown the message on the front door. A dark, scribbled chinagraph pen message read: 'Do not go inside at all. Call the squadron first.' I hadn't seen the message in the dark; I wasn't looking for one. And I had no means to call them. They had been trying to get a message to me for days. A team from the squadron had apparently isolated the water supply and tried to salvage things. My wardrobe! I suddenly panicked. They hadn't mentioned anything. I went back to my bedroom 'to fetch something'. The wardrobe was still locked; my bedroom was the only dry corner of the house, so the salvage focus had been elsewhere, thank goodness. The house was wrecked, but my secret was still safe, unbelievably! There was some luck left in my world – only a little, but for once it had hit the right place.

The boss and his wife Liz, and Russ and his wife Kay, were amazingly supportive, as were many other people, especially colleagues off the squadron, who all helped sort the debris out over the coming weeks. After an overnight stay with Russ and Kay, I returned to rebuilding my home, rather than the leave I had eagerly anticipated.

9

THE LONGEST DAY

1997–1999

In 1997, the Wessex was beginning to be removed from RAF service to make way for a new helicopter, a state of the art troop-carrier known as the Merlin HC Mk3. I, meanwhile, was remaining at Benson: I had been recommended for a job with the Tactics and Trials Flight (TTF) at RAF Odiham by Ian, who now worked there. The job was to look after the introduction of the Merlin, but TTF were moving here and becoming the Rotary Wing Operational Evaluation and Training Unit (RWOETU), responsible for the operational evaluation of all RAF battlefield helicopters and for the tactics development and training of all the crews. I became the first aircrew posted to the RAF Merlin, and to RWOETU, a great accolade, and it was a role I was eager to take on. I needed to remain Combat-Ready on a helicopter type, so, because the Merlin was still being built, and the Wessex was going out of service, I was given a full conversion course on the Puma HC Mk1. It was unusual to do such a course without being posted to the aircraft type, but little did I realise how important this would become. For now, it meant I could maintain my flying role, help with aircraft trials, teach on the tactics instructor course and still liaise with the Westlands factory about Merlin introduction and operations issues. Soon I was joined by a Chinook pilot, New Zealander Tony Ballantyne, and a Chinook crewman, Dave Coombes, also posted in as Merlin crew.

My first job was to join a small exchange team of flying instructors visiting the USAF Special Operations Squadrons at Kirtland Airbase, in Albuquerque, New Mexico. Here, I got to experience US Air Force tactical helicopter operations in combat search and rescue (CSAR) work-up training, flying on MH-53J Pave Low and HH-60 Pave Hawk. I flew on helicopter air-to-air refuelling sorties for the first time. It was great to experience, if a little unnerving at first, seeing rotor blades and armoured refuel hoses in such proximity, especially at low level at night; not as comfortable as refuelling in Phantoms, where the wings stayed safely behind. I also flew on a Hercules HC-130P Combat King for a night-time low-level and helicopter air-refuelling sortie, seeing it from the tanker aspect. It was all experience that might prove valuable in the future, as Merlin came with an air-to-air refuel capability, and CSAR was a role it was suited for. My professional life was moving forward as I wanted, but my personal life was in turmoil.

I wasn't sure if it was the hormones, but my brain was constantly buzzing now, with dreams and hopes for change. I wanted to do this, I needed to do this. What about my family, though? Change would destroy them … but it was my life, I couldn't go on living it like this, I had to stand for who I was. And surely if they truly loved me, as I loved them, they would stand with me? In my heart, I knew that wouldn't happen, but I had no choice: I had to be true to myself, or accept the consequences. The opinion of a gender identity specialist would help.

I had a computer now, and there was a lot of information about 'transsexuality' on the internet. Some was confusing, but I was building up a better understanding of the significance of my life's struggle. I hadn't been alone all this time. If this information had been available earlier, where might I be now? I needed to get out, beyond the house. I already knew of Manchester Village; perhaps the gay scene there would afford protection. It was rumoured that military police teams randomly targeted such places, though, and it would be just my luck to choose such a time.

I booked an appointment at the Albany Gender Identity Clinic. After a chat with the doctor, I knew I wasn't jumping to false conclusions. She offered to prescribe me female hormones and I was so tempted to say yes, but I worried they would add to the breast development I already had and I would be discovered before I was ready. I was a little surprised, however, that after just one meeting I had been offered a life-changing prescription. I would find a different clinic next time, so I could compare their practices and make sure it was the best way to proceed.

Next I joined an 'introductions agency', to see if I could put aside my own convictions and form a relationship with another woman. I was nervous, but it was an essential part of my test: could I continue to live like this? I got on well with a couple of 'introductions', but I never felt like I was on a date. It always seemed like I was meeting a friend who was a girl, not a girlfriend. We would meet for lunch in a pub, chat about ourselves, then go our separate ways. But I did decide to meet one again, as I enjoyed her friendship. I invited her to the summer ball at Benson Officers' Mess, but suggested she bring a friend, to avoid any awkward one-on-one company. I also invited my brothers Rich and Stan, and Rich's wife Sandy. The girls all looked fabulous in their ball gowns, I was so jealous. I had always attended summer balls with friends and their partners. It was saddening never having a partner of my own to take, but the socialising and entertainment soon took my mind off such things. A few weeks afterwards, my 'date' invited me to a BBQ at her house. Stan was visiting, so I took him too; it also gave me an excuse should I be offered a 'stop-over'. After a while, I sensed that she wanted a kiss; I kissed her on the cheek and left. It was time for our friendship to come to an end. I had my answer.

Now it was time to see my senior Desk Officer, the Wing Commander responsible for the career management of junior officer navigator aircrew on fast-jets and helicopters. Sat behind his desk in the Personnel Management Agency, he read through my military record, then looked up and remarked, 'You haven't really done enough yet to warrant promotion.' He seemed very lethargic, uninterested. I had clearly disrupted his day managing people's careers.

'What do you mean enough?' I queried.

'You don't have a broad enough career.' I couldn't believe he had the discourtesy to say that. I asked how two tours defending the UK in fast-jets, one tour on a Tactical Weapons Unit, with an aircrew management responsibility, one tour as a tactics instructor on battlefield helicopters, one currently on the Operational Evaluation Unit working to bring the latest battlefield helicopter into service, and eight operational tours, including one managing the whole helicopter programme in a war zone didn't count as being 'broad'. It was likely far more than he had ever done, though I didn't add that. I had seen people promoted who had only flown one aircraft type and never been on operations.

'What do you mean?' I repeated.

'Well, you haven't done any noteworthy secondary duties; you haven't been on the Mess Committee, for instance.'

'I have been on the committee! I've been the Bar Officer in the officers' mess at Chivenor, and at Benson, several times!'

'That doesn't count, you need to be the Mess Secretary or similar.'

I was getting angry now, but I didn't dare show it. He was just coming up with excuse after excuse.

'What about my recent tour in Bosnia?'

'What about it?'

'That was seven months out of area, I got an exceptional report from the General, and written up by the senior RAF Officer there!'

'Well, I haven't seen anything.'

'I did plenty of voluntary duties there, and there was a war going on around me, wasn't that good enough?'

'No, it counts as your primary job, and we haven't seen it anyway.'

I was trying to hold back my anger now. Everything above my normal call of duty was being shrugged off; he seemed more anxious to get on with a coffee break. The RAF promotion system made no sense. What other company bases its personnel promotions on jobs they weren't paid to do, extra jobs they did as a 'volunteer'? Army and Navy promotions, to Major or Lieutenant Commander, were based on time served as a Flight Lieutenant equivalent. The RAF made it selective, secretive and blinkered, and assumed doing your 'primary job' was a given, which clearly wasn't true, given some of the people it had promoted. I was infuriated. I had worked harder than anyone I knew on my squadron to work the crews up in operational skills, the most important part of being military aviators. I was proactive in everything I did, I had people skills, and I had proven I could su-pervise and lead others. Why was that not good enough to give me a glimpse of a career, or at least some hope of progression? My face clearly didn't fit. I couldn't commit to another seventeen years of this: enough was enough. But before I burnt my bridges, I set myself my final test. I already knew I stood to lose my family and friends; if I couldn't even walk down the street without being humiliated, then what was the point of living?

I had seen an advert from a lady who offered a 'dressing sanctuary' for cross-dressers, including the opportunity to go out in female company. Her name was Krystyna and when I phoned she had immediately come across as a caring, genuine, understanding lady who would be discreet and confidential. I made a booking for three nights.

'Normally guests staying that long like to get into male clothes, every now and then,' she suggested.

'I live in female clothes as much as possible; I really just want to be Caroline if that's OK?'

She had a great sense of humour and put me completely at ease. I grew my nails in anticipation and nobody at work seemed to notice. I was still worried about my car being identified and linking me, so I parked nearby and walked the rest of the way. The house was a large, double-fronted property set back from the main road, behind a small car parking area. It wasn't as private as I had anticipated, but I felt secure. Krystyna greeted me and introduced her friend Elaine, who would be my companion for our visits to Manchester. Over the next few days, I was hosted as a female guest. We went into town for dinner, to a few bars in Manchester Village, and for an afternoon walk in nearby Dunham Park, on a bright, sunshiny autumn day, amongst other members of the public. I wasn't noticed, let alone harassed or humiliated.

There was one moment of worry when Krystyna's son arrived home to collect something. I was ushered into the cellar, as she explained he was an officer in the RAF and she didn't want to chance the fact we might have met before. She recognised I was 'different from their usual customer'; she sensed my pain. She was a spiritual healer and offered to use her gift to help. It was an extraordinarily emotional experience, but I felt a lot of worry channel away. I felt more positive about the future. I told her of my plan to confide in my sister first, and we had a long talk about how that may go. I felt reassured, and was so grateful to her and Elaine for giving me the opportunity to be myself, openly in someone else's company. I drove home confidently, as Caroline.

I made a plan: get medical help, tell Sandra, resign from the RAF, begin transition. At Krystyna's, I had read a magazine that mentioned a gender psychiatrist called Dr Russell Reid, who worked at the London Institute, so I started with that. I was disappointed to find he was fully booked until November; I wanted everything to happen immediately now. Three months seemed an eternity, but being a private patient was still the quickest route. In the meantime, there was plenty to do. I learned about the use of lasers for hair removal and found a clinic in Northampton. Apparently, I would need a course of four to six treatments and that would cost nearly £2,500, but that would be worth it if I never had to shave again.

The first draft of my letter of resignation reflected my anger, so I rewrote it several times, until I had calmed down a little. I wrote that I was no longer happy with remaining in the service and wanted to pursue a new life outside. There was no reason they should know what that new life was going to involve. I confided in Ian that I was submitting my application for PVR (Premature Voluntary Release, a formal means of resignation). He was very supportive, but I couldn't bring myself to tell him the real reason.

Soon after submitting the formal paperwork, I received notice from my Desk Officer that I couldn't leave: I was required to 'amortise training costs' for three years, for the Puma helicopter course that I had done. But that was crazy! I didn't have a Puma job, so even if I stayed in, I wasn't going to amortise the cost of the course. I had flown Puma tasks and I had instructed on it, but my posting was to Merlin, I was merely 'helping out' with Puma. This was difficult for me now, because I had already begun the steps to transition. I couldn't just stop. But I knew the moment I explained my reasons they would throw me out, or they might assume I was trying an extreme excuse to get out quicker. There was a difference between leaving and being thrown out: leaving left me in control of my future. I could no longer wait three years – but what could I do? Now more than ever, I needed somebody to talk to. It was all becoming too stressful. I had to confide in Sandra, and an opportunity presented itself when I was given a couple of days tasking with a Puma helicopter, up in Scotland, operating from a base near where she lived.

28 October 1998 had been a long day; it was about to be my longest. We had spent the afternoon tasking with troops in the Scottish Highlands and it was 9 p.m. before we finally shut the aircraft down at RAF Kinloss, on the southern shore of the Moray Firth, near Elgin. After completing post-flight servicing checks and debriefing the day's mission, it had already gone 10 p.m. We were here for two nights, but I explained to Steve and Oz, the pilot and crewman, that I was visiting Sandra for the first night. It was a long way north and our usual contact was by phone, so it was perfect timing.

'I have some very important news to tell you,' I'd said on the phone. She grew worried it was a life-threatening illness. 'No, it's nothing like that,' I reassured her – though I knew it could spiral me into a dark place if this meeting didn't go well. 'It is exciting news, it is a new chapter in my life and I want you to be with me for it.' I didn't want to give anything away; I had to explain it face-to-face.

I wasn't waiting long before I saw her dark blue Ford Escort swing into the entrance road beside the main gate. Katie and Iain were in the car too, my favourite niece and nephew. I wondered how they would cope. They were wonderful children, caring and sensitive, especially Iain.

Katie was the eldest at twelve and Iain was two years younger. Children were so much more adaptable than adults, as long as they saw their parents understanding. We didn't get to the house until just before midnight. It was in a remote location; my sister and her husband preferred it that way. Sat on the side of a gently rolling valley, the sheep just visible in the dark of the fields surrounding the house, this would be where I would be saved or broken. Stuart, my brother-in-law, worked as senior engineer on an ocean-floor survey ship. He would be away for the next four weeks, somewhere in the Gulf of Mexico. I was extremely nervous: once I had said a couple of vital words, there was no going back. I would be exposed and vulnerable. Sandra would be the first family member to know; the power would be in her hands.

Iain gave me a quick tour of the house while Sandra put the kettle on. It wasn't a big house, but it was a warm family home. Soon it was gone 1 a.m. and we had to insist the kids went to bed. It was lovely to see them; I worried it may not last.

We sat on a low sofa in the snug lounge, a fireplace flame keeping the cold night at bay. Sandra sat close by, handing me a large white mug of coffee. We spoke for a while, about usual things, about family, about work, about nothing. I was trying to drag the time out, delay the possibility of rejection, and then the moment came.

'So what is your exciting news?' She had played her part, not rushing me, helping me relax as much as I could.

She could tell it was big news, or I was being unnaturally overdramatic. I suddenly felt awful. I was about to shatter all her illusions about her much-respected eldest brother, and there would be no going back.

I looked at my watch. It had gone 2 a.m. and we had to be up early, to get me back to the base.

'I'll tell you tomorrow night,' I offered.

'Noooo, I want to know what it is that has you so worried. Go on, you can tell me.' She moved slightly closer. I felt awkward, scared, embarrassed.

Would it matter if I told her tomorrow, next week? Perhaps on the phone would be better? But I would have to tell her soon anyway, or even worse, she would find out from someone else. This was a lot more difficult than I had anticipated.

'So, are you going to tell me then?' Her need to know was so apparent in her face now.

'Shall we have another coffee first?' I was stretching time, maybe it would get easier.

'You can tell me... Are you ill?' Now I felt bad, I didn't want her to worry unnecessarily about such things. 'I can cope with anything else if you're not seriously ill. Tell me... Trust me,' she added.

'I'm not seriously ill, honestly... It's possibly worse than you think, though.' How was I going to say this? She was so close, and so focused. It was the most uncomfortable place I'd been in my whole life. It would break our family apart. I knew that. I'd had all my life to see how unacceptable my news would be to my family; Sandra was the only one I had hope in. 'You may not like me after I tell you,' I said, softly now.

'Whatever it is, I will be OK with it, I will help you. I said to Stuart that the worst thing it would be was that you are very ill, anything else is better. Are you emigrating...? 'Cos if you are, we're coming with you!'

'No, I've had a problem for all my life now... and...'

'Are you gay?' It was the first time she had interrupted.

'No, I'm not gay...' I could feel that the time to tell was so close, yet I still didn't know how. I had lived through this meeting in my mind so many times. Now it was here and I was lost.

'Is it a sex change?'

I practically gulped my now cold coffee, suddenly beginning to feel emotional. Still I didn't know if I should say, but she had presented an opening and it was now or never.

'Sandra, for the past thirty-four years… every night when I went to bed, I wished that I would wake up… as a girl.' I looked into her eyes.

She had remained ever so calm, and somehow appeared totally unfazed. She began to talk and I tensed up, ready for the worst.

'That's OK, honestly that is OK, I love you and I was worried you were very ill. If that's all it is, there's no problem. I love you and I will be there for you… I will help you through this.'

This was unbelievable. My lifelong dream was to be Sandra's sister, not having to live falsely as a brother, and this was wholly acceptable to her. 'I've always wanted a sister, and now I have one, and it's great!' she said so loudly, so unreservedly. I could see her face was no longer saddened by the fear of bad news, of worry; it was happy, surprised still, but happy surprise. I asked her for a hug and we hugged for a long while. 'I'll put the kettle back on,' she said. 'This is so exciting!'

Sitting back on the sofa, with our coffee fresh and hot, I reached into a small green rucksack I had kept by my side, pulling out some photos, hoping she would want to see the real me. I passed a few into her hands. She looked through them, pausing to study each one, taking in the detail before placing it to the back of the batch in her hand.

'I'm impressed, you look great! I can't believe how pretty you look!' I blushed, but when I looked into her eyes I could see she meant what she was saying. 'I still can't believe it is you in these photos.' She turned a photo so I could see which one. I still couldn't believe what was happening. All my fears and woes for this moment had been unnecessary.

I reached into the bag again and brought out a plastic A5-sized album, decorated in red and green flowers, bursting from being overfilled with papers and even more photos. They were mostly Polaroid pictures, dating back many years, a record of my true self in the world.

'Oh, I get a portfolio!' she giggled. I laughed too.

'I thought pictures painted thousands of words!' Some of the photos gave me the opportunity to introduce other facts about my life.

I told her about my hormone creams, my laser treatment, my ever-growing wardrobe. I confessed to wearing her clothes, and we had a long laugh about that. I recounted my disastrous attempt to venture outside in her green flowery summer dress on her bicycle, and we tried to work out which dress it was. I told her of changing into a nightie underneath my bedsheets so I could sleep better. I still couldn't believe this was happening. Then our thoughts turned to the rest of the family. She agreed that it wasn't going to go well. This wasn't a time to dwell on the gloom and dark, though, this was a time of joy and excitement. Of two sisters meeting for the first time. Of chat and advice, of confession and dreams. It was a great time, the best time, a new beginning.

I slept well that night, though briefly; I had to be back at the base a few hours later. I planned to return once I had finished the morning's tasking, moving troops from Fort George around a simulated battle-field. We were also night-flying, so there was a break in the afternoon when I could see Sandra and the children again. Steve and Oz asked how my meeting had gone and all I could do was grin. 'Great!' Great was an understatement, but I couldn't tell them why.

When they arrived back at the main gate, Katie and Iain ran from the car to give me enthusiastic hugs. Sandra smiled.

'I told them… I hope you're OK with that? They were in tears be-cause they didn't want you get hurt, or for people to be nasty, or to not love you because of who you are.'

I didn't know what to say, and even if I did, I couldn't have said it.

'They want to call you Auntie, they'd love a close auntie.' Tears were forming, clouding my eyes. 'When I told Katie your name was Caz, she said, "Trust her to have a cool name!" They are happy for you.'

Time was too short to go to the house, so we went shopping in Elgin. Katie had many questions.

'How many skirts do you have? How many dresses? I liked your photos, where did you get your boots?' There were many more, together with advice on colours when we passed a cosmetics counter. It was a wonderful afternoon. I was feeling like the luckiest person in the world. Back at the main gate of RAF Kinloss, it was hugs all round. As Iain sat back in the car, he looked upset. I touched his hand through the open window, asking him not to worry. During the evening's flying, I began to feel fatigued. It had been the longest of days, but the best.

The following morning, after further troop tasking, I planned for us to route home past Sandra's house. Steve agreed, so I made the arrangements and appropriate flight bookings. I phoned Sandra to tell her when we would be overhead.

'Caz, I know you asked me not to tell Stuart until he came home, but he was concerned that I hadn't been in the house whenever he tried to phone or email. I had told him I was worried you might be seriously ill, so I had to tell him you weren't, and I knew he would be OK. He said, "Oh, is that all, why didn't you mention anything before?" I told him how big a decision it was, and he said it must have taken a lot of courage. He is quite all right about it, and wants you to stay with us. He has sent you an email. I didn't want him to because I hadn't spoken to you, but he said it would be OK.'

At home, I found Stuart's email waiting. He offered support and understanding, and wished to remain a good friend. It was wonderful, but I still dreaded telling the rest of our family.

My self-confidence had been re-energised and I began to review my decisions. If I quit the RAF, as someone who was questioning gender identity, what employer would be open-minded enough to give me a job? Why would anyone else be any more tolerant of difference? But I had already told everyone I was leaving. If anyone discovered the reasons behind my PVR, it would surely be processed as a priority, to get rid of potential embarrassment. Being gay or transgender was still illegal in the military, but I was 'financially' bonded for another three years. I had to move my life forward, there could be no delay. How would that work? I was going to transition come what may, but how should I tell the military that? And who should I tell? It was a nightmare. Sandra agreed I should see how my first appointment with Dr Reid went, but whatever happened she would support me.

Soon afterwards, I saw an article online that had originated in the *Express* newspaper. It was about a Sergeant-Major who 'wanted to stay in the Army as a woman'. I had to track this person down; her given name was Joanne Rushton. I found her listed with a network provided by a charity called the Gender Trust. Their confidential membership directory, GEMS, provided the means to contact listed transgender people anonymously. They wouldn't release contact details of members, but they would forward a letter on. It was encouraging that there might be someone else in the military feeling the same way I did. I needed someone else to talk to, someone who understood; someone who was on a similar journey would be perfect. I hoped she would receive my letter, but as the weeks went by I gave up hope. Perhaps she had already been dismissed by the Army and wasn't open to communicating. I wrote to Stonewall to ask for their help and guidance. I knew they were specifically an LGB charity and lobbying group, but I thought they might be able to help, to at least advise me on where I stood legally with the military. They said they didn't deal with transgender people. I was on my own.

My appointment with Dr Reid arrived, finally, in November 1998. The clinic receptionist had recommended a hotel nearby known to be 'LGBT friendly', and sure enough nobody batted an eyelid when I went out dressed as Caroline. It felt fantastic to be out walking in London, though I was still worried that I could be outed. Dr Reid was a relaxed, clearly very caring man, who sat on the edge of his seat as he listened patiently to my story, then offered options. He wouldn't offer direction; that was my choice alone. Hormones were deemed a good 'diagnostic test for transsexualism'. If I found the changes they brought comforting, then I could follow that path; if I found them distressing, then that would indicate a different solution. Not every patient found them comforting, for many reasons. He didn't know where I stood with remaining in the military – the timing of my transition was a decision I had to make alone – but he urged caution. When I left, I had a prescription for oestrogen hormones. I walked to a chemist on Earls Court Road and swapped it for my eagerly anticipated treasure. Back at the hotel, I excitedly began my medication. I had been invited by others in the clinic's waiting room to join them for dinner, in the same hotel as me, and it was an enjoyable evening, chatting for the first time to other people who were in the same situation as me. We spoke about clothes, about hair, makeup, shoes, weather, work, the day's news, but we also spoke of our day at the clinic, where we lived, how we were doing, relationships with family members, with friends, good experiences mixed with bad. It was all useful chat for me, just starting out on this part of my journey. We all had the same wish, though: to be accepted for who we were. I excused myself after dinner, as I had an early start in the morning. I was up at 5 a.m. to get to work on time, but I checked over and over for traces of makeup and nail varnish.

The following day, I was off to Yeovil, in Somerset, the home of the Westlands factory, for a roll-out ceremony of the RAF's very first EH 101 Merlin. It was more than a roll-out ceremony for the aircraft; it was my first full day on oestrogen hormones. It couldn't have been the medication working so quickly, surely, but I felt unbelievably happy. I met the UK Defence Secretary, several MPs, VIPs and senior RAF officers. I stood beside the aircraft, along with Tony and Dave, to answer questions and represent the RAF crews who would be flying the aircraft, then we joined them for a buffet lunch and a chance to interact further. The Merlin was looking amazing, and I was dismayed that I wasn't going to get to fly her. Even if I could stay in the service, it was less likely I would able to keep my job as aircrew.

The first thing to do was rescind my PVR. Although LGBT personnel were still not permitted in the military, it would be a harder argument for the RAF to dismiss me if I had a contract to the age of fifty-five, rather than a submitted application to leave. I phoned my Desk Officer, who said he hadn't received the formal paperwork yet but reassured me that the process would be halted once he did. I wasn't out of the woods yet: that paperwork had to disappear before I could reveal my cards.

Then, out of the blue, Joanne Rushton got in touch. We had a long chat on the phone, and it turned out she hadn't received my letter at all, but had been given my details. She had been fighting the Army system for a while and had been put on 'sick leave', waiting on the decision as to whether she could transition. It was a big comfort for us both to have someone else to discuss matters with. I agreed to meet her nearer Christmas, at an LGBT club in London.

Two months later we met. Apparently I 'looked far better' than what she was expecting – I took that as a compliment. Jo was celebrating: she had been given permission to formally transition in the New Year. I was so envious; my second appointment with Dr Reid was still six weeks away. As much as I wanted to transition now, everything had to be carefully primed. A letter from him, addressed to the medical officer at RAF Benson, could help sway the Air Force's decision process.

Nightclubs weren't my thing, but I was so pleased that I had shown the strength to go out as myself and mix with other people: it helped me to believe in myself. I had a fabulous time dancing into the early hours, though I found it very noisy and difficult to hold a conversation. I met Jan Cobb, a retired Squadron Leader who had transitioned after leaving the RAF and now worked for a public information bureau. Competing against the music, our necessarily loud and fragmented, though reassuring, chat ended abruptly when she was dragged onto the dance floor, returning briefly to announce she had 'pulled'. I was a bit disappointed that I wasn't even chatted up at all, but it was early days, I was happy with that. I wasn't concerned about sexuality for the moment.

At Christmas, I took my Land Rover up to Sandra's for her and Stuart to use over winter. They frequently got snowed in, but the main purpose was to spend Christmas and New Year together. It was the first Christmas that I received the most wonderful presents, all gendered correctly. When Stan invited himself up, offering to give me a lift back home, we considered whether to tell him, and how. Once he had settled in, Sandra introduced some hypothetical scenarios. Someone her children knew well had been outed as gay, how should we deal with that? Someone in the family was gay, what then? Someone in the family had a friend revealed to be transgender, what did we think of that? His answers weren't good. Sandra and I went to the kitchen 'to make tea', and agreed it would be bad to tell him now. The family would need to be told soon, but it would be best all together, in the New Year.

Back at work, I decided I should tell Ian. He had invited me to visit his house in Essex for a weekend, and I thought that would be the best opportunity. He was a trusted friend, but I worried that this may be too much, even for him. In nervous anticipation, I arrived at his house and met his wife Kristien and daughters Laura and Philippine. I was invited to help the girls with their homework before we went into town for some supplies. They made me feel so welcome. Later in the evening, once everyone else had gone to bed, Ian and I sat down for a chat, over a few drinks. It was like telling Sandra all over again. I didn't want to lose such a good friend, but he would find out soon anyway and I'd rather it came from me. Eventually the time felt right, and I couldn't believe how unfazed he was. It just seemed to be so matter-of-fact, he remained so calm, I couldn't have hoped for a better reaction. We chatted into the morning. He suggested there was a new senior medical officer (SMO) at Benson who would be very helpful; her name was Katie Geary. This was incredibly valuable to me, and when I finally got to bed I couldn't sleep. At breakfast, he told me he had already told Kristien. She had replied, 'Is that all?' Laura and Philippine just wanted to paint my nails, and said it made perfect sense – 'Who would want to be a boy anyway?!' I had a fantastic weekend in their company, and drove home with a huge smile on my face. My support circle was small, but stronger now.

I decided it would be best to offer my family some protection by changing my surname, so I wouldn't bring attention, or 'shame', to the family name. Katie and Iain contributed some lovely ideas, but in the end I chose one that had no links to people I knew, so I didn't offend anyone. My new surname would be Paige.

I was almost ready to inform the RAF. Jo was now working for a Colonel in the Army's Directorate of Manning Employment Branch, who had agreed to help where he could. As much as the three services all worked to the same standards and regulations, laid down by the Ministry of Defence, they all tended to 'interpret' the rules differently, or provide reasons why some rules weren't appropriate for them. Service law was binding, but it could easily be argued that, due to the medical and psychological stresses involved in transitioning gender, it wasn't appropriate for me to remain as aircrew. And if I couldn't do my job, then there would be no reason for me to be retained. As much as Jo had found budding support, my future remained uncertain. 'Dismissed on medical grounds' was an easy quick-fix for the RAF.

Finally, on 2 February 1999, I had my second appointment with Dr Reid. I explained my need to take a letter to present to my medical officer. He agreed the time was right for me to transition, and he would forward a letter as soon as he could. I wanted it to take with me, but the letter arrived by mail just three days later. I placed it on top of the pile of research information I had downloaded from the internet, happy, excited, worried, scared. I couldn't assume Katie Geary would know what this was all about, and I wanted her to be able to read it all after my appointment, so she would understand. I wanted her support for when I told the Station Commander, and I had made an appointment with him in three days' time. I had pushed the timelines right up; I didn't want any unnecessary delay. It was time to show the military my true colours.

I phoned the medical centre, asking for a double appointment with Dr Geary soonest. 'Dr Geary is at lunch, I can make you an appointment for next week, or with a different doctor?'

'No, thank you, when will she be back?'

'I don't know, but she has appointments for this afternoon.'

'I need to see her urgently, is it possible for you to call me if she has any free time after lunch?'

'I can pass that message on.'

At 1 p.m. I received a call: she would see me now. I was in the waiting room for only a few seconds before being called through to her office. My briefing pack remained in a small rucksack at my side. I sat down at the desk opposite her.

'Please excuse me if I get a little emotional when I tell you this, it is very difficult, but it's not something that I have just decided, this is something that has been with me from my very earliest days, but it has become far too much now, and I've accepted that. I need to move on, and I need your help. I'm hoping I can do this and stay in the Air Force, and I'm hoping that you will understand… Basically… I have been seeing a gender psychiatrist… and I have been diagnosed with gender dysphoria… I have a letter from him here.' She sat patiently listening, until my last few words grabbed her attention. Before she could say anything, I pulled the paperwork from my rucksack and placed it on the desk.

'All this information is for you. I don't know if you will have come across this before, but this is yours to keep hold of and read… and that's it really… I need your help!'

She reached for a telephone. 'Cancel all my appointments for the afternoon.' I breathed a huge sigh of relief. I had become a little emotional while telling her, and my voice was all over the place, but she reassured me that I had her full attention and support. Ian had been right; Katie was exactly the right person to tell. We spent the next three hours chatting as I took her through my life history and my hopes. I explained I had made an appointment with the Station Commander, that I needed her support for that, that I was worried I wouldn't be able to stay in the Air Force. I didn't know what the policy was, but Jo had transitioned in the Army three weeks ago and her Colonel was willing to speak to anyone, if requested.

I was asked to go back to work and wait. She had phone calls to make. An anxious hour or so later, I was back in her office. She was angry. The Wing Commander at RAF Medical Policy had broken her strict request for confidentiality. He had already phoned RAF Odiham and spoken to the Station Commander there, telling him that he would 'soon receive a request from someone to change sex, but that should be ignored, it was just a bloke who wanted to wear a dress, it was a phase he was going through, and that come Monday it would all be forgotten'. Fortunately, Katie had not revealed any clues to my identity, and this person had gone to the wrong Station Commander. She was livid that he had such an outrageous attitude: she had explained it certainly was not a phase, that I already had a medical background of assessment, and it was something that had taken me over thirty years to come to terms with. Then she explained that she had spoken with our own Station Commander. My stomach fell to the floor as I waited for the outcome. Katie sensed my concern. 'He wants to help where he can. He is already making enquiries regarding your future employment. He would like to see us both together tomorrow, and you should have a plan for where we go next... He doesn't have your name yet.' I already had a plan and Katie was keen to listen.

'I'd prefer to keep this on a need-to-know basis, until it comes time to actually change my identity. I'm happy for my Flight Commander, Ian Rose, to know, because he directly supervises my flying duties, and he is a friend I can trust.' I explained I had already told Ian Wright, and he was the only other person in the military who knew. Katie checked her diary.

'Can you tell your Flight Commander he has an appointment with me for Monday at 10 a.m., to speak about a medical condition that will affect your employment?' I nodded happily. It was a great plan, and it made it easier, when the time came, to tell people that it was a medical matter. She continued, 'I knew it was a serious matter when I heard you had asked several times to see me. I pulled up your medical records and, apart from your annual aircrew medicals, you haven't had any medical events since you joined!'

I laughed, 'The first time I do, it has to be something so big!' I thanked her for her amazing support, and went home excited for my future.

The next day, the Station Commander invited us to his office. As I entered, I saw his jaw drop. He motioned me to a chair. 'I wasn't expecting it to be you!' he said. Katie briefed him on the latest developments, then he reassured me that the RAF was keen to keep me, and that he had been 'given clearance from the very top, to do whatever I can to help you remain in service, and transition'. Apparently, the RAF was 'keen to get it right first time'. I wasn't expecting that; how wrong I had been.

Over the following days, I met regularly with the Station Commander and Katie. The few people we told had all taken it tremendously well. A management team was set up at the RAF Personnel Management Agency, a Group Captain and a female Wing Commander from the Equal Opportunities office. Over the coming weeks the Wing Commander was a great source of friendly chat. They were both working on where I could be based to transition. As nobody had ever done this before in the RAF, we were making it up as we went along. It had been necessary to downgrade my medical category because of the medication, which meant I couldn't fly until it was upgraded, and that wasn't going to happen until I had completed my medical transition. The minimum time permitted before I could undergo the reassignment surgery I wanted was set by care standards to one year living in a female role.

The management group suggested they needed a minimum of six months to find a posting and change all my paperwork. I understood, but my hair and nails were already longer than normal, and my shape was changing; people would notice soon. With Katie's help, we ne-gotiated it inside four months. I asked if I could take medical leave in the meantime, to begin my transition, to settle into my new life before starting at a new workplace. They authorised two months, which would help with their timelines for getting everything in place. Knowing that the RAF was happy to retain me in service could help the rest of my family understand. It was time for them to know.

I travelled north to see my family for what I knew could be the last time. Dad sensed something was amiss, but he wouldn't ask. I felt awkward in his company, embarrassed even. I knew the news that was coming, I knew this moment would never happen again, the family would never be the same, and that burden was difficult to carry. I had kept this secret for a lifetime. I had shown them clues since that first day in Malaya, but they hadn't seen, they only saw what they wanted to see. I was trying to enjoy their company, but I felt like I was be-traying them. I knew it wasn't my fault, I knew this had to be done, I had to live my own life, but that wasn't making it any easier. Maybe I had got them all wrong and they would be supportive, but decades of experience told me that was a hopeless dream. I resisted the temp-tation to say something. Sandra and I had discussed this at length, we had agreed the best way to do this, the only way to do this, and it was already unfolding. She was on her way down from Scotland with Stuart, and as they arrived I would leave.

Back at home, I sat waiting by the phone, waiting for the inevitable call, but not knowing who would make it. Breaking this news with me in the room wasn't in the interests of any one of us. Ears would close and explanation would be futile, anger and revulsion would override any emotion, and the risk of someone getting hurt, as unintentional as that might be, was too real.

Time passed slowly, I saw every second. Sandra was breaking the news gently: she carried letters from me, one for Mum and one each for Stan and Rich. I thought Mum would receive a letter better than Dad would, if she would receive it at all, so I wrote one between the two of them, but addressed to her. Each letter poured out my heart, reassured them of my love and tried to explain why it was that I had to do this, why my love for them had stopped me doing this long ago, and why this couldn't be the deciding factor for our future happiness.

The phone rang and it took all my strength to answer it.

'Is this true... what Sandra has just told us?'

'Yes,' I replied softly, scared for what was about to come.

'In which case you are dead to us... Do you understand?'

'Yes, I do... I'm sorry, I love you... Goodbye, Dad.'

Tears filled my eyes as I placed the phone back on its receiver. It had gone exactly as I feared; my life of worry had been for good reason. I had heard Dad's words before, usually as a warning or a threat. 'If you do this, you are dead to us... If you do that, you're dead to us.' He used it as emotional blackmail: any unacceptable behaviour and we would be cast out from the family. Threats to Sandra should she 'come home pregnant', to us all if we dared have mixed-race relationships, or if we took drugs, or, worst of all, if we 'became' gay. Transgender wasn't on the usual list; it wasn't even a considered possibility. The words had become more familiar as we reached teenage years, and they were words I believed, words that had been central to my need for secrecy. I had become the first to learn that they weren't just words.

I was torn between the confirmation that I had been right to guard my dreams and the guilt of relief. At least I was to be spared the eternal regret that would have come had I misjudged my parents, had their love and support been waiting when I needed it. One hour later the phone rang and, after a quick chat, Sandra handed over to Dad. He

Mum and Dad's wedding, September 1958

Me, aged six, with Rich, Stan, Sandra and Dad, Malaysia 1966

My favourite hobby, writing. Aged eleven in Lippstadt, Germany

My first Jet Provost solo, aged twenty. RAF Linton-on-Ouse, 1980

111 (F) Squadron with F4 Phantoms, RAF Leuchars, 1989
© MINISTRY
OF DEFENCE

Amongst a four-ship of Hawks during a Mixed
Fighter Force exercise, Germany c. 1992

ABOVE Flying high in Wessex 'Quebec' of 60
Squadron, Oxfordshire c. 1994

RIGHT UN Medal Parade, Kiseljak, Bosnia,
November 1995

RRFOS HQ, Kiseljak, winter 1995

ABOVE LEFT Christmas with Sandra in 1997, my last as her 'brother'

ABOVE RIGHT Flight Lieutenant Caroline Paige, RAF Cranwell, June 2000

LEFT Back on a Squadron. With Pip Harding at RAF Benson, 2001

A Merlin and Puma in formation, Oxfordshire, 2002
© MINISTRY OF DEFENCE

Christmas draw, RAF Benson, 2002
© MINISTRY OF DEFENCE

ABOVE Preparing for a mission with a US Army Apache in Bosnia, January 2004

LEFT Sarah, me and Val on holiday near Lake Maggiore, Italy, 2004

ABOVE Me and Penny
with Merlin 'X-Ray'
at Camp Smitty, Iraq,
April 2005

LEFT Operation Agile,
after an overnight ambush
mission, Al Muthanná
desert, Iraq, April 2005

LEFT Santa and Rudolph
visit Michelle and me
after our Christmas
Day mission, 2006

My first 'Stonehenge'
IDF shelter, Basra, Iraq,
April 2008

Me and Kat with Merlin
'Tango' in her new
protective revetment,
Basra, February 2009

A 'final tour' crew pic:
me, 'Tennis', 'Winnie' and
Simon. Basra, March 2009

With some of my belated fiftieth birthday celebration spa team. Kat, me, Helen and M-C, January 2010

With Sandra in the QDJ muster lunch marquee, May 2012

Invited to 10 Downing Street, July 2012

Christmas Day comes to Afghanistan. In my accommodation, 2012

International representation at the conference on transgender military service, Washington DC, October 2014. L–R: Alexandra (Sweden), me (UK), Nata (Canada), Catherine (Australia), Lucy (New Zealand)

Me, Kat and Michelle at Michelle's wedding to Andy, May 2015

'Dry Your Eyes, Princess' exhibition image, Museum of Liverpool, December 2015
© STEPHEN KING

OK! OK! SO MAPREADING'S NOT ONE OF A WOMAN'S STRONG POINTS

LADY ON BOARD

The cartoon that appeared when I was outed in *The Sun*, 14 August 2000
© DAVE GASKILL / *THE SUN*

was clearly upset, he didn't understand and admitted he couldn't deal with it, but he didn't want to expel me from the family either. I spoke to Sandra again. It had taken her a while to explain as no one believed her. Stan responded by declaring himself 'the new male heir'. The feeling amongst them had been consistent: what would their friends think of them? How could I do this to them? The rest of the family would laugh. They would be laughing stocks. No one considered what I must have gone through to make such a decision, why I had held it back so long. Support wasn't the question; hiding this 'scandal' from others was the real concern. My letters weren't opened.

After a while, I was permitted to phone my parents, but not to mention my 'problem'. Mum would answer the phone and suggest Dad was sleeping. He was always 'sleeping'. Stan and Rich refused to talk to me at all. I told Mum my timescales for changing my life, and it was agreed that I should visit home before that happened, one last time, but I could only visit as their son.

A few weeks later, I arrived home. Dad was sat back in his favourite burgundy button-holed leather armchair. He muted the TV with his remote control as I sat down on the sofa. Mum had already gone through to the kitchen.

'How was your journey up?'

'OK.'

'So… any news?' Before I could reply, he added, 'Before you talk about that… I don't want to talk about it at all… about your problem… Understand?'

The TV was unmuted and we sat in uneasy silence, re-watching the repeats he always said he'd never seen before.

The following day, I'd woken early and sat in the living room, thinking, worrying, hating myself. After a few hours, Mum came downstairs.

'You're being really calm about this,' she said, accusingly.

'Trust me, I don't feel calm.'

'It's so hard to take in, Dad gets really upset... He feels really guilty that his comments in the past stopped you talking to us... We could have got you electric shock treatment.'

Later that day, Rich phoned up. He had read my letter. 'Is what you wrote true?'

'Yes, all of it is true.'

'We'll have to talk, you'll need support.'

For a moment I saw a glimmer of hope, but that was all he wanted to say for now.

Dad came down and sat in his chair. 'Are you doing the right thing?'

'Yes, it is something I have to do.' The TV came on, the volume made talking difficult. They weren't able to talk, they didn't want to listen. I knew it was time to go. I never heard from Stan or Rich again.

10

ALL THE THINGS I HAVE GIVEN YOU

1999–2000

It was agreed that the best option for me was to move to a new base, where nobody knew me, so I could transition with the least disturbance to me and to my colleagues. I didn't want to put them under pressure by turning up one day wearing female uniform. It didn't feel right to expect them to cope with that; nobody had transitioned gender while still serving in the RAF before, and we didn't have any real idea how it would work out. So I was posted to RAF Innsworth, near Gloucester. I decided the best option was to move straight into private accommodation, rather than the mess, for the same reasons.

I was thirty-nine and I had finally begun living full-time as Caroline. It was a day I never thought would come, but one I had always dreamt of, and it was absolutely brilliant! But I wasn't confident enough to 'out' myself to my local friends and neighbours yet. Until I found new accommodation in Gloucestershire, I had to remain discreet moving outside the house. It was frustrating me, but I had come so far and I didn't want to jeopardise that in a last-minute rush. My distinctive twelve-year-old Toyota MR2 identified me locally, so, in preparation for transitioning, I had bought a second-hand dull-purple Ford Fiesta, so nobody would look twice when I drove by. I had told the salesman I was buying it as a present for my girlfriend, but I wanted it to be a surprise, so could we do all the paperwork in her name? He was happy to do that, and added, 'I did wonder why you were buying that car in that colour. It's a bit girly, isn't it!'

What I didn't need was the additional stress when, two weeks later, on my way to visit friends in Milton Keynes as the newly transitioned Caroline, a hit-and-run driver crashed into the back of the car while I was stopped at a red traffic light. When I made an emergency call, I couldn't convince the police operator that my name was Caroline. Unfortunately, the driving licence in my new name hadn't arrived yet, and when I was required to produce my current version, at my local police station in Wallingford, the officer on desk duty excused himself to 'pop into the office a second', shortly after which, two other officers peered around the doorway, one at a time, sniggering openly as they returned to their seemingly less amusing work. I wondered how they would respond if I ever needed to summon help in any emergency.

Moving jobs can be stressful for anyone. Moving home is a big event too, more so moving home on your own. Doing both, and transitioning gender all at the same time, alone, wasn't easy. Sandra was way up north in Scotland and busy with her own family, my parents and brothers didn't want to know, and what friends I had were busy with their own lives, or they didn't know yet. It was a period of huge excitement, mashed up with the most stressful time of my life. There were administrators and medical professionals trying to sort out the additional pieces of my life, new documentation, the finer details of my employment, who my boss would be, who else needed to know. But the rest was all down to me.

I had found a flat to rent in Cheltenham, a Regency spa town of wonderful character, with everything I needed on my doorstep, but the property's landlord believed that, to be 'legal', I had to sign in the birth name my background checks had revealed. A formal letter from my gender psychiatrist wasn't enough, so I had to provide two identities; the fact that these rental checks would always reveal my background wasn't a reassuring prospect. It was a small two-bedroom flat, close to the town centre, home until my Oxfordshire home sold. After that, a cheaper house would leave money to cover relocation costs, and pay my anticipated medical expenses.

I didn't know anyone locally yet, but not long after I had settled in I was paid a visit by people who would be looking after me when I began my work. Flight Lieutenant John Martin commanded Personnel Holding Flight, a small unit that managed people who weren't administrated by their parent base. He quickly came across as the kind of person I could trust. He was accompanied by his boss, Sarah, someone else who quickly put me at ease. I had been nervously expecting their visit, and although my wardrobe wasn't very full, I had tried everything on more than once, wanting to make a good first impression. Over a cup of tea, they reassured me that I would be looked after and that John would be taking on the responsibility of managing all my paperwork and administrative matters. Not long after they left, John phoned me to say they had both been very impressed, and the only discussions in the car were complimentary. I was thrilled he had thought to phone and tell me that; I had been worried about what people thought. Very few people had seen me as Caroline, and they were the first in the RAF to do so. Their reactions gave an important insight into how I would be welcomed returning to work in a female role. My next visitor was Group Captain Martin Stringer, a tall, lean, respectful man, equally quick to put me at ease. We chatted about the job I would be doing for him, and whether I had any concerns, and that his aim was to do what was best for me. I realised how fortunate I was to have such people on my side and going out of their way to help me adjust to my new life. These two visits allayed so many fears and lifted much stress from my shoulders.

My relationship with Sandra had broken down and I had been going through a bad patch. I had wanted to tell her how amazing it was to be starting work as the true me, and how helpful people had been, but all my calls were going to voicemail. Then I received an email saying she was too busy to talk, and that I should write an email. When I did, it became apparent she had totally misread my message. I only wanted to tell her my exciting news, maybe get some tips on what to wear for my first day at work, but when I added that I was nervous how that might go, it evidently triggered alarm that I might be wanting to unload emotional distress and problems on her. She was having doubts about our relationship; she said she 'needed time'. Our relationship was on the verge of collapsing totally. I was distraught; she was the only family member I had, the only one who would talk to me. I didn't know what I had done wrong. I didn't know she was struggling with family matters, that she felt additional worries might overwhelm her. It got worse when she added, 'Even Katie and Iain are having doubts... I still love you, but I'm not sure where it can go from here.' I suddenly felt very alone. I became depressed, and the only safe way I could deal with that was to sleep. Getting to sleep wasn't easy, but it kept my dark pessimism at bay. It took a while to realise that Sandra was finding my transition as stressful as I was. She was having to deal with our parents and brothers, and she was the only one who had been taking my side, speaking on my behalf. They were constantly arguing about what I had done, how embarrassing it was for them, how difficult it was for them, asking whether I realised what I had done to them. Sandra argued, 'If it's difficult for you, how difficult do you think it is or was for Caz? She's the one who's had to deal with this, on her own, for so long, she's the one who kept it all bottled up, out of respect and love for you!' But it was getting to her. She had her own young family too, and Stuart worked overseas much of the time. I hadn't foreseen how hard it could be for her. Being in the middle of all this had clearly broken her. I decided to leave her alone for a while, hopeful that she would bounce back. For the moment, though, I was on my own, and that was hard.

One of the things I hated most about my life was having to shave. It was unfair that I had to do so every day, especially when I had never developed much body hair. I would have gladly swapped, for the hair to be where it could be easily covered up. Living openly as Caroline had made it an even more intolerable burden, a painful reminder of what was wrong with my body, my life. Unfortunately, facial hair was seen by the National Health Service as a 'cosmetic inconvenience' and therefore it wasn't willing to cover treatment or cost. It was a financial burden I knew I had to bear, and was another reason for my decision to sell my house, but all these extra costs were adding up. I was recommended an electrolysist near Congresbury, in north Somerset, which offered a discreet facility to access but meant a two-hour round-trip by car. Closer options were too public. To have electrolysis required hair long enough for tweezers to get hold of, which, for me, meant three days of visible hair growth, and that was incredibly distressing. It also meant taking a day's leave, on top of a weekend each time, so I wouldn't have to go to work with facial hair! It would have been far too embarrassing to bear, especially when regulations stated that personnel were to be clean shaven, and that was only ever expected to apply to males. Visible hair would only be a trigger for mockery and confusion. Another issue was getting to and from my car without being seen closely. I hadn't realised how painstakingly slow the treatment process was, or how painful. Being ginger with fair skin was proving to be particularly cruel: the new laser treatments promised to remove hair in a five- or six-month treatment cycle, but not if that hair was red.

Now I was living openly, it was appropriate to let some valued friends know about my new life before the rumours reached them first. I wrote individual, open and honest letters, by hand, and was delighted to receive some comforting offers of support and continued friendship in return, but I guessed that those who didn't reply didn't want to know. It was heartening to hear from Frosty, and more so when he phoned up and we chatted for hours.

My first day at work had arrived. Nervously, I stepped out of my car and walked over to the building that housed the Personnel Flights. I was dressed smartly in a beige two-piece suit, with a knee-length skirt, single-breasted jacket and brown court shoes. My hair had become overly curly, with hair extensions adding the length I needed until my own hair could grow long enough for my liking. The RAF had agreed I could wear civilian clothes for the first few months, as my body was still developing, complicating the uniform issue, and this allowed me the added touch of femininity that would present a softer image and boost my confidence. A young senior aircraftwoman showed me around the building and then the station, before leaving me with Sarah and Group Captain Stringer. We chatted for about forty minutes before I was led over to the headquarters building where I would be working. I was disappointed to learn that everyone in my new office had been briefed about my arrival and my background. It had been decided it was the right thing to do, without my involvement, but for me it was a disaster. A key reason for me beginning my life in a new workplace, where nobody knew my background, had just been destroyed.

From behind a desk in a long, open-plan office, I observed a mix of twenty or so civilian and Air Force employees, all busy working at computer screens. My desk was beside a window, in the corner of the room, my back to a wall. Walking into that room, I knew that everyone in there knew I was a transgender woman. I had wanted them to get to know me as a person first, as a woman, not as something unusual or different, so there wouldn't be any worries about how to interact with me, they wouldn't prejudge me. When the Group Captain left me to 'settle in', I felt self-conscious, on show and lonely. I knew that wasn't the intention at all, and they would have been upset I felt that way, but I did. There was an awkward silence in the room. People were doing their best not to look at me, in case I should think they were staring. I couldn't help but think, had a female worker started in a new office she would have been introduced to all the staff as herself, and the ice would have been broken. I felt like I was sat behind a full continental ice-shelf, not a small plastic and metal desk.

I tried to keep busy, reading the work my boss had placed in the in-tray, glancing up occasionally, observing the people in the room. What were they thinking? Were they happy with me being there? Normally, I would have been the first person to welcome a 'stranger' to a group or a room. But I couldn't make the first move here; I had to know if they accepted me, if they wanted me to be here. They had to offer that welcome freely for it to mean anything. After a very long thirty to forty minutes, a middle-aged civilian lady in glasses, with a nice smile and prominent rosy cheeks, approached my desk.

'Hi, I'm Rose West, welcome to our office. Would you like to join me for a coffee?' The ice-shelf had been cracked, and a good friendship began. After Rose said hello, a few more people came across and introduced themselves. Finally I began to believe I would be safe working here. All it takes is a 'hello'.

My boss invited me to join him for lunch, and we were joined by the Command Press Relations Officer, Glynn. Apparently the rumour network was already busy, especially in the Flying Training Office in the same building. Another fallout of pre-briefing people about my background. It didn't surprise me, because that office was full of aircrew, mostly fast-jet aircrew, so if the rumour said I was an aviator they would have a strong urge to know who it was. Glynn felt that if the press got hold of my story it would go to print, so I should be prepared for a media-led invasion of my privacy. It was agreed I should go to London to meet with the Ministry of Defence press relations team and they could give me advice. I was also introduced to Jennifer Griffiths, the Deputy Command Press Relations Officer. Jennifer offered me plenty of good advice and we quickly became friends too. I was often invited for a weekend's stay with her and her partner, Jack, a veteran RAF senior officer Nimrod pilot, at their home near Gloucester. I learned a lot of useful information in London, though the principal lessons I took away were 'Only say things you would be OK with seeing in print' and 'Control the interview: you don't have to answer every question.' We considered pre-empting any sensationalised 'outing' with a positive release, demonstrating open diversity and inclusion, but all the evidence, at that time, suggested it would be unwise to trust in the press.

Back in my office, something disturbed me. I must have sensed staring eyes, hungry for recognition, and as I looked up I saw a familiar face, looking awkwardly backwards over a dropped shoulder. A wide grin appeared, then he hurried away. I recognised him as surely as he had recognised me: Fozzie, an ex-Buccaneer navigator I had known since nav school. He had no reason to be walking through our corridor, but his mission was successful, and now everyone would know my identity. I waited for the phone calls and further 'lost' aircrew walking by my desk with straining necks, but that didn't happen. For the time being, they appeared content with just knowing the secret.

Working at Personnel Headquarters was a perfect opportunity to help evolve the first draft of a document written to provide 'Guidance to Commanders, Supervisors and Personnel Regarding the Retention and Recruitment of Transsexual Personnel'. It was evident the MoD was committed to retaining such individuals, yet the ban on lesbian, gay and bisexual service personnel was still in force.

Through my work with equality and policy staffs, I developed two further very close friendships, with Val Marden and Gail Kinvig, two ladies who would play an important part in my confidence as an individual and my inclusion in things everyone else would consider routine. Val was a similar age to me. She was an eccentric five-foot-three lady with a passion for historic houses and collecting antique toy bears and other furry creatures. We were like-minded and her taste in fashion became a handy attribute for advising me, though unlike her, I never wore trousers. I had had enough of those, and skirts added confidence in my appearance. Her petite frame initially made me feel conspicuously tall when we stood together in public view. I'd become self-conscious of my five-foot-ten height, which made me stand out amongst a group of girls, but as our friendship grew, that anxiety faded. Besides, I wasn't always the tallest girl in the room; Gail was a sociable, athletic lady who enjoyed adventurous sports such as skiing and offshore sailing, and she was proud of her Harley-Davidson motorbike. John Martin was also helping my confidence to grow. He and his

wife Glenis had invited me to their family home, and their two young
daughters were just as positive and accepting. He was a dark-haired
Welshman, about five foot eight, who wore black-rimmed glasses and
had a sharp wit and wonderful people skills. He frequently bantered
with me, 'One day you'll write a book, and I probably won't be in it!'
Occasionally, at weekends, he would arrange to meet up for coffee or
lunch. I still had no family to call on and he was an open ear with a
total respect for confidentiality. One night, I was invited around to
Val's home. It was her husband Andy who had suggested it, and I got
on very well with both. With Val, I gained the close friendship and
respect of a female friend who had only ever known me as Caroline
and that was an important milestone for me. Andy was a six-foot air
traffic control officer whose work happily favoured his passion for
military aircraft spotting. He remembered meeting me before, after
joining an exchange visit with my Phantom squadron to a Belgian Air
Force F-16 fighter squadron at Beauvechain Air Base, near Brussels.
Thankfully my image was a seemingly distant one to recall. It didn't
mean I valued my longer-standing friends any less because they had
known my previous life, but the closest of these friends were male,
and that had changed things. I had to respect that. Andy knew how
to boost my confidence: when I left their house, he would voice his
opinions to Val; apparently, I 'scrubbed up well'!

My work with the Group Captain was focused on Ethnic Minority
Recruitment Policy; he was the 'Policy Desk', which in practice was
just him and a desk! He had snapped up the opportunity to have a
junior officer to help with the routine matters of policy administra-
tion, though he included me in some of his visits out into the commu-
nities too. We were trying to understand why the recruitment figures
for ethnic minority personnel were below the national average percentage of ethnic population. It was a busy job, but he was also trying

to give me the best chances too – I could see that, and I was grateful. He detached me to work with Val on equalities matters and I was sent to RAF Cranwell to work at the Department of Recruitment and Selection, known as Doris.

At Cranwell, rumours soon began to spread. It didn't help when I was stopped by the RAF Police and taken to the guardroom for an identity check. I still only had a paper representation of an ID card, so they wanted to know who I worked for and who could vouch for me. They had remained polite throughout, and I was content they were doing their job, but my boss wasn't happy they had taken me to the guardroom. It made me think that maybe I wasn't blending in as much as I thought I was. Then, walking to breakfast in Daedalus House Officers' Mess one day, I stepped into a corridor just behind two young officers. They said 'Good morning!' to me, then continued their conversation as we all walked towards the dining hall.

'Did you hear there's an officer who's had a sex change living here?'

'Yes, I saw her the other day. She's living in a caravan on the mess carpark... looks like a bloke.'

I wondered if they would be shocked to know she was living in the same mess accommodation as them, and was walking alongside them, but at least they were using the correct pronouns. If, for some reason, a female officer was living in a caravan outside the mess, which was highly irregular, I couldn't think of a worse misunderstanding for her to suffer.

I met a young officer called Mary Jones, and she became a great mentor. I'd never had to put my hair up before, into a regulation bun, so she taught me how to do that. Playing with hairstyles and accessories was a gift most girls learned well before they reached their thirties. It was a simple thing but it gave me great pleasure, though I still preferred my hair down and long. I was very conscious of my neck:

it wasn't as slender as I'd have liked – in fact, it seemed more like a tree trunk to me. It was the product of twelve years of neck muscles straining to hold my head high while pulling high levels of G during air combat in the Phantom and the Hawk.

The Careers Information Recruiters Training School was commanded by Squadron Leader Stephanie Johnson, a lovely lady whom I knew from her time as an admin officer at RAF Leuchars. She had sent a positive message of support after Val had discussed my working with her, and now we had a good catch-up over coffee. I would be observing one of the courses she ran, from the back of their classroom. Any person posted to serve in an RAF careers office had to do this course, so it was a mixture of all ranks and trades. I interacted with the commissioned officer students during coffee breaks and we all got on OK. Then, one day, the mood of the course changed. I didn't catch the trigger but they all downed tools and demanded to know why there was someone in the classroom who had changed sex. 'Why was that allowed?' 'Why were they still in the military?' I was asked directly, with an angry tone, 'Why are you in my Air Force?' I was surrounded by a cacophony of demands and complaints. They were genuinely aggrieved that I was serving in the same Air Force as they were.

I was shocked and disappointed: what had changed their attitudes? Stephanie invited me to go for a coffee while she had words with them. It wasn't great timing: just the day before, I'd been called to Stephanie's office. 'I've received a message for you to call your sister as soon as possible. You can use my phone, dial 0 first.' As she stepped out, I knew it wasn't going to be good news. Thankfully my relationship with Sandra was back on solid ground; whatever had unsettled it was gladly forgotten.

'Don't worry but…' – too late, I was worried – '… Dad has had a heart attack and is in the intensive care unit at Arrowe Park Hospital. He is OK at the moment, they're going to keep him in… They have told me not to tell you, they don't want you to visit.' 'They' were Stan and Mum. I was worried before, but now I was angry and upset. How dare they tell me I couldn't visit my own dad in intensive care! I agreed with Sandra that it wouldn't do him any favours if there was an argument at his bedside, so I reluctantly agreed not to go, but I didn't want that to sound like I didn't care. I couldn't send flowers or a card, as I wasn't meant to know. Sandra reassured me he was awake and talking, and feeling very sorry for himself, and that I would be told the minute there was any change in his condition. I knew my transition had been hard on him, but if I thought for a moment that it could cause his death, that would destroy us both.

So, when the class at Cranwell had downed tools and demanded I leave 'their' Air Force immediately, it was the straw that broke my back. After dealing with the group, Stephanie joined me in her office and we had a chat for a while. She was appalled that they had reacted the way they did, and had questioned their own fitness to serve in careers offices with such attitudes. As with all incidents like this, though, it proved to be a vocal minority who had caused such strong negative responses. They had taken advantage of the shock and confusion caused by revealing something without all the facts. They made everyone else think it was wrong and unlawful to 'have a transsexual in the military'. I could see why that argument would be offered, as, incredibly, it was still against military law for someone to be LGB in the Armed Forces, and people still believed being 'transsexual' was a matter of sexual identity. I didn't like the word for that very reason: 'sexual' frequently drove people to that conclusion. The term 'transgender' wasn't in common use at this time, but I didn't like that word either. It implied I had crossed or changed gender, but my own gender had always been the same. I hadn't changed; it was other people's perceptions of my gender that had changed.

The outspoken students in the room were quick to back down when they realised their careers were now more questionable than mine was. In the mess bar later that evening, some officer students explained that the views expressed weren't theirs, and I enjoyed a nice evening in respectful company, with best wishes offered for my dad. But I had seen evidence now that my acceptance wasn't going to be straightforward within the wider military.

Two days later, Dad was allowed home from hospital. Mum answered the phone but said nothing about his heart attack. I couldn't mention it because then they would know Sandra had told me. Mum said only that Dad was tired and would call me back when he was rested. A month later was his birthday and this time he did speak to me, but all he said was, 'Listen, all the things I have given you I want back. They belong to the male side of the family, you have to give them back, they're not yours any more, understand?!' He was talking about a few books and bits of memorabilia from his Army days. That was the only thing he ever said that almost acknowledged my gender. The fact that he wouldn't talk about it made it more difficult for us both: I couldn't help him to understand, I couldn't tell him it wasn't his fault, it wasn't my fault, it was nobody's fault, it was just the way things were. Not talking about it was eating him up.

Back at Innsworth, I was finally issued my photo ID. The photo wasn't great, but it was far better than my previous one. I never expected I would see this day; it was just a fantastic feeling. Just as pleasing was my new passport – better, in fact, because it had a nicer photo. I was excited when Val suggested we should get together with another friend of hers, Sarah Duffy, a Wing Commander dentist, and all go on holiday together, somewhere abroad. It was a great excuse to use my new passport.

Uniform issue didn't go well, though. The Officer Commanding Supply had sent an open email out, cc-ing many people who had no right to know. What was worse was that he wrote: 'Flight Lieutenant Paige will be visiting Clothing Stores tomorrow at 10 a.m. He is to be issued female uniform in accordance with the following list, in replacement to his male uniform.' When I showed Group Captain Stringer, he was outraged, immediately phoning the author of the email and dismissing me while he gave him a thorough and frank debrief. The gossip network was growing – but my social network was growing too. Rose West's young adult daughter, Sarah, proved to be a great shopping companion, and when I was invited to a family home now, it was nice just talking about everyday things.

Conversation on telephones was a different matter, however. Hormones made no difference to a 'male' voice post-puberty, and on the phone I was constantly being called 'sir'. Saying my name was Caroline always raised questions, sometimes rudely put questions, so I began to use 'Caz' as my default name. Caz was gender-free, so it became the easy option. It had been used first by Krystyna and Elaine when I had stayed with them in Manchester; they'd joked that Caroline was too long a name to say all the time. It was painful being reminded that I was different; simple things hit harder than most people would realise. Simple things added up, and people didn't see that what seemed like something of no consequence to somebody briefly in my company would be a cumulative event that became insufferable to me. I asked my doctor if I could try speech therapy again. I had already tried it very briefly in Oxford, but it hadn't made any difference.

Dr Hannam was a civilian doctor contracted to provide healthcare on the base. He was a very understanding person, but just being a doctor didn't mean he was automatically familiar with what it meant to be transgender, or that he understood, or that he was supportive. I had already suffered senior medical people who weren't supportive by any means. Gender dysphoria was now a recognised medical term, replacing the old label of 'gender disorder', which had wrongly implied a mental illness. The transition process and psychiatric assessments were there to protect any people with mental illness from making the wrong life-changing decisions. The old assumptions that equated a desire to transition with a mental disorder had engendered an ignorance and a misunderstanding that were very difficult to shake off.

But being transgender meant knowing exactly who I was, and being in full control of my mind: it was my body that was incongruent. No one chooses to be transgender: it is a card that is dealt before birth. A person might not come to realise that for a while, for many different reasons, but it's not a choice. The only 'choice' involved is whether you choose to live your life to its fullest or not, just as anyone else does. If that means having to reveal you are transgender, then the consequences of that have to be endured for ever. Who on earth would freely choose something that would likely take away everything that they loved, their family, their friends, their job, their life? It is a soul-destroying realisation, and for me it was important to make it right, as much as I could.

However, there was still a lot of resistance to helping people who had gender identity issues, and one of the biggest stumbling blocks was healthcare. After my local primary care trust (PCT) had unequivocally rejected any possibility of funding surgery, Dr Hannam had tried so hard to find a way. He tried Cheltenham because I lived there, and Gloucester because I was posted to a base within its duty of care. Neither PCT would fund 'sex reassignment surgery', as it was known then, even though gender dysphoria was listed as an NHS medical condition. All NHS treatments are supposed to be provided equally for members of the armed forces, wherever they are based, but both of these PCTs disagreed. Selling my house had been the only option. Consequently, Dr Hannam was keen to help in any other way he could. Speech therapy was an NHS option that could be provided with a doctor's recommendation. I only had a few appointments, but I learned to 'speak from my stomach', and projecting my voice as though it was coming from just in front of my mouth, rather than from my throat. This did round my voice off slightly, but it didn't improve on the pitch and that was disheartening. It meant I would still have issues using the phone and speaking out loudly in public. It sounds daft, but I decided I could never own a dog, because I might need to shout out and that would attract unwanted attention.

I was beginning to miss my flying. I hadn't flown for five months by now, so I joined a local flying club at Gloucester Airport. The owner of Staverton Flying School, Jennie, encouraged me to join the British Women Pilots' Association (BWPA), and that led me to some fun social activities with like-minded ladies. Soon I was back in the air flying Cessna 172s – a larger aircraft than I needed, but I liked the extra room the four-seat 172 had in the cockpit, and it was a bit faster than the two-seat 152. It made me more determined to get back on a squadron, but there wasn't any point rushing back just yet. My medical needed upgrading first, and there was reluctance to do that until I had completed my planned surgery, set for June 2000, seventeen months after I'd informed the RAF of my intentions. It was a long time, but this was all still new territory for personnel and medical management teams, and for me! It was trial and error. In the future, transgender aircrew would be able to upgrade their medical status after a short settling-in period on hormones, until the next trigger for review, and remain on a flying unit if they wished; that would only come from the lessons we learned now. But anyway, the aircraft I wanted to go back to, the Merlin helicopter, hadn't come into service yet. If I went back to flying a different aircraft now then I wouldn't be able to swap to the new one for a few years, so the timings could all work out just nicely.

On my next visit to Dr Hannam, I was told that I was required to visit an RAF psychiatrist at RAF Brize Norton in Oxfordshire. When Katie had previously enquired about this, we had been told it wasn't required because they had no gender specialist psychiatrist. Now, apparently, it would help to get my flying categorisation back – and they felt they needed to learn from me about concerns specific to being transgender because another transgender individual had now made themselves known. I was aware of this because I had been asked to become her mentor, and to advise her personnel management staffs on the intricacies of managing any possible transition. I was beginning to realise the importance of getting things right for those who would be following in my footsteps.

The Wing Commander psychiatrist reassured me that there was no reason why I shouldn't be able to return to a flying career, as long as a medical board judged my medical assessments to be good enough. He spent the rest of the appointment trying to understand the complexities of being transgender, and how relationships with my family, friends and colleagues had changed. I had to be very careful not to endanger my flying career. Many people in his field of expertise didn't understand, or even accept, what being transgender meant – my previous experience bore that out. It could be easy for him to jump to the wrong conclusion, especially as he had admitted to not being practised in such matters. He was keen to learn from my experience, however, so I agreed to further appointments. Then I got a phone call from Oz at the Rotary Wing Operational Evaluation and Training Unit. Oz had previously tracked me down and offered his support;

now he explained that they had recently become inundated with calls from other units, asking if the rumours about me were true. Surely a media invasion wasn't far behind.

By now I had bought and moved into my own brand-new two-bed apartment in the heart of Cheltenham. I became well acquainted with the sales team and made friends with a lovely lady called Dianne King, who kept inviting me over to her on-site sales office for coffee and a chat, or popping over to see how I was settling in. Before I knew it, the officers' mess Christmas draw was calling, a black-tie event that gave me the excuse to go looking for a beautiful dress, with Val's help. We met up in London when I was having some hair extensions taken out; my own hair was long enough now. In a local charity shop we came across a cute Merrythought bear looking for a home. Val bought him with her collection in mind, then thoughtfully presented him to me. His given name was Fred Bear, though he was in great condition! It was so nice being able to display cute things openly in my own home. He joined my Thornton's Toffee bear, whom I'd named Vasco, after the famous Portuguese navigator, because he had his own backpack and always accompanied me on my travels, as well as 'Bear', a bear I'd had since I was born, and they all became uplifting companions. I found a beautiful metallic-silver ankle-length evening dress, too, and when I went to the draw, with my hair and makeup all done, another of my childhood dreams had, unbelievably, come true.

I couldn't believe the year had gone so quickly – and what a year it had been. The unthinkable had happened, and 2000 promised to be even better. I was invited to Val and Andy's to celebrate the New Year, where I finally met Sarah, Val's Wing Commander dentist friend, a five-foot-four lady with a bob of thick black hair, and a soft Edinburgh lilt. After a fun night, we all went into the crowded streets to join the neighbourhood in counting in the new millennium. As the clock passed midnight, I was kissed on the lips, by a young man I had never met before. I didn't dare say anything, lest he hear my voice and get upset, but he moved quickly on to the next lady to kiss. 2000 would be an incredibly important year for me.

It was meant to be a minimum of twelve months from formally beginning my transition to the earliest date for surgery, but when the surgeon's office phoned to say he couldn't make the original appointment but they could offer an earlier one, I leapt at the opportunity. I had to arrange a referral agreement from a second gender psychiatrist, and from the surgeon himself, so, with three formal assessments, my mental wellbeing was certified the fittest it could ever be. Had I gone down the NHS route, I would be waiting at least a couple of years more. As the day approached, I became nervous, but excited at the same time. There was always risk associated with major surgery, but I would soon be able to get back on with my life. Two days before, I received a phone call from Mum; this was unusual. She asked if there was anything exciting happening. 'Well, I'm off to hospital on Monday, that's quite exciting!'

'What's that for?'

I told her – she knew, but had chosen to forget – and the phone went quiet. 'I'll call back tomorrow.' She never did.

I was delighted when John and Sue Hunter offered to drive me to the hospital. Sue was a lady from SSAFA (the Armed Forces charity Soldiers, Sailors and Airmen's Families Association) I had got to know well. We arrived at the hospital in West Sussex, after a brief stop for a pub lunch, and I was greeted and taken to my hospital room for the usual paperwork to be completed. The surgeon called by and made me feel at ease. There were blood tests to do, and all the usual pre-meds that go with major surgery, but when John and Sue left, I suddenly felt all alone. I vainly tried to sleep, against the noise of birds chirping away outside my room, and early the next morning, after more questionnaires, I dressed in a white surgical gown and waited on my bed. Now I felt frightened. Even though I knew this was the right thing for me, emotions were running high, and there was a deep sense of loneliness. Unfortunately, Sandra was too far away in Scotland, and the rest of my family didn't want to know, or hadn't been told about me yet. It was confusing being so scared when I wanted this more than anything. Was I doing the right thing? Yes! Why was I even thinking that? Will I be OK? What happens if it goes wrong? I'll have to deal with that! I had so many questions; thank goodness a cheery med team appeared and I was wheeled away on a trolley.

I woke up in the recovery room feeling cold, even though I was covered in several blankets; my body temperature had apparently dropped to almost hypothermic levels. I slept for a while. The next time I woke up, I had some lovely flowers from Sandra, then the phone rang, over and over. It was so nice to hear people's voices: Val and Andy, then Sandra, Sue, John, Dick and Liz, and more, even my boss. More flowers, from caring friends. And I had visitors, Jennifer and Jack, who had driven over 150 miles, and Penny and Kate, two transgender friends I had been visiting in Milton Keynes when my car had been hit, had driven 100 miles. Oz and his wife Trish, and Joanne visited too. Gail was on her way but had a car crash, so sent her apologies – thank goodness she was OK. The nursing staff were wonderful and the surgeon was happy, so I was happy. For several days, I couldn't see much more than bandages covering my genital area, but when I could see, all I saw was me: this was how my body should have looked when I was born, though a lot younger! This would have triggered a whole different life; I would have had the treasured childhood joys and cares of any other girl.

Not all people with gender dysphoria want, or can have, such surgery, for many reasons. There might be financial, medical or age-related issues, family pressures, social pressures, personal or other factors – but it was right for me. I was held in a few days longer than expected, mostly because my temperature was now too high and I was needing tablets to sleep, besides a couple of other 'need to know' factors, but eight days after my arrival I was collected and driven home by Val, then I was left to sleep. I had a few weeks to recover fully before returning to work, and I had plenty of visitors in that time, though sadly no family. I hadn't heard from my parents or brothers at all. With no follow-up interest from local healthcare units, I became totally reliant on the goodwill of friends, and they were marvellous. Why had it taken so long for me to do this? It was wonderful. There was no celebration; now my body matched my identity, and I could get on with my life properly. Now I could return to flying, it was time to see my Desk Officer.

Three months later, I was summoned to Group Captain Stringer's office.

'Caz, close the door.'

'Uh-oh!' I thought.

'MoD Media Ops has been on the phone. *The Sun* newspaper has your details. They have asked the MoD for any comments before they go to print.'

I was shocked. I had been a serving female officer for sixteen months without any press attention, and it had lulled me into a false sense of security, neglecting the ever-present risk of public exposure.

'What are they going to say?'

'They say you are a Squadron Leader about to go to Northern Ireland, and they have your name; the rest is just made up, I believe.'

'Well, it sounds like it's all made up, sir, unless you haven't told me about a promotion and posting!' I laughed. But this wasn't funny: if it was being made up by *The Sun* that meant it was going to mock and shock, coercing unaware readers into believing a transgender person was nothing more than a laughing stock. I had seen it before, others falling foul of the same prejudiced and hurtful narrative. I would be considered an embarrassment – and that would sway military opinion too. Anywhere I went, animosity would follow, or even precede, my arrival. But worst of all, what of my family? They would be outed too, and humiliated in the worst possible way. I had told them this day would come, but they had taken the ostrich approach. They were embarrassed to tell anyone about me. As far as the wider part of our family were concerned, for the past sixteen months I had been living in Canada and I wasn't coming back.

'Is there any way it can be stopped?' I asked. I wondered who might have exposed me.

'No, I don't believe so.'

'Would it be possible to speak to them then… put my side of the story across, at least it might balance it up a little, make it more positive, more informative?'

'I can have words with the press and media team if you wish?'

'Yes please, sir.'

An hour later, the boss called me back. 'The MoD is happy, we need to get you prepped. They're going to provide support, so it's going to happen at the MoD Main Building in London. I've had a word with Jennifer and Glynn, and Jennifer will go to London with you.'

The MoD Main Building is a 1915 design, eight-storey stone detached building, set in the heart of London, off Horseguards Parade and Whitehall. After clearing security, Jennifer and I were escorted up to the Media and Corporate Communications section, where we were met by an Air Commodore and two other senior officers, who each reassured me they were there for support and advice, and to make sure I wasn't persuaded to say anything I didn't want to, or wasn't meant to. After a short while, I was introduced to John Kay, the chief reporter from *The Sun*. He was a friendlier man than I thought he would be; we had a good chat about travel, weather and London, and we even shared a few laughs too. Then everything became more serious and we got down to business. After a few questions about how I knew myself to be female, he put his notebook aside and relaxed more into his chair. He looked at me, pausing, seemingly looking for inspiration as to where he was going to go with the questions.

'OK... I think I'd like to do this as a human interest story... if I may?'

I was happy with that, as were Jennifer and my mentor team.

I felt more confident, that he was being more positive, more sensitive. I was pleased because I thought I must have made a good impression. The questions and the time flew by, then he closed his notepad. 'I would like to go back to my office now and write that up, then I'll fax over a copy for your perusal. If you're happy with that, we'll go to print.'

I was totally taken aback. I wasn't expecting him to make such an offer, but I wasn't going to turn it down. After a short while, he was as good as his word. There were a few statements I thought didn't read right, so I was even more pleasantly surprised when he agreed to edit them as requested! After I suggested a second couple of changes, I was advised by the Media Ops team that I 'should allow him at least some journalistic freedoms'! The following Monday, I received an early morning phone call from Val. 'Caz, you're on TV!'

'What do you mean on TV, how?'

'They're reviewing the front pages of today's papers, and you're on one!' I missed the TV show, but I pulled into a petrol station on my way to work and there, in the plastic weather-cover facing me, was my face and the headline 'Sun Exclusive: Sex Change for RAF Top Gun'. I felt so embarrassed buying the paper, but thankfully the till operator didn't pay any attention. I couldn't believe it was front-page news. Inside it covered two other pages, and on page seven was a cartoon by Dave Gaskill, the paper's cartoonist. A Phantom, flying over some moon craters, with the Earth in the distance, had a sign on its tail saying 'Lady Onboard'. The navigator was holding up a map, and a speech bubble said, 'OK! OK! So map reading's not one of a woman's strong points!' It made me laugh. There were a few lines in the article that read differently to what I meant, and media use of the term 'sex change' had always inferred deviation, or that someone had just whimsically chosen to be a different gender, encouraging people to ridicule those it identified in this way, making it a hurtful term. But, given this newspaper's track record, the article was thankfully positive. However, now I was at the mercy of the public, and my life became a rollercoaster again.

I had phoned my parents to warn them, but they still wouldn't contact my aunties and uncles to explain. How could they possibly believe no one would notice?! Front-page headlines destroyed that idea, and soon their phone rang hot. My Auntie Val was particularly angry, and not at me. She wanted to know why she hadn't been given the opportunity to support me, and she was shocked my parents weren't doing so. I wrote a letter to her explaining why I hadn't spoken with her myself, then we spoke for hours on the phone. She was so understanding, and I was so saddened that I had never had the courage to confide in her before. The paternal side of my family stood at Dad's shoulder, and their love and respect for me had turned to hate. I had 'ruined my family, destroyed their good name'. I was devastated that they felt this way, yet from most of the maternal side of my family came love and offers of support. I had gained a closer relationship with aunties, uncles and cousins that I hadn't seen for a long time. The positive and negative sides of exposure now split my family in half; it was just what I had feared. My biggest worry was the counsel my parents were now getting: it was going to drive us even further apart. Had Dad's siblings persuaded him it wasn't a bad thing, I know that would have helped him.

Then Group Captain Stringer said those immortal words: 'Caz, have you seen the comments on the PPrune website?'

'No, what is that?'

'Nothing, don't go on there!' Easier said than done – now I had to know!

PPrune stood for the Pilots Rumour Network: it was an unofficial online forum, and its members were mostly RAF aircrew, but others could join. And it wasn't good. I was being ripped apart. I could see why I had been told not to visit the site, but it was too late. It was all overly negative and demeaning; challenging my mental fitness for flying and military service, presuming a shocking 'man-in-a-dress' appearance, predicting unwelcome receptions on squadrons. Their own identities, of course, remained hidden behind their log-on character nickname or call sign. What hurt more was the female fast-jet aviator joining in; I somehow imagined more respect from her. Although outspoken criticism of my continued service wasn't the preserve of male voices, they were dominant. Now I was truly seeing what people thought of me. Not just that – it was my peers, and it looked like a flying unit was going to become an unwelcoming place to be.

'Experts' began coming out of the woodwork, all over. A retired Army Colonel was wheeled out, declaring himself an 'expert', questioning my retention, insisting that people like me 'had no place in the military', I 'would be a liability on operations', I 'couldn't be issued a weapon', because I had 'a mental health problem', and if I couldn't bear a weapon I 'had no place in the military'. He moaned that the military was short of equipment, yet it was paying for sex changes for people with 'serious psychological issues'! Actually, it wasn't paying, and besides, even though equipment and healthcare were two completely separate budgets, training someone else to do my job would cost millions, rather than the thousands of pounds to help. And a replacement would take years to train but still have none of the military experience-based skills that I had. If his statement had been true, and the military had been paying, they would have been saving money, in more ways than one. People came first; the military had taken a long hard time to learn that 'if you look after your people, they look after the job in hand'.

I had already served in war zones, concealing my 'issues', yet I hadn't allowed it to affect my expected performance, which surely demonstrated a tremendously resilient mental health. And, now that I was free of my distress, if anything, my performance was going to be even better. I could focus 100 per cent now, not having to worry someone was going to knock on my door and invite me to a disciplinary hearing, followed by humiliation and dismissal from my job. He highlighted his true bigoted nature when he followed up by attacking military women 'who get pregnant and have the audacity to fight to keep their jobs afterwards'. However, what made his denigration of me worse was that people who didn't understand listened to him, and more 'experts' joined in, all voicing opinions on why a 'transsexual' person had no place in today's military. And this was the gist of PPrune.

It was demoralising, and I feared for my future on the front line. I had spoken with my Desk Officer about my move back to a front-line squadron, and he had kindly offered me several options, some of which offered less demanding roles, but I only wanted one: the Merlin HC Mk3. It would be coming into service in the next year and I was keen to be reacquainted. As a tactical battlefield helicopter, Merlin was going to be as frontline as you could get with aircraft. It would also give me the opportunity to prove these voices wrong, to show that I could serve on the front line, that being transgender was of no consequence. I knew that being 'good enough' wasn't going to work now. Just over 2 per cent of the 4,246 aircrew in the RAF were female, and I was the only openly transgender one. To be deemed 'as good as a man' in the military, a woman had to be better; to be 'as good as man' as a transgender woman, I would need to be exceptional. Anything less would be regarded as 'average'. But doing this would be impossible without the support of my colleagues.

Then, finally, after a week that had seemingly stretched to eternity, PPrune began to transform: positive comments were being posted, referring to my professional ability, or positive experiences individuals had shared with me, arguing that doing the job was all that mattered. The negative opinions were still coming, but they were becoming overwhelmed now. It had taken just one bold voice to take that first stand. Perhaps there was reluctance to be first, to be seen standing up for something so 'controversial', but whatever the delay, others now followed, and each one inspired more, and good wishes too, mostly from the helicopter world. The bullies were being put back in their box. I was beginning to see hope. Maybe I did have a future back on a squadron. It was time to find out.

11

THE FINAL NAIL

2000–2003

On my arrival back at Benson, a young senior aircraftwoman helpfully showed me to my room in the officers' mess. I never dreamt I would be back here as a female officer. It was unreal, almost as unreal as my posting. I was back on a squadron, and it was the one I wanted, No. 28 Army Cooperation (AC) Squadron RAF. My room was bright and modern and, most importantly, en suite. I had a few days' leave, so I was depositing some basic belongings before visiting Tony Ballantyne, my colleague on RWOETU before I'd left here. His support was calming my nervous anticipation of the week to come, my first week back amongst people I knew, people I had worked with before I transitioned; he had been one of them. If everyone was as supportive, I would have nothing to fear.

On the evening before my first day on No. 28 (AC) Squadron, I was visited by Andy van Balaam, a friend from my Wessex days. I was nervous because he knew my 'old image' well, and I wondered what he would think. When he arrived, he appeared amiable and advised that he would meet me at the squadron's main entrance in the morning and that I shouldn't be worried. But I was. I appreciated that he'd taken the time to do this, but regardless of his good intentions, I still didn't get a moment's sleep. My brain was active all night with anxious anticipation. At 8.55 a.m. on Monday 4 December 2000, I arrived at the squadron, in the very same hangar I had worked in before I changed my life around. In the squadron's crew room, I met the other people I was going to be working closely with, all male. We stood in the crew room having tea or coffee, an obvious gap separating me from the guys, talking in a closed group, that awkward moment of finding a way to break the ice. They seemed unsure how to say hello, or else they didn't want to. They were talking about names that parents shouldn't have given their children.

'If your name was Head, why would you call your son Richard? It's bound to be shortened to Dick!' This conversation went around for a few minutes, with various paired names being laughed at; then I saw my moment and chipped in.

'If you think those names were bad… my parents gave me a boy's name!'

They all fell about laughing. The ice had been smashed. They would all become good friends. Pip Harding I knew as a kindly and courteous character from my Puma OCF in 1998; Simon Reade, a friendly character who was more 'soldier' than anyone I'd met previously, following an exchange tour with the Army Air Corps; 'Dinger' Tennant-Bell, a good-natured man with a permanently cheeky grin, would become a strong ally; Phil Miller was a tall, slim, down-to-earth individual; Andy, who would be my Flight Commander; and Squadron Leader Tim Fauchon, who was the Squadron Second-in-Command, a kind-hearted soul held with high regard for his experience and pleasant manner. Apart from Tim, we would all be on No. 1 Course of the Merlin HC Mk3 OCF, when it started in July 2002. Until then, we each had jobs that involved getting the squadron ready for its reformation, and preparations to accept the aircraft when they arrived from the factory.

After being shown around the squadron, we were invited to the Squadron Commander's office for individual welcomes. Wing Commander Dave Stubbs, a stocky, ginger-haired man, welcomed me to the squadron and said he valued my experience. I thanked him for accepting me, because he could have said no. It wasn't up to him if I was posted to his squadron, but he could have influenced whether I would be accepted or not. I knew my Desk Officer had discussed my posting with him and he had given it some thought before saying yes, so I already respected that. He explained that the only people who had been told about my background were the Station Executive Officers and the Squadron Executives. That was unexpected, but explained why no one had paid any attention as I toured the squadron facilities. It was so much nicer to arrive as a female officer, than a transgender officer: it gave me chance to be accepted as me, before being judged for what I was. Of course, my colleagues in the crew room knew, because I had worked with two of them before.

The troop-carrying version of the Merlin was not due to begin arriving into RAF service until March 2001, and the squadron's reformation deadline was a royal parade and celebration just seven months away. My role was to become the squadron helicopter tactics instructor, and I needed to learn the aircraft systems to do this; the Merlin was coming into service with one of the most technologically advanced defensive aids systems in the world. This was an important role, so I decided to use my time learning and relearning as much about tactics, electronic warfare and defensive systems as I could. In the space of three months I had been on three major courses, plus two tactics conferences at the Air Warfare Centre at RAF Waddington, in Lincolnshire, and I had gained a higher security clearance to help. In the past, revealing my personal distresses, in order to remove any risk of being open to blackmail, would have been a big worry; not any more.

The courses were exactly what I needed: they gave me purpose and more credibility. I was the first transgender person to be posted to a frontline unit in any of the Armed Forces, and there was a lot of pressure that went with that. Unhappily, Joanne hadn't been allowed to return to her unit, and, without promotion to Warrant Officer First Class, she would only serve for a couple of years post-transition before her service came to its natural end. She wanted to stay, but she had done a great job trailblazing transgender service in the British Army, ensuring the policy was adapted so that others in the future would have a far easier journey and be far more easily accepted. I knew that once the squadron had formed and we began operational flying, I would be scrutinised just as the first female fast-jet aircrew were ten years ago. All the outspoken critics who had forecast disaster and weakness would be watching so they could say, 'Told you so… this kind of person has no place on the front line.' If I failed, then I failed for all transgender people following. I needed a skill that was respected, and important to operational capability: my role as a tactical expert was perfect for that. There were few helicopter tactics instructors (HTIs), and there were even fewer female ones, but there was only one transgender one, and I couldn't afford to be the weakest of HTIs! For the moment, I had the relative protection of working with a small group of people who accepted me, but that would change as the squadron and the base grew. Volunteering for these courses was taking me away from my security blanket. It would help, but my self-confidence was still fragile, and I had to get over that to succeed.

In June 2001, I was invited to my cousin Lorna's wedding, at Leasowe Castle, near my family home. I was so grateful to Lorna and Wayne for inviting me to their big day. It demonstrated the love and support that existed in my wider family. I hadn't been able to go home for over two years now, but, out of the blue, Dad agreed I could stay there. Conversation had been rare and difficult by phone; perhaps a visit would let them see me happy now, and perhaps it would help them to understand. Maybe my invite to a family wedding had given them cause to see me too.

It was twenty-seven years since I had last walked down the pathway to my parents' house as a girl. Memories of that fateful day on my sister's bicycle, when joy had turn to fear, sprang to mind, but this time I wasn't scared of being caught, though I had plenty of other worries. I was home. This was in my dreams, but the day wasn't going to be easy, for any of us.

'Let's do this,' Dad said, as he gave me a brief hug. Mum didn't say anything. I handed her a bouquet of flowers, and she went off to put the kettle on. I sensed I had pleasantly surprised them both: I knew they would have envisaged a drag-queen identity; instead, I wore a plain though smart skirt and blouse, with subtle makeup, and I'd been to the hairdressers before I set off. I wanted to look nice for the wedding, but this moment was more important. This was all about first impressions – would they accept me as their daughter? We talked of my work and where I was living. They were surprised I had been accepted by people in the Armed Forces. I hoped that would help, that if they could see how positive my workplace was, that might influence their attitude. It was more of an interview than a family discussion. My future in the family remained on a knife-edge, my acceptance was not yet won. Soon it was time to get ready for the wedding, and when I came downstairs wearing a fawn-coloured knee-length skirt and matching jacket with low brown heels, once more I saw genuine surprise on their faces. I was overjoyed when I got a compliment from Dad. 'You look smart,' he said.

The wedding was a wonderful day, and family I met there were openly supportive. I was only ever treated as a female guest, a female cousin and niece. I stayed overnight in the castle and went back to my parents' the next day, where the questions continued. This time it was more about who I had met at the wedding. What did they think? What did they say? It was like my parents were looking for an excuse to accept me: if everyone else accepted me then it might be all right for them to do so. I wasn't blind to the pain that still existed; I stayed as long as I dared, then bid my farewells while the atmosphere remained positive.

I had arranged to visit Lorna's mum, my Auntie Dee, at her home just a few miles away, but I knew I couldn't tell my parents this. Auntie Dee behaved exactly like I always dreamt Mum would. She and Uncle Bernie participated in amateur dramatics and sang songs from shows, and she had a spare bedroom full of the most amazing costume dresses and accessories. I would have had an absolute field day growing up in such a house. I was treated to a marvellous fully costumed performance of Marlene Dietrich's 'Lili Marlene'. The new bride and groom appeared for lunch and we had a lovely afternoon before I had to say goodbye and return south. The contrast between their unquestioning acceptance and the struggle my parents were undergoing burnt in my heart.

Hope that my visit home had been a positive influence soon began to fade. Phone contact became even more infrequent and strained; conversation with Mum was limited to the weather and what was on telly, while Dad quickly resumed his previous posture whenever I phoned: 'Sorry, he's asleep, he's only just gone… Maybe next time.'

Something had changed following my visit. Sandra and I suspected the hand of Stan. My brothers still wanted nothing to do with me, but I knew Rich would follow others; if my parents were accepting then he would be. The key was Dad, the locked door was Mum, the loaded shotgun was Stan – and he was now exerting his opinion as the 'heir apparent to the family fortune', a former council house and a collection of military toys. Dad had previously suggested I write a letter to Stan explaining why I hadn't told him my news first, instead of Sandra, seemingly an important issue to him. So I wrote the letter and I wrote the truth, as delicately as I could: that his bigotry wasn't nice, it had made it feel unsafe to tell him first, that needing a supportive ally when I told the rest of the family meant Sandra was the better choice, and that his reaction proved I was right to not anticipate his support. His response was a letter of spite and anger. Our estrangement was almost sealed, but there was worse to come – literally the final nail in the coffin.

On 1 July 2001, No. 28 (Army Cooperation) Squadron officially reformed, with Prince Michael of Kent taking the salute. Several aircraft had arrived from the factory now, all shiny and new, almost as polished as the hangar floor on which they would be parked and maintained. Soon after, I was approached by a friendly face from my past and asked if I would like a sortie in a Merlin. I naturally snapped up the opportunity. It was John Coxen; he had been posted to Benson as the boss of the Merlin Operational Conversion Flight, the team who would teach us when No. 1 Course began. He was taking an aircraft to RAF Coningsby for their Station Families' Day, and on the way back he offered me the left-hand cockpit seat. It was a very comfortable seat for me: the Merlin was an amazing aircraft, far different to anything I had flown before. It was fast, quiet and could cover 600 miles between refuels, further with extra fuel tanks fitted, or air-to-air refuelling. A perfect vehicle for Joint Personnel Recovery (JPR), or Combat Recovery (CR), a division of CSAR, recovering friendly forces trapped in enemy territory. The Americans were the experts at this, so in September I visited the 21st Special Operations Squadron (SOS) based at RAF Mildenhall, a US Air Force base in Suffolk. They flew the MH-53M Pave Low, a later model of the version I flew in Albuquerque. Pip and Simon came with me.

I provided a presentation to our hosts on the roles and performance capabilities of the Merlin, and in return they did the same regarding the MH-53. I was a little nervous, but this was the first time I'd had close contact with American personnel as Caroline, so it was understandable. Not once did they question my gender or make comment. I knew they knew, from the looks I got when I began talking to them; quick glances at each other looked for acknowledgement that this Brit was 'different', but then they just paid attention to what I was saying. I was in a flying suit, I wore unit badges, and I was speaking with knowledge; we just naturally moved on.

As we made our way to the crew room for a coffee break, we passed their squadron operations room. Something was wrong. Half a dozen aircrew stood around a television screen, staring with disbelieving faces at what was unfolding thousands of miles away, in New York. We watched as it appeared a light aircraft had crashed into one of the World Trade Center buildings. We wondered why or how that could happen – an accident perhaps, a suicide maybe. Then a second aircraft hit the adjacent tower, and we saw it wasn't a light aircraft at all, it was much bigger than that. We couldn't believe what our eyes were showing us, or what we were hearing. I didn't know what to say to our American colleagues. It was clear there was a lot of distress in the room. Today was 9/11 and the world had changed for ever. Little did I realise how much that would influence my future, the future of my friends and their families, the future of the military, of the civilised world.

Then the station went into lockdown: there was considered to be a threat to all American units overseas. Security and alert levels were raised to their highest possible stages and all non-American personnel were asked to leave the base immediately. As members of the British military, we were welcomed to stay but asked to return to our on-base accommodation, for our own safety. I watched as road signs were covered over, building names too, even the church sign was covered; measures taken to cause disorientation to any threats who may already be on the base.

Back at our accommodation, we sat down and watched the news unfolding. American single officers' quarters are so much more spacious and comfortable than the UK equivalents. Each room contained a large double bed, a widescreen television, a desk, a telephone and a minibar. We drank the contents of the minibar in my room, then moved to Pip's room and did the same, then to Simon's room; it was a day that needed alcohol. The following morning, we returned to the 21st SOS's operations room, but after a short while we decided it would be best to leave them to it and return to our own base. We would have to continue our exchange another day.

Towards the end of October, John Coxen approached me with another invitation. He was taking a Merlin to Northern Ireland, to be part of a Tiger Meet celebration. Tiger Meets were business and social exchanges between military aviation units, usually NATO units, that had a tiger in their squadron badge or identity. This was to be a 'mini-meet' hosted by No. 230 Squadron, flying Puma helicopters at RAF Aldergrove. As part of the event was intended to show off our new helicopter and to brief other aircrew on its capabilities, John wanted me to do the presentation. It was quite nerve-racking standing up in front of so many aviators and talking about a helicopter I'd only flown once so far, but my talk was very well received, and when the Squadron Commander stood up and personally thanked me, I was completely surprised by what he said.

'Courage is something we respect and strive for, being aircrew. Caz is certainly displaying courage in abundance… Thank you for being here today and speaking to us, Caz… Best wishes for your time to come on Merlin.' He then led the room in a round of applause. I was blushing, but felt cheered that he'd said this. I wondered if I was displaying courage. I hadn't thought of my transition in that way before. I guess in a way I was, but it was something that I had to do, to live my life to the fullest I possibly could. If that was courage then, yes, I guess I did display it in abundance. It was a pleasantly reassuring start to the weekend.

The first social evening was in No. 5 uniform, or mess kit, military formal evening wear. For me, this consisted of an ankle-length skirt and a short-waisted jacket, all in the same Air Force grey-blue of the boys' uniform, with miniature versions of entitled medals worn above the left breast. A white winged-collar blouse with pearl buttons and a pin-tuck front was tucked in behind a squadron cummerbund in blue and gold, and black court shoes and barely black tights completed my uniform. Two broad gold-foil bands wrapped around my sleeve, above the cuff, denoted my rank of Flight Lieutenant. This was the first opportunity I'd had to wear my mess kit, and it was a wonderful feeling not to have to wear trousers and a shirt with bow tie. After I got changed, I went to Sarah Bird's room. Sarah was a cheerful young Aldergrove-based admin officer who had made me feel welcome, and we had arranged to do our makeup and hair together before we went for pre-dinner drinks in the mess bar.

After dinner, we all gathered for the usual social celebrations and, as the evening passed through midnight, I was approached by one of the German visitors, a pilot from a Tornado squadron. We were

chatting for a while when I noticed his comrade stood watching, leaning against a pillar in earshot, a silent wingman. I was taken aback
when the pilot asked out of the blue whether I'd had 'full surgery'
or not. He added, 'I can see why you did this, why you made this
change, it suits you.' It wasn't what I was expecting to hear. I took
it as a compliment, though wondered if something had been lost in
the German translation to English. I certainly didn't 'change' through
choice, I changed through necessity, and there was a big difference.
Just then, his wingman approached, seemingly concerned. They had a
short, sharp dialogue in German, then the wingman tried to drag his
colleague away, pulling at his elbow. The pilot wanted to talk to me
more, but his colleague was having none of it. They both staggered
away and presumably retired for the evening. I wondered later whether the wingman thought his friend was going to make a big mistake,
having had too much alcohol. He was perfectly safe, I only ever had
conversation in mind, but I realised that for the first time, as Caroline,
I may have been chatted up, and it was a nice feeling, even just the
prospect of it happening.

Recently, I had passed my medical board; now I could do my job
without any medical restrictions. It meant my future as aircrew was
more secure. Things seemed to be going very well, but, away from the
security of my job, life was proving much harder. I had been welcomed
into a good circle of female friends in the mess: Lynn Powell, Sally
Barber, Natalie Beck and Jane Gillespie, to name but a few. But out
on my own, my confidence remained fragile. When shopping, I was
just another woman queuing at the till, and nobody would pay me any
attention until the till operator asked me a question. As I spoke, some
of the surrounding heads and eyes would turn and stare, followed by
whispered chit-chat or muffled sniggers. It was better when I was in
company, because I felt the strength of support, and people tended to

pay less attention to a woman in company. Some people would even laugh and point, and one woman followed me around a clothing department, blatantly staring, not even shopping herself, just staring. I didn't know what to say, or whether saying anything would just trigger a worse scenario, so I went home. Just one bad experience would destroy my confidence in being in town for a month or more.

Then, as Christmas approached, it was time for the traditional officers' and sergeants' mess 'exchange drinks'. Officers weren't routinely allowed to enter the sergeants' mess, and vice versa. A sergeants' mess included all senior non-commissioned officer (SNCO) ranks from Sergeant to Warrant Officer. At Christmas, these rules were waived for one night, but there were still protocols and traditions to be followed.

I was quite happy to be socialising with the SNCOs – why shouldn't I be, my dad had been a Staff Sergeant, and I worked and socialised with SNCO colleagues and friends. At work, formal respect for rank was expected, though on board the aircraft, most crews respected first name use, except the Army. This year's invite came from the sergeants to the officers: we would be guests in their mess. At first, the evening went well, but slowly it became evident that some people resented me being there. They had remained silent until the alcohol began to fuel their 'bravery'; now they just had to say something.

'Can I ask you a question?'

'Sure!'

'What are you? Why are you in the Air Force? ... I have a team of engineers... What do I tell them about you? ... You're an officer but you're... How can they respect you?'

I was never asked these questions in the company of friends, be they officers or not; it was always when I'd been cornered, out of earshot of those who might object on my behalf.

The questioning became persistent and I tried to answer with reason, but it wasn't working, it was too confrontational, and eventually I began struggling with emotion, tears began to well. I didn't want them to see that, so I made an excuse to go to the toilet. Behind the safety of a locked cubicle door, I checked my eyes and considered whether to stay or go back to my own accommodation. If I went, they had won; if I stayed, I had to face more hurtful judgements. I decided to return and face up to my critics. There were very few people remaining, but my brave questioners were amongst them. I asked if I could buy them a drink, then, shortly afterwards, I left, before it got out of hand. I had done enough purely by going back.

The following day, I confided in a friend, who informed my boss. It was probably the best thing he could have done. I hadn't reported it, but he was aware now and asked if I wanted any action taken against them. It was a difficult decision: if they got in trouble for harassing me, then I had lost – they would never respect me, and likely their peers and subordinates would think I 'got their friends in trouble'. But if I didn't report harassment, then the military would sit back thinking it didn't exist. Worse still, as a qualified Equality and Diversity Adviser, I had been trained on procedures for dealing with harassment and bullying, to encourage people to stand against it and report it where appropriate, but I knew I couldn't follow those procedures. I stood to win more by not doing so. If I was labelled as a cry-baby or tell-tale, then transgender people following in my footsteps would be tarred with the same brush. So I let it be, but I decided I would never go to the sergeants' mess again for Christmas drinks, which was a great shame because there were many wonderful people who lived or socialised in that mess, and it would have been nice to accept their genuine invitation. Many of them would have been devastated that a guest in their home had been treated with such disrespect. I had learned a valuable lesson about mixed social events that involved alcohol. As my first year back on a squadron drew to a close, I reflected on what a year it had been. Generally, it had been positive but with a long way to go, and it was going to get a lot harder.

Soon it was time to begin No. 1 Merlin Course. There were twenty-four aircrew, six crews' worth, including the Squadron Commander and two Flight Commanders. We would be the backbone of No. 28 Squadron, and that was a big honour. The course provided training and familiarisation in aircraft handling, emergencies, navigation, night flying, instrument flying and tactical flying. Ironically, it was during the tactical flying phase that my acceptance ran out. The instructors wanted to use my own experience as a tactics instructor, so I was dispatched to RAF Leeming to liaise with a Hawk squadron for evasion training against fighters. They flew the Hawk I was familiar with from my time at Chivenor. They would simulate enemy aircraft and attack our Merlins so the crews could practise defensive tactics.

I had already spoken with their squadron training officer on the phone, so when I entered the busy Squadron Operations Room, I wasn't expecting the aircrew to make me feel so unwelcome. I was wearing my flying suit with my squadron badges, and it was unheard of that visiting aircrew weren't made welcome on any squadron. I recognised a good friend from my Phantom tours. I knew his family, I had dined in his home, we had shared good times and bad times. As I walked around the room, he deliberately spun to keep his back towards me. When I went to the crew room, everyone there finished their drinks and left. I got the message. I wasn't welcome, at all. That meant I couldn't do the job I had been sent there for, so I phoned a course instructor to explain. Marco was the mellowest instructor I had ever come across, he was a much respected ally – and he was infuriated. He suggested I leave, but I didn't want to do that until I had done my job. Not long after our conversation ended, I was joined by a Hawk representative in the crew room. We agreed the appropriate arrangements, and then I was summoned back to my own squadron. It was a disappointing experience and upsetting too, particularly that a good friend felt the way he did. It was another knock to my confidence, but I hadn't run away, and I had experienced valuable support from my own colleagues.

As part of a squadron work-up, we got involved in as many Army exercises as we could, and that meant time operating in the field, living in tents. I had no problems about operating in austere conditions: it went with the job, even though it exposed me to the risk of indignity. Laser and electrolysis treatments had had very little effect on my facial hair. I tried any new treatment advertised but none would work on red hair. The communal wash tent contained two rows of trestle tables and a small supply of black plastic washing-up bowls. Water was provided from a small bowser trailer parked nearby, and hot water was provided by pouring it through a small stand-alone fuel-burning heater, if it was working. To reduce the risk of someone entering when my face was covered in tell-tale shaving foam, I produced a flip-over cardboard sign for the entrance saying 'Females Only' on one side. But that only reduced the risk, as I wasn't the only female on the squadron. Penny Grayson had joined me on No. 1 Course as a pilot, and there were female engineers, ground support and operations staff. Not many, but enough. I got used to using the tent in off-peak wash times, alert to the signs of someone approaching, ready to rapidly wipe my face. The fact that I still had to do this was soul-destroying.

I had just landed from a sortie moving paratroops around a 'battlefield' on Salisbury Plain exercise area, when I was approached by the boss. I was having a successful exercise: just the night before, as we approached our tented base, I had spotted three suspicious shapes on the ground perimeter by using the forward-looking infra-red (FLIR) camera fitted to our aircraft. I initially thought they could be sheep, stood together. We couldn't make them out using night-vision goggles, so I asked Simon to fly a quick orbit while I examined the monochrome-green FLIR display, manually controlling the camera as we turned, keeping it pointing at them. There was something that didn't look right. I called it in over the radio; a security patrol would investigate. In the debrief, they would be confirmed as concealed special forces troops, tasked as enemy, waiting to infiltrate our camp in the early hours of darkness.

The boss asked me to follow him, then asked for my rifle. He handed it to Amanda, our training officer, walking alongside. It seemed odd; I looked at him, something was wrong.

'I have some bad news…'

'It's my dad isn't it?' I interrupted, saving him the words. I just knew. Tears began welling, I wiped my eyes.

'Very sorry, Caz, he passed away this morning. It was a heart attack. We'll get you home soonest.' My tears flooded now.

I sat in a tent, spilling the tea that had just been offered by the boss, as arrangements were made to fly me home. If he'd remained critically ill, a Merlin would have flown me directly to the hospital – the military was good under such circumstances – but because he was already dead, any urgency vanished. I was flown back to RAF Benson, where I could make my own arrangements to get home. I was met there by Lynn. We had been sharing a house together for nearly a year now, after becoming good friends while living in the officers' mess. With property prices so high, neither of us could afford our own houses, so we had co-bought a four-bedroom mid-terrace house. Lynn worked in the Support Helicopter Force Headquarters; as the Admin Staff Officer, she had triggered my notification after my sister had called.

I phoned home, and Sandra answered. Dad had been taken into hospital for observation after being unwell, and while there he had a fatal heart attack. Then Sandra sensitively added that I 'shouldn't make plans to come home', that 'a hostile reception' awaited – though not from her. Nobody else wanted to talk to me. I got the impression they were blaming me for his heart attack. A paternal auntie had threatened that she would kill me if I went home. Then I was told I wasn't welcome at his funeral either. It was my dad – how dare they try to bar me from his funeral! He would never have wanted that, regardless of our strained relationship over recent years.

I phoned my Auntie Val and we spoke for a long time. She had one of the wisest and most understanding heads I knew. With great sadness and reluctance, we agreed it would be bad to trigger a disturbance at my dad's funeral. But I would only stay away out of respect for him. I could not believe they would not let me go, but the message was clear.

At Benson, I often spoke with Padre Stan Jones whenever our paths crossed in the mess – not about religion, just life. He was a tall, thin, highly regarded Army veteran whose sparkling character belied the fact that he was in his eighties. I asked if it would be possible to hold a small service on the day of my dad's funeral. When I explained, he immediately offered to help. I attended in my No. 1 uniform, with medals, and Lynn came with me. It was a beautiful service in RAF Benson's small church, with just the three of us. I said a few words and Padre Stan did too. But banning me from my own dad's funeral was unacceptable: there was no way to turn back from that. I gave them what they wanted: we would never speak again.

I believed Dad had been slowly beginning to understand, even though he was the one in the family who was hurt the most. Other than his outspoken opinion, he was a lovely man. As a child, I had always been the one who accompanied him to watch his regiment play rugby, to the Remembrance Day parades and church service. I'd visit him in his office at work, I would go with him in the car if he was 'going on a message', I would always chat to him when I visited home. He would always contradict me about what I was doing – he knew my job better than I did, or so he thought – but I really loved him, so much that I didn't want to hurt him, I didn't want to ruin his life. As much as he struggled to accept me now, he loved the person I had been, though he could never tell me that. He was the single biggest reason I'd had to live my secret life, but I didn't hate him for that, I couldn't hate him, and that was my problem – because if I did, I would have gone my own way many years before. I wondered if there was a way we could have worked this out earlier in my life, but when I looked back, the message was clear: it was unacceptable to have someone like me in the family. I knew that, he knew that, but I still wondered if we could have found a way.

He had grown to be a giant, but in the past few years he had grown old. The last time we'd met, he was grey, his hair and his skin, and his once crushing handshake had grown weak, like a politician's. All he did was sit in his favourite throne and watch television, complaining about every channel being rubbish or showing repeats. Occasionally he'd admire his collection of painted soldiers of the Napoleonic era, his cabinet of aeroplanes – some of them once my toys – and another cabinet full of his latest hobby, collecting miniature metal warships. Brass shell casings either side of the gas fireplace triggered memories of his glory days in the Artillery. I heard he sometimes cried, so far removed from his old character. I knew, from Sandra, that he regretted making it impossible for me to be open. Dad had come across the letter I had written to Mum, over a year after Sandra had given it to her. He'd asked her, 'Have you seen this?'

'Yes,' she had replied.

'Have you read it?' The letter had evidently struck a chord in his heart; it had been an emotional outpouring of my love for them, an explanation of my dilemma, a plea for them not to turn away. Mum had just put it away, in a drawer. I suppose she could have destroyed it. In Dad's death, the estranged side of my family had shown themselves, the ones who were making it hard for him to accept me, and they were tearing apart the family he had made. They were given an opportunity now to turn back the clock, to bring the family back together, but they didn't. It wasn't me who'd destroyed my family; I saw that now.

12

CLOUDED SKIES

2003–2004

War was in the air again. The USA and the UK were putting pressure on the world for action against Saddam Hussein and Iraq, suggesting that weapons of mass destruction there could 'fall into the wrong hands', perhaps used against opposing nations and their populations. Military action in the Middle East had once again become a possibility and preparations had begun for UK forces to mobilise. But our aircraft wasn't Combat-Ready yet: it still lacked many clearances. The boss briefed us: 'War is imminent, and although we might not be there at the start, it is inevitable we will be there later. We are going to Norway. For training purposes, snow landings provide many of the same issues as desert sand.' Helicopters are good at creating significant dust or snow clouds during take-off and landing, denying crews visual references at an already hazardous stage of flight. The risk increased significantly when taking off or landing over an unprepared surface, especially one confined by trees, wires, terrain or other obstructions.

On a cold February day in 2003, we set off on our first major overseas exercise with the Merlin, Exercise Cold Lion, a winter-warfare and survival-training exercise. Some of the squadron had already

deployed with a pair of aircraft. My flight there was as a singleton
Merlin, with two crews on board, swapping responsibilities for alternate legs of the route. I was in the left-hand seat, with Al Dale as the
aircraft captain in the right-hand seat, for the first leg to RAF Man-
ston, in Kent, then from Eelde Airport, near Groningen in north-east
Holland, through Germany and up to Aalborg in Denmark for an
overnight stop. Everyone was keen to enjoy the famous hospitality of
Aalborg, and soon we were downtown. I was quite comfortable in the
restaurant and bars – I felt safe in a group of people – but then we
ended up in a club. The problem with clubs is that the guys like to
check out the girls, and while that is only natural, it meant that I came
under closer scrutiny than if I was elsewhere. Also, they tend to be
crowded places, people stand closer, and alcohol is involved. All three
of those together made me uneasy, and that also drew attention. It
came as no surprise, therefore, when I noticed customers, sat at a large
table near the bar, staring at me, then leaning in to friends, their heads
turning, indiscreetly, smirking. After a while I tired of it, and advised
Al I was returning to the accommodation. He suggested I wait a short
while, because taxis would be expensive and we'd all go together, but
time passed by and the unwanted attention persisted. I tried to believe
they were laughing because I had red hair, or I was older than them,
but I failed; it was in their faces, their mannerisms. I approached
Al again and explained that I was happy to get a taxi alone, but he
immediately began rounding the crews up. I was impressed that he
responded so positively, but the others weren't happy to be leaving
'early'. I didn't realise how much it would upset them, but an awkward
silence fell between us.

Our destination was Fagernes, a small regional airport in
south-central Norway, surrounded by wooded hills, covered in deep
snow. On arrival at our accommodation, a wooden chalet-style hostel,

we were given time to find our rooms before having a brief on what would happen next. I was sharing a room with Penny; the guys were in rooms just down a corridor. It was a cosy building with its own bar and small restaurant, but first, we were told, we would 'be out for three days'. Within an hour or so of landing we were disembarking from a BV tracked all-terrain vehicle on a forest track in deep snow, wearing Arctic survival clothing, carrying a Bergen backpack containing a sleeping bag, survival aids, a snow shovel and a pair of white tennis racquet-style snow-shoes. We were given a grid reference to set up camp, but it wasn't a long walk. The days were about survival, rather than route marches. Our first night was in a tent. Simon was told to share with me and Penny, I wasn't sure why, but he voluntarily became our chef, and chief tent putter-upper. Penny had been an officer in the Adjutant General Corps before she began pilot training, transferring to the RAF when she preferred the flying opportunities. They were quick to get on with things, leaving me to make a brew or fetch items to help raise the tent.

The temperature on the first night dropped to −25°C and, even with three of us in the tent, it became unbearably cold. I couldn't get to sleep for shivering, inside my green standard-issue winter-weight sleeping bag. Contrary to expert advice, I decided to put another layer of clothing on, then after a while another, and another, until eventually I stopped shivering and slept. The following morning, we broke camp and hiked to our next location, to build snow holes for the night. After a demonstration, we chose our team snow banks then spent the afternoon digging 'three-bed lodgings'. It was so much warmer in the snow hole than the tent. We had to take it in turns to be awake as 'safety sentry', should snowfall block the air shaft, but otherwise it was actually a better night's sleep. Our final day of survival training involved ice-breaking drills on a frozen lake, how to get out if we fell through the ice. I was exempted from the task: I had turned forty and the cold-shock was deemed a risk to older hearts, so I got to watch instead. Most of the guys were in their twenties, they could take it! I could have volunteered, at my own risk, but then if I did have a medical issue, the MoD would declare it was my own fault, not an accident in training, and it would become my financial liability.

Since the club incident in Aalborg, I had sensed an awkward atmosphere between me and colleagues whom I considered friends. They seemed to snap at me for no obvious reason. After we had returned to the hostel accommodation, Penny would be invited to a room for drinks with the guys each evening, but I wasn't. Penny and I shared a room, we both knew them well, we were the only two girls; why leave one out? I couldn't believe this was still about the club, but neither could I see any other reason. I began skipping meals, and retiring to bed early.

I had only flown two short trips in snow conditions, both to practise snow-landings not navigation in an unfamiliar environment, when the boss decided to do a Combat-Ready check on me and my Flight Commander, Barty. It was a full day of tasking, with challenging flying and equally challenging navigation; one snow-covered mountain looked just like any other. We made plans, which we had to change when the boss added complications. Then we had to change the changed plan, and so on. It was hard work, and the final task was to get a 'simulated casualty' to Bergen Hospital. We needed to speak to Bergen Air Traffic Control on the radio, before entering their restricted airspace to reach the hospital. But the mountainous terrain meant we would have already 'trespassed' before we could get close enough, or high enough, to communicate. Going around the mountains meant adding hours to our flight time, with a casualty requiring urgent care. I decided no airliners would be flying below 100 feet above the ground in the mountains, so we could approach at low level until we could raise them. It was a fail! It was always going to be a fail, if it was assumed Bergen would file a complaint for infringing their outer airspace, regardless of the circumstances. I didn't think so, for an emergency; the boss disagreed, but he gave Barty a pass, as the aircraft captain. We had been working as a team, but my decision was taken in isolation. I couldn't argue, but I would have made the same decision in any life-or-death mission. I wasn't fitting in on the squadron any more, socially or professionally. I could see my future crashing down. Where did I go from here?

I met one of the guys in a corridor. We hadn't been on speaking terms for days, it all seemed a little childish and I decided to try to fix it. 'Look, can we have a talk?' I asked. He nodded.

'This is silly, we were good friends and we're not speaking, can we draw a line under whatever has happened recently, and start again?' He looked at me for a while, just staring, then nodded again.

'Can I ask you a question…? Do you all think of me as one of the girls, or something else?' It was a dangerous question. 'It's just that I get the impression you all treat Penny totally different to me, I always feel like I'm something else… Do you see me as female at all?' He shrugged his shoulders. Enough was said. We rekindled our friendship, but my fragile confidence and respect in myself as a female was crushed.

I paid more attention to how I was regarded. If I was standing in a group, with a female friend, and someone approached that group, they would greet her with a kiss on the cheek, or shake hands with her and the guys, but just nod and say 'Hi Caz' to me. There were only two aircrew who would greet me in the same fashion as they would greet any female friend: Pip and Al. It seems such a minor thing, but it constantly reminded me I was different, and few people knew how to respect difference. All anyone had to do was greet everyone the same – a handshake would have been perfectly acceptable for male or female colleagues, and they wouldn't have to feel awkward, as to whether they should kiss me on the cheek or not. But they couldn't see that.

Back at Benson, I was summoned to my Flight Commander's office; he was worried about my state of mind. I convinced him I was OK. There was too much to lose: if my medical category was downgraded I would be removed from flying duties, and there might be no way back from that, but only time would tell. I was having an extraordinarily hard time, but I wasn't going to give up.

I went to see Val. It was great just to get away, but there was also a young soldier working on her unit who wished to transition gender, and Val had asked if I could offer reassurance and advice. I met the Padre there first. He had been trying to help, but acknowledged he didn't have any experience of dealing with transgender issues. We all met over a coffee and then I had a chat with the soldier alone. I was able to provide some appropriate advice, but I couldn't help worrying that 'she' wanted to rush things. I remembered how keen I was, but this seemed to be different. Arrangements were subsequently made for her to begin her transition, but, soon after changing accommodation blocks, she decided it was all a mistake and returned to a male existence. Nothing had happened that was irreversible; some people have doubts and they need to explore their gender identity. It isn't as clear-cut as many people think, and the whole care and psycho-analysis process involved in gender identity 'dysphoria' is designed to prevent people from misinterpreting their own feelings and emotions, to realise what it is they are actually going through, and what needs to be done about it. A diagnosis of dysphoria means a state of being uncomfortable or unhappy; it doesn't mean that everyone diagnosed with it needs to, or wants to, 'change their sex'. No harm had been done. I had mentored several individuals now, and it was something I would never refuse to do, even though I was fighting battles of my own. It was demanding, but I remembered what it was like for me not having anyone to turn to in what was the hardest time of my life.

Regardless of what my supervisors thought of my state of mind, they still valued my skills as a tactics and platform protection specialist. I was tasked to evaluate some tactical missions in the simulators as pre-deployment training. The squadron was off to Bosnia next, as part of NATO's Stability Forces (SFOR). I had to laugh when I went to get my Bosnia equipment from stores, only to be told they didn't have any left. It reminded me of my deployment there in 1995.

As hostilities in Iraq were announced, I set off for Bosnia with Dinger. We were to be crewed together, and I was happy with that as I got on very well with Dinger and his wife Sarah. Our new home was a base centred around a disused metal processing factory near Banja Luka, known as the Metal Factory, or BLMF. My accommodation this time was in a two-storey block of white Corimecs, a prefabricated flat-pack modular room that can be joined together in a line, or placed on top of each other. Everything was behind a barbed wire security fence, but the threat level was low enough for our weapons to be stored in an armoury, ready to be signed out for flying tasks. Although an attack with a MANPADS missile was considered highly unlikely, the threat couldn't be ignored, given the number of weapons that were unaccounted for following the war. So the aircraft had its first outing with the directional infra-red countermeasure (DIRCM) fitted, a high-tech missile detection and crew warning system.

In June 2003, we were tasked to fly with Rapid Reaction Force troops on Operation Eleison, to be ready for any security contingencies during a day visit to Banja Luka by Pope John Paul II. Our own escort was provided by Apache helicopters from B Company of the 1-149th Aviation Regiment, a US Army unit based at Tuzla. In the weeks leading up to the visit, we worked together, two Merlins escorted by a pair of Apaches, becoming familiar with each other's capabilities and operating procedures. The papal visit passed without incident and the next day Pip and I, together with our crewmen Dave and Jon, flew the Apache engineers back to their base in Tuzla, with our escort. We met with an American General there who presented us all with his coin. American units and senior officers carry tribute coins, which they sometimes present as a token of respect or gratitude. I had no problems while working with the Apache crews, and they never questioned my gender. Unfortunately, UK soldiers hadn't been so free of prejudice. When I climbed in or out of the cockpit and walked past soldiers we were carrying, I would hear sniggers and muttered comments, like 'Don't touch it, you'll become one!' I decided I wouldn't touch them: I wouldn't wish this on my worst enemies.

It was nice to get home, and Val had booked us both a relaxing spa weekend at Radcliffe Hall. I was invited to my cousin Michelle's wedding on the Isle of Wight. It was a lovely day and I got to spend time with family who were very special to me, particularly Auntie Val, her three daughters, Michelle, Kathy and Nettie, and their families, as well as the wonderful bonus of catching up with my Uncle Fred and Auntie Mary, visiting from the Isle of Man. My cousin's partners, Steve, Kris and Ian, were incredibly welcoming and respectful, and it was all such a welcome contrast to my experiences with the troops. It was a perfect summer's day, and I got to wear a big hat at a wedding. Then I went back to work.

The pressures on me had been growing and my airborne confidence was beginning to be damaged. I was regularly flying with one particular flying instructor, prior to a second Combat-Ready check, but we were mismatched in the cockpit. It is rare, but it happens. I had a lot of experience and I had a certain way I did things; he was younger and wanted to do things differently. Flying instructors liked things 'by the book'; tactics instructors didn't! I tried, but it wasn't working. He was a widely respected flying instructor and a well-liked character, and he was assessing me, so it was assumed to be my failing. Then the boss informed me I had an appointment to attend the station medical centre. Dr Naidoo was fortunately a lady with whom I got on very well. She explained that the boss had suggested I wasn't coping with life, particularly after the loss of my father, and this was influencing my performance in the air. I didn't believe this was true. Dr Naidoo listened to my explanation, and understood, offering her support. She declared me fully fit and offered to have words with my boss, but I thought that might make matters worse, so I knocked on his door myself. I explained that he would see the evidence himself if the flying programme was managed so I didn't fly with that one person. He accepted my request, but now I began to question myself. I was in danger of losing trust in myself. My relationship with my friends had broken down in Norway. It was fixed again now, but being failed on my CR check, and the question mark on my subsequent airborne performance adding to that, had flagged an assumption that I wasn't coping with personal issues. The recourse to send me for a medical assessment was proof of that. There is no place in the cockpit for 'personal issues'; the option would be to remove me from flying duties. Perhaps this would be temporary, but there was real risk of it becoming permanent. If that decision was made, my flying would stop immediately and I would be removed from the squadron.

I was crewed with Al, as the squadron's senior qualified helicopter instructor (QHI), and my assessments returned to normal. After a short while, he flew my pre-CR check, a day-into-night sortie, tasking with troops on Salisbury Plain then instrument flying to Cardiff Airport, and finally low-level night navigation home, some of which I got to pilot myself. I earned the highest grade possible, but as much as Al's positive attitude had restored confidence, if I failed a second check with the boss, I would most definitely be removed from the squadron, and possibly from flying altogether. That was an unbelievable amount of pressure.

The day came and I was flying with Jock Brown, with the boss tasking and assessing us from the centre seat. I knew Jock well from flying Wessex together in the '90s. He was a good pilot to have on a check ride – lots of experience and an excellent cockpit manner. I planned the mission, knowing most of it would be changed as soon as we got airborne, as no-notice or short-notice re-plans were revealed. As we were in transit to our first pick-up point, we had a malfunction in the aircraft and a warning light lit up, requiring us to land as soon as possible: this meant no panic, but don't dawdle. We selected a suitable field close by.

An hour later, another Merlin arrived, with engineers to fix the fault. It was going to take a while, so the boss decided to commandeer the other aircraft and continue our task, leaving the other crew with our broken aircraft. By this time, a small crowd had gathered on the road adjacent to the field, and some of them were being shown around the aircraft. I was busy re-planning the mission, seeing where I could regain timelines and where we could get to with the fuel load our new aircraft had. I entered the aircraft to do some pre-start cockpit checks. As I walked up the ramp, I heard a young girl shouting excitedly, 'Look, Mummy, look, Mummy, it's a lady, it's a lady, she's flying the helicopter!' I was overjoyed, firstly that the young girl had identified me as a lady, and secondly that I had made her day, and hopefully inspired her in some way. I didn't want to ruin that impression by turning around and talking to her. I feared that, on hearing my voice, she might decide otherwise. I wanted her to leave with the idea that a lady was flying the helicopter. I was busy anyway, though I always liked to acknowledge people who were interested in the aircraft.

The rest of the mission was 'uneventful', though extremely challenging, as we were diverted from one task to another, to another, to another, all with time constraints and implications on fuel, rising in complexity, until finally the last task took us back to Benson. To be told I had passed was an incredible weight off my shoulders, and it was graded B++ – not quite an A, but plenty of pluses to make it better than a B. I wasn't sure when pluses had become so fashionable, but I accepted them as a confidence boost. Now I was fully qualified, now the worst pressure was released, now I could focus on my job in full.

Over the next few months the squadron went from exercise to exercise, and we got to know field conditions and tents intimately. A new Squadron Commander arrived, and his focus was getting the squadron fully Combat-Ready. I was moved to a new flight, D Flt, a small group of experienced aviators, each with different responsibilities; my contribution remained tactics.

My second flying tour in Bosnia came in the winter, and what a contrast. The missions were quieter due to the weather factor, but that made them more challenging in other ways. It was a great place to operate the aircraft in environmental conditions we had never experienced in the UK. On one mission, with one of our 'young' first tourist pilots, Mike, and two experienced crewmen, Dave and Jon, we were tasked to pick up the US Ambassador from Sarajevo. The forecast hadn't been too bad, but as we got closer, the weather got worse and worse, and then the airfield declared it was 'closing due to heavy snowfall'. I called the air traffic controllers on the radio; they didn't understand how we could be flying in such weather. They kept telling us it wasn't fit to be flying. I would have laughed, but I was working too hard trying to find a route through the mountains. Each option we took closed in. Eventually we accepted defeat, and then the battle really began. Running into white-out conditions, everything merged into a pure white canvas. The sky joined the ground, the mountains became one, and it was incredibly disorientating, with no visible navigation features, no horizon. Were we turning? Were we descending? My brain's gyros were at odds with the aircraft's. I had to believe the aircraft's instruments. Air traffic was right; no one should be flying in this. I always enjoyed the challenges of navigating a helicopter in poor visibility, but this was different. I took my hat off to Mike's flying skill; the whole crew got a good workout that day. But our time here was coming to an end. It had been a valuable proving ground for the aircraft, but now we were due elsewhere.

PART THREE

RED IN
THE SAND

2004–2013

13

DISCREETLY HOSTILE

2004–2005

In August 2004, our Squadron Commander announced that we would be deploying to southern Iraq in the New Year, in support of Operation Telic, providing support to coalition and Iraqi troops. I was disappointed when I wasn't included amongst the first crews selected to go. I was the lead squadron tactics instructor, and I knew the protection systems fitted to our aircraft better than anyone else, a responsibility I took seriously. I had been doing a lot of work with the Air Warfare Centre, but during one visit I was shown some unsettling news. An essential part of the on-board system wasn't working as it was meant to, making the aircraft unsafe to deploy to a war zone. I was confused when the boss wouldn't believe me, saying all the reports he had seen said everything was fine. But I had a responsibility to make sure the crews were as well prepared as they could be. If I didn't get this right then I wasn't helping to minimise the risk, not just for my friends, but for colleagues and anyone else who would be flying on our aircraft. I had begun giving a set of morning briefs on tactics subjects, and during one of these I revealed what I had learned. The boss wasn't happy. I tried to reason with him, but I was told to shut up and sit down. I did. I was happy though, that the crews knew and they could make their own minds up. I took it up with with my Flight Commander but he just decided the boss knew better than me. The whole purpose of my speciality was that he didn't need to: he had someone who was dedicated to knowing such detail, who could inform him. That was my job: I had a responsibility to be the expert, and an adviser to senior commanders. Did he not trust me?

The boss had a lot on his plate, trying to get the squadron ready for its first major operational detachment. Iraq was a major step up from present-day Bosnia, in terms of threat, enemy intent and environment. The enemy would put a lot of resources into trying to shoot a helicopter down: they had already done so, far too many times. As the deployment day drew closer, I arranged a two-day briefing programme for the squadron aircrew. It included briefings on expected weather and environmental conditions, role and capability briefs from representatives of the key Army units they would be working with, and a brief from the helicopter Tactics and Trials officer from the Air Warfare Centre (AWC). His talk highlighted what I had told the boss, who now became angry. He summoned the briefing officer, my Flight Commander, the Detachment Flight Commander, the Squadron Second-in-Command and me into his office to discuss the problem. There were some crazy solutions offered, from some supposedly respectable sources.

There was a solution, though it would take a little work from experts in the AWC and the Defence Science and Technology Laboratory (DSTL), a government-funded body of scientists, military and civilian specialists and other clever people. The boss was happy with the solution, and I was happy. I had done my job, and now I was included on the first detachment of Merlin going to Iraq! I would have gone anyway, that was inevitable, on the second or third detachment perhaps, but my place was on the first detachment. I had to experience the environment first-hand if I was going to learn and teach how to survive there.

As I prepared myself to go to Iraq, the country was preparing for an upcoming general election. I'd seen on the news that a new Act of Parliament had been proposed, which would give transgender people new rights of protection, and permit amendment to birth certificates, but MPs were arguing about it. As things stood, the law allowed me to change my driving licence and passport to identify as female, yet I was considered legally male in all other respects, so I could be sent to an all-male prison if I was given a jail sentence. That would be a threatening place for any woman to be incarcerated. I wanted to see how my local politicians felt on this matter. If I was willing to put my life on the line for the country, what respect would it show me? I sent hand-written letters to local representatives of each of the three main parties, Conservative, Labour and Liberal Democrats. They were very long letters and each said basically the same thing, in short:

> The UK is only one of two countries in Europe, along with Eire, which does not recognise the rights of transgender people. I am a transgender officer in the British Armed Forces and the government intends to put my life at risk by sending me to Iraq. I am prepared to do that as my duty, but if your party wins the election, what is it going to do about its own duty, to its own citizens? What is it going to do to ensure that transgender people have the same rights for liberty, legal protection and respect that anyone deserves?

The answers, if any, would come only while I was away.

It was decided we would fly four aircraft to Iraq, rather than transport them; it was going to be a long trip. The first two Merlins took six days to get there, after resting in Jordan to acclimatise to the temperatures, but I was in the second pair, and we were told to get there as soon as possible: we were to aim for four days. I was flying in 'X-Ray' with Penny and our crewmen Dave and Winnie, and we carried three engineers.

A light covering of snow lay on the fields of Oxfordshire as we departed. Everyone was wearing dark-green sea-survival immersion suits, apart from the engineers, who brightened the cabin on a cold grey day, wearing their orange passenger survival suits. As we coasted in to France, 1,000 feet above the Channel, the snow-covered ground blended into the grey horizon; then, as we got further south, the weather got progressively worse. After a brief refuel stop at Châteauroux, the visibility became dangerously poor and we had to separate to climb through cloud to a safe height. With the temperature below freezing, and our high-tech anti-icing systems still limited by partial clearances, it wasn't a good place to be. Crawling out of the cloud above 10,000 feet at −19°C, it was just like my jet days: the sun was always shining on top. However, the Merlin isn't pressurised and flight above 10,000 feet required breathing equipment. I always felt uncomfortable being that high without wings or a parachute; if a fire broke out we would be unlikely to reach safety quickly enough. Helicopters can't expedite a descent in the way that fixed-wing aircraft can. Fortunately, as we approached the Alps, the cloud began to break up and we became visual with the ground once again, allowing us to descend.

From there on we were plagued with giant thunderstorms as we routed from Nice to Rome, then via Crete to Rhodes, and Cyprus to Amman, in Jordan. Early starts rudely following late finishes; aircraft preparation, flight documentation and customs clearances all left little time for sleep, and no time for exploring our night-stop locations. Between Jordan and Kuwait lay endless miles of open desert. Bedouin camps and shepherds tending their sheep would appear out of the middle of nowhere. After seeing our umpteenth herd of camels, the novelty began to wear off, and the vast monotonous landscape soon denied us even the most obscure of I-Spy subjects. Following a welcome halfway refuel at the remote oasis airstrip of Al Jouf, strong headwinds and giant thunderstorms forced us low, hugging the desert floor, reducing our already tight fuel supply to even shorter margins. In rapidly falling light, we made our approach into Kuwait City International Airport, overstretching the aircraft's four-hour flying endurance by a good ten minutes, as the 'fuel low' warning lights reminded us. Here we met with our escort into Iraq, the other two Merlins, and after a quick brief we flew a four-ship night tactical, lights-out, formation transit to our final destination, Basra. We had crossed ten countries and over 3,500 miles within four days. It was 8 p.m. local time and all the food tents had closed, with 'absolutely no exceptions' for providing two very hungry crews a late meal. It was just as well I had accepted an orange from a local at Al Jouf. In the chaos of the dark, our bags went everywhere and I wasn't to see one of mine for another three days.

Basra Air Station was located just west of the city of Basra. It was the main operating base for British and Danish forces in the MND (SE), the Multi-National Division (South East) region. Our allocated area of operations covered approximately 20,000 square miles, from the Kuwaiti border in the south, along the Iranian border to the east, into the Maysan province north of Al Amarah, and west, along the Saudi Arabian border, into the Al Muthana province, as far as a Merlin could reach.

Domestic accommodation consisted of several tents grouped together, either side of an access corridor, under the cover of a semi-circular desert-sand-colour outer tent. Each inner tent could sleep approximately ten people on camp-cots, allowing for some personal space. Penny and I were allocated bed spaces in a girl-only tent. Each camp-cot was inside a two-tier mosquito net and had a black plastic trunk for storing personal items. On the hard black plastic floor lay electrical extension leads, providing power for a small bedside lamp and laptops or CD players. The ablutions areas were across the small corridor separating the internal tents: a separate ablution for the women contained a few showers and stainless-steel toilets and sinks. The lack of any privacy was going to be a challenge for me; being caught shaving would be demoralising. The main tents were allocated to different units. We were part of Joint Helicopter Force (Iraq), or JHF(I), but due to the small number of females in this unit we'd been separated to a general tent, sharing initially with four young servicewomen. The girls already occupying our tent were very helpful and had already sorted out our bed spaces before we arrived. In the early days we felt separated from the guys, occasionally meeting for meals in a communal dining tent or at work. Once we had completed the initial training missions, Penny and I were allocated to different crews, which meant that we didn't get to see much of each other either. From tent to work was about quarter of a mile. Sometimes a crew would be allocated a Land Rover to get backwards and forwards for meals and to carry equipment out to the aircraft, but otherwise it was a walk along metalled roads. JHF(I) consisted of a group of Portakabins joined together under a thin desert-beige metal shell, forming briefing rooms, an operations room and various offices. A separate Portakabin was provided for our flight and to be used by the duty crew. An adjacent ISO container was used to store our personnel weapons and ammunition securely.

My first operational sortie in Iraq was straight into the heart of Basra City, with the boss and crewmen Dino and John. Flying at fifty feet above the ground was the safest option for the short hop from the airfield to the city. It provided an element of safety based on surprise and the buildings provided obstructions that would make it difficult to track us with guns, rocket-propelled grenades (RPGs) or MANPADS heat-seeking missiles. Our mission was stopping random vehicles for no-notice searches. As we approached our first briefed drop-off point, the troops readied themselves for disembarking rapidly.

The roads were incredibly busy, often with four lanes of traffic going each way on a dual carriageway. The only way to get that amount of traffic to stop was to block the road with the aircraft, which meant easing a 72-foot-long helicopter down into the busy traffic. With Dino and John manning the machine guns, drivers seemed willing to stop, though some did try to drive around. I imagined them getting to work and trying to convince an angry boss they were late 'because a British helicopter blocked the road'. The troops were off in seconds, lining each side of the road, looking initially for vehicle occupants that roused suspicion, warranting further attention.

Back at a safer height, we maintained top cover, with the guys protectively observing from behind the aircraft's guns, and the boss and me scanning for possible signs of trouble further afield or for other aircraft to avoid. After ten minutes, the troops radioed they were complete. Now we would move them to a different road, in a different part of today's area of interest. Short times in random places prevented us all from becoming predictable, or a static target, and drivers carrying illegal or wanted cargo never knew where they would be stopped. There was no option of seeing a barricade and turning around: the barricade came to them. And if they did turn around then the 'barricade' chased them from the air. It was a simple way of denying insurgents their assumed security of unrestricted movement, a successful part of Northern Ireland tactics.

Our first day was a long one, finishing just before midnight. By the time we had unloaded the aircraft, debriefed the mission and returned rifles to the armoury, it was another hour before I saw my camp-cot, nearly eighteen hours after I'd left it. The problem for me working such a long day was facial hair growth. Speaking face-to-face to people became very uncomfortable, though arriving back at my accommodation so late usually meant I had privacy in the ablutions to deal with that.

A few days later, I received replies to my letters to the politicians. The letter from the Lib Dem parliamentary candidate was positive and supportive. The Labour man said he wasn't my MP, even though he continually posted notifications through my door saying he was, and the Conservative candidate 'disagreed personally' with my 'life choice', but wished me luck on my tour of duty! However, contrary to the Conservative Party's predominant attitude of rejection or indifference, a Gender Recognition Bill had become law on 4 April! When I got home I would be able to amend my birth certificate so that my sex at birth would be listed as female, in accordance with my gender, finally giving me full protection in the eyes of the law. This was the much-appreciated result of a long struggle by determined champions of equality for people with an even longer experience of persecution and discrimination. But being recognised in law and being respected or supported were two very different matters.

As well as operations out of Basra, we would detach for several days at a time to Al Amarah, an hour's flight time to the north, or Camp Smyth VC, seventy minutes' flight to the west, to provide an airborne reaction force (ARF) with fifteen troops on standby with us, or a medical immediate response team (MIRT) with two combat medics, able to treat casualties as we rushed them to the nearest appropriate medical aid.

Camp Smyth VC was a Queen's Dragoon Guards (QDG) base,

known as Camp Smitty, near As Samawah. Its lasting impression was its infestation with flies, and the overladen sticky fly-trap tapes in the lunch tent. On our first mission from Smitty we picked up some troops from a town sixty miles south into the open desert, nestled in a small gully. Nearby stood the tall castellated walls of a fort, built by the British in 1912. En route we flew low over a patrol group of Land Rovers of the QDG, letting them see there were 'friendly forces' above them. At our pick-up point, an Army Major called Chris explained that they were looking to use the area as a FOB for Merlin. It would give patrols extra reach along the border they had been unable to get to with Sea King or Chinook. Once we were airborne, Chris directed us via Camp Miner II, a collection of Portakabins, surrounded by desert, marking the scene of an appalling mass murder. The desert was being excavated to locate and identify thousands of bodies. 'Up to 15,000,' Chris had said; some of the many Kurdish people allegedly murdered on the orders of Saddam Hussein. They were driven out into the desert where they wouldn't be found, and they were executed beside excavated pits, then covered over by bulldozed sand. A six-year-old girl feigned death and dug herself out afterwards, revealing her story after she was found by Bedouins in the local desert. Many such graves still lay undiscovered. The debate over the dubious legalities of invading Iraq will always be argued, but there could be no denying that at least our being here had halted crimes against humanity like this one. It was an emotional encounter, reminding me of Bosnia. We were keen to help the QDG explore this area further, but Divisional Headquarters was very short of helicopter assets and held them close. One day we would get to do some long-range desert patrols, but for now, other tasking was coming thick and fast.

Al Amarah was regularly rocketed and I got used to wearing body armour and a helmet, but, for me, ablutions were a much more stressful time. Toilets, two rows of sinks, and ten shower cubicles, some with shower curtains, were available in a large open-plan shower block 200 metres from our accommodation, beyond the aircraft. But I always planned my visits when it was unlikely that anyone else would be using them, such as at meal times, at shift changeovers or in the early hours of the morning. Our sleeping space here contained four camp-cots, each with a mattress on top, in a mosquito-net pod. The walls were covered in naked centrefolds, but when I was alone I would remove those beside my bed. I felt ugly enough as it was. One day we were watching a DVD in the IRT crew room – the guys 'had to choose the movies' and, ironically, it was *Scary Movie 3* – when there was a loud, sharp bang from very close by. For a moment it went very silent, minds thinking the same thing – 'Was that what I thought it was?' – looking at each other, until the shriek of the mortar alarm settled any doubt. It was standard procedure to get the aircraft airborne as soon as possible: it was our casualty evacuation means, and with an ARF we might catch the rocket team before they had got too far. We scrambled to our aircraft, 'Foxy', but unfortunately, the batteries for the management computers had failed, which meant we couldn't start the engines or get the radios to work to tell anyone. We expected troops to have been at the aircraft by now, but everyone else was clearly still sheltering from the attack. John dashed back in to fetch an engineer and we still managed to be airborne within twenty minutes of the explosion. A Lynx took off before us and was patrolling overhead the stadium in west Al Amarah, the suspected firing point. We took over while he went for fuel, but it was likely the attackers had escaped into the city crowds by now. The rocket had hit the perimeter wall next to our aircraft – fortunately, on the other side of her protective concrete blast-pen. An explosive ordnance device (EOD) team just happened to be twenty-five yards from the impact point and were showered in debris, though not hurt. This was our new routine.

My experiences in Iraq had been a mix of positives and negatives: professionally it was going well, but personally it had been very difficult. It wasn't so much about the personal stresses I had encountered, but the more public ones. I had seen that personnel who didn't know me were quick to mock, to snigger as I passed by, to point me out to colleagues so they could join in. I was skipping meals and I stayed away from the gymnasium tent for the same reason. It reinforced my Bosnia experiences, showing me that people didn't understand what it meant to be transgender, and, away from the reassurance of my own colleagues and friends, the wider military still found a way to be discreetly hostile. While the policy supported diversity, the workplace threatened any idea of inclusion. I could hide from this, or I could try to raise awareness, to show them that I was worthy of respect, that transgender people in the military was a fact now – a forever fact. I was the first, and currently only, openly serving transgender person on frontline operations, and while it was a lonely place to be, giving in would be failing; persevering could make it easier for others following.

14

A FAMILIAR DREAD

2005–2007

On my return to the UK, the boss asked if I would consider a posting back to RWOETU, the very unit I had been on when I made my decision to live my life openly, back in 1998. There was a need for someone with my experience. I had mixed feelings about this idea: I was happy being on the squadron, it meant a lot to me, but it also made a lot of sense to be part of RWOETU, with the knowledge, skills and current operational experience I had gained. There was a lot to be done to help evolve the protection of aircraft flying in war zones, and I wanted to be part of that. RWOETU played a vital role in enhancing that capability, being responsible for evaluating everything from operating software and control systems to personal equipment, and also had a responsibility to develop procedures and provide guidance and training for the crews, so I agreed. Although I was on RWOETU, I was still declared part of the squadron's Combat-Ready aircrew allocation, which meant I needed to keep my skill levels and knowledge to the highest of standards, more so because now I was looked upon by the squadron as an expert on all matters. The Merlin desk was a team of three, and my speciality became tactics, electronic warfare and platform protection. Perfect.

Once a year, RWOETU personnel also organised and ran the

seven-week Helicopter Tactics Instructor Course, and my role would be to train the student instructors that each helicopter squadron sent. The Army Air Corps (AAC) and RN Commando Helicopter Force (CHF) were participating too, so I got to instruct on Merlin primarily, but also Puma, Chinook, Sea King (CHF and SAR), and AAC Lynx, amongst others.

At the end of each course was a graduation dinner, where the spirit of military aviators meant all sorts of shenanigans happened. The 'work hard, play hard... and pay for anything you break' ethos had been tamed somewhat, due to rules being enforced more strictly. We dined formally, in uniform, at heavy oak tables, dressed with mess silver – silver ornaments belonging to the station, squadrons or units present. The squadron standards (beautiful silk banners, in Air Force blue, with gold tassels and silk embroidery), listing historical operational honours bestowed by the King or Queen at the time, were formally paraded and placed unfurled in a stand at the foot of the tables, with everyone stood to attention in respect and honour. After grace, a four-course meal would be served by mess stewards, also serving wine, in organised formations, sweeping by each of the four tables extending singly from the top table. And then – but only after a toast to the Queen – the speeches would start and the mischief would begin. I had been enjoying the evening at the 2006 dinner when I felt a tap to my leg. 'What was that?' I exclaimed, curiously. 'Something just hit my leg!' I happened to look at Danny, a graduating AAC Lynx pilot sat opposite me on our table, four feet away; he was looking straight at me, his face white. An inordinately loud explosion was followed by several hundred kilograms of oak table shaking: my left leg was thrown violently up against its underside, mess silver shook as wine glasses jumped, my ears were ringing. I looked at my leg: my tights were torn – no, burnt – my otherwise pale white skin had black and red flecks. 'Ow!' was my understated reaction, rubbing my leg.

Danny's face was now wearing an eyes-wide-open look of shock and embarrassment. 'I'm ever so sorry, Caz… that was meant for that lot!' He pointed at the table behind me, whose occupants sat covering their ears, looking at the faint wisp of smoke around my chair. Danny had smuggled in an exercise-grade 'Thunderflash', a pyrotechnic training aid, a small explosive device with a six-second fuse used for battle training, not meant for direct contact with people. He had decided to throw it beneath the tables, so no one would see it arrive. I had never seen anyone so apologetic, so innocently concerned, after attacking someone with an explosive device, albeit accidentally. I had got off lightly, with just a large bruise and a few minor marks, but it would cost Danny a drink every time we met from then on.

Shortly after, on Saturday 6 May 2006, I switched on my television to watch the morning news, disturbingly showing the burnt-out wreckage of a helicopter with a familiar rotor-blade shape. The Berp Blade – it could only be a Merlin or a Lynx. It was Iraq, and there were fatalities. I phoned Dave, a Squadron Leader who was standing in for our boss while he was away in Iraq on a recce. Dave knew only the same as me, so I phoned a few other friends. We all waited, worried. Then the news came: four dead, three crew and a passenger. It was an 847 Naval Air Squadron Lynx, shot down over Basra City. As guilty as this made me feel, I did ease a little on hearing that news. Of course I was distraught that UK personnel had lost their lives, but the only thing that made it just slightly less distressing, personally, was that it wasn't a Merlin. To lose people close to me, people I was working to keep safe from such losses, was unthinkable. But aviators had lost their lives in a violent way. We knew it was always a risk, but that would never make it any easier to hear.

By Monday morning, the names still hadn't been released. Dave called me into his office. 'Caz, I have some really awful news.' A familiar dread descended, the same as when Dad's death was about to be revealed, and when I'd heard the more recent news of Dinger's tragic death. 'John Coxen and Sarah Mulvihill were on board that Lynx. There were five fatalities, including them.' It was heart-wrenching news. Both were amazing people who had done more than most to make me feel accepted. John had been my Wing Commander boss for the past year. He was next in line for a six-month tour of duty, as Officer Commanding (OC) JHF(I), and had only gone to Iraq to build essential awareness for his role, to prepare him better for when he returned as the commanding officer. His role would make him responsible for the Lynx detachment too, and they had been tasked to show him the normal operating areas within Basra. Sarah was the Merlin Operations Officer on 28 (AC) Squadron, and she was coming towards the end of a tour of duty in Iraq as the Adjutant to the incumbent OC JHF(I). Hers was a ground tour, but when her boss couldn't go on the task, she stood in, for operational experience and as a familiar face from the Merlin Force, to continue the hosting of John's visit. The Lynx had been operating east of Basra and pulled up to cross over the city at a safer height on their way back to base, via one final recce: the Old State Building, known as OSB, a name that would become familiar on my next tour. Shortly after reaching height, they were engaged from behind by a MANPADS heat-seeking missile. The Lynx exploded and fell into a residential area, in a bad area for recovery forces to be on the ground, and not far from the OSB. It was such a heartless reminder of how dangerous those skies were.

• • •

My responsibility for Merlin meant working very closely with the Air Platform Protection Operational Evaluation Unit (APP OEU), a team of experts who conducted the trials and research into counter-measures and missile warnings systems. RAF Merlins were fitted with a state-of-the-art 'directional infra-red countermeasure' (DIRCM), a system that no other UK helicopter had. It could detect a missile, calculate its position in three dimensions, and then point a beam of coded infra-red energy into its heat-seeking eye, so the missile became confused and missed its target. The problem is the missile's 'eye' is very small, and travelling at twice the speed of sound towards the target aircraft.

Defences had to respond immediately, faster than a human could, and they needed to be accurate. But DIRCM was new, and it was American (though built to a British design requirement). We needed to understand the system in more detail than the manufacturer would give us. It was what we did with every single piece of equipment, re-gardless of where it had been made. It wasn't acceptable to just believe what was put in a glossy brochure when lives were at stake. But the USA wouldn't release classified information that their own forces relied on – understandably, though very unhelpfully for us. The UK had tried, at the highest senior management and political levels, to obtain a device to help us to understand the system, a data acquisi-tion unit (DAU), a specialist laptop that plugged into critical systems and provided detailed information to help understand and tune them for peak performance. At a DIRCM UK Users Conference held in the UK, I was given the opportunity to stand up in front of directors from Northrop Grumman, the primary manufacturer, and explain powerful reasons why we needed this equipment, and how they would also benefit from us having it. I was amazed when they agreed on the spot. As the two-day conference progressed, they wrote the case for permissions, in a US/UK memorandum regarding military equipment procurement. Within weeks we had our own DAU on long-term loan. The AWC and DSTL were particularly happy; it would help tremendously with their work.

In November 2006, I deployed to Iraq for the second time. I was happy I was going to be crewed with Kat – she was already a good friend and it would be great having a female cockpit; we were tuned together better. Our crewmen were Andy and Alex, both good guys. There was no one on the squadron I didn't get on well with, but it made a big difference to fly with a team that worked well together from the start. Technically, I was a guest: I was invited by the squadron to bring my tactics experience and my knowledge as a specialist on the aircraft's defensive systems, and it felt good that they trusted me to provide this – and little did we know how much it would be required. Six years had passed since critics of my military service had voiced their opinions to the press that I shouldn't be allowed in the military, that I would be a liability on operations, yet here I was deploying on my fourth operational tour in four years, demonstrating otherwise. I had volunteered for this tour, mostly because I wanted to do my job to its best, but also because I wanted to prove that those very voices of spite were completely unfounded.

While UK trials and evaluations were priceless, the real proof of any system would come in the hostile environments endured on operations: that was where I needed to be, doing my job, as one of the Combat-Ready crews in theatre, flying the same missions in the same environment the squadron crews did.

It was no surprise that RWOETU Flight Commanders preferred to keep their personnel in the UK, where possible. Deploying to Iraq wasn't just for the duration of the tour: each tour rotation required months of work-up for crews, engineers and support staff. Everyone deploying as a unit had to work up together. As well as our own tactical flying training, we practised downed-aircraft drills, road convoy and ambush drills, mine detection and clearing, combat First Aid, conduct-after-capture training, survival training, the law of armed conflict, weapons handling and range tests, mission training in the flight simulators, and environmental flying training in friendly-nation dust environments – the deserts of Jordan or Arizona – by day and by night. Crew training is vital and flight simulators just can't replicate the real world accurately enough.

To justify such a long-term commitment away from my UK responsibilities, and especially because I had also been nominated as the Merlin desk lead, I performed a cunning two-pronged attack. I reasoned with my Flight Commander why I needed to go, and I presented my 'unquestionable value' to the Officer Commanding 'B' Flight, and Commanding Officer of 28 (AC) Squadron, knowing they would then also reason with my Flight Commander why they needed me. So when he called me into his office and asked, 'Would you be OK going to Iraq with "B" Flight?', I replied, 'Sure, no problem, when?' with a smile. Going with 'B' Flight meant being there over Christmas, so he offered to delay my departure. It was a nice thought, but I was happy to go. It would be my second Christmas in a war zone – and although I didn't know it, there would be more to come. Christmas and New Year had long meant visiting friends, and I often shared it with Val and Andy, or Helen and Bill Bacchus, and their two young sons, Matt and TJ. TJ once innocently asked me if I was a girl – my voice let me down again – but his straightforward acceptance of my answer was wonderful.

Squadron Leader Mikey Kay was my Flight Commander now, a tall lean blond Puma pilot with an amazingly lively, positive and buoyant character. We had first met on our Puma helicopter course in December 1997 and his friendship survived my transition without any questions or concerns, offering just the kind of support anyone could wish for. One night we were walking from the officers' mess to a dinner night at the Station Commander's house. It was a cold night and the pavement was a little slippery with frost, so Mikey wrapped his arm around mine as we walked. Not many men would do that so visibly, regardless of their strength of character; to be seen walking arm-in-arm with me was still something that was somehow embarrassing, and therefore a rare treat for me, a simple act that meant so much more than Mikey would have realised. I knew it would never have even crossed his mind – it was a natural extension of his arm to a female in his company.

The job I was doing now demanded a lot of attention in the UK that was vital to the safe operation of our aircraft in Iraq. Having already completed one Iraq tour, nobody would suggest that I should be doing more. The RWOETU policy was: CR aircrew should aim to do one operational tour in any one RWOETU tour, nominally a three-year period. But I believed I needed to be there more frequently than that: tactics evolve, the threat evolves, the enemy was always seeking weaknesses in our defences, trying different techniques to shoot an aircraft down. But this time the threat wasn't just in the skies or on the roads; within hours of our arrival in Basra, a noise that would soon become far too familiar interrupted all conversation.

The distinctive sound of the attack siren filled the air, wailing from wall-mounted speakers, from mast-mounted speakers, from distant speakers. All around the base the same tune, a mixed cacophony as echoes and time delays modified the warble, a sound that generated fear, pressure and instinct. The focus was on survival now, bodies diving everywhere, controlled commotion. A rocket attack was in progress. Indirect fire, known as IDF, was inbound and the warning system was giving life-saving seconds of notice. Lying prone minimised the risk of shrapnel and blast damage. Training was fighting instinct: people would instinctively reach for their body armour, but there wasn't time for that now; at this stage of attack, the training said 'get down!' Rockets had no precise target, they just fell from the sky when they ran out of energy and gravity took charge. The shooters would set them up on improvised launchers or shaped ground in the middle of nowhere. Some firing teams made better guesstimates than others and we would get to know that. Sometimes they would be set on a timer, allowing the shooters to escape before their firing position was given away. The rockets were simply pointed in the right direction and angled for the required range; where they landed was more down to fate than judgement. Hopefully fate was on your side but we had to wait, lie and wait, wait for the noise, wait for fate.

No one heard the explosion this time; a small insignificant crater would be added to the open desert surrounding the base. Movement was advised only when absolutely essential: to move away from fire, for instance, or to reach a seriously injured casualty. The danger radius from shrapnel following a rocket explosion typically increased with height above the impact point; hence lying down significantly reduced the risk of being hit. The alarm stopped as sharply as it began. Now was the time to put on body armour, if it wasn't already being worn beforehand. The all-clear siren sounded, permitting post-attack drills to check for casualties and damage. Rockets weren't new – their use goes back centuries – but still we learned old lessons over and over, sometimes in the worst possible way.

The rest of the day was filled with arrival briefings, re-zeroing weapon sights, in case they had been jarred during our journey out, and preparing personal equipment for flying. I completed a flight 'check-ride' by day (a sortie with no troops on board to refamiliarise me with the operating area and remote landing sites, and to refresh me on desert landing techniques), and a night refamiliarisation of the local area, combined with troop tasking. Our first destination was Basra Palace, an impressive complex on the western bank of the River Shatt-al-Arab, once a holiday home for Saddam Hussein and his family, now the home of hundreds of British troops. Forty seconds after we lifted off, a radio operator shouted out, 'Palace Red, Red, Red, mortar attack in progress!' We were already accelerating away, into the darkness: the Palace was used to such attacks but it didn't need the added incentive of a large helicopter vulnerable on its landing site, full of fuel, ammunition and people. Our best protection at such sites was to minimise time spent on the ground. Troops and cargo had to be off or loaded in thirty seconds – any longer and the defence of surprise was lost.

Shaibah was our next destination. Passing the small town of Az Zubayr, random lines of tracer reached into the night sky, a luminous tell-tale of the bullets it marked, perhaps blindly aiming towards the noise of our helicopter; then Shaibah went 'Red'. With rockets in-bound, we broke off our approach and looked for somewhere safe to hold off. It was going to be one of those tours.

The following day, I was united with my own crew. Our routine became two days of tasking by day, two days of night tasking, two of immediate response team – usually a medical immediate response team, though it could also be with an airborne reaction force of sol-diers or an ammunition technical officer (ATO), colloquially referred to as bomb disposal, though they did much more than that. Two days would be spent as the duty crew, available for air tests, ground duties, and any additional flying tasking as required, then the cycle repeated. There were no 'off days', but that was the way it was. We had enough crews to run the programme, no spare – this wasn't a place to have more people than need be.

Accommodation for the IRT crew was close to the aircraft, in a Portakabin to the rear of the main JHF(I) building, containing a small crew room with a television and DVD player, a fridge and a water boiler for hot drinks. There were two sleeping areas, each with four camp-beds inside their own individual mosquito-net frames; one room was allocated for female occupation. For washing, there was a sink in the toilets of the headquarters block, though it was pot luck whether the water was running from the tap or flooding the corridor outside. The JHF(I) Operations building was open and used 24/7, so using the sink there didn't offer the guarantee of privacy I would have liked. Regardless of where I was, and even if I tried 3.15 a.m., someone would walk in.

Day two of our first IRT duty began with a very loud bang, followed by the sirens as a rocket hit close to the runway nearby, providing an early morning wake-up call. Rocket attacks were daily now, and frequently more than once a day. One day a truck arrived at our tented accommodation and deposited hundreds of individual breeze-block type bricks, so we could build a protective wall around the outside of our tents, six bricks high and double skinned. A couple of weeks later, the Army vacated some Corimecs at an alternate accommodation site and we were moved in. Corimecs looked like they should provide more protection from rockets but they weren't reinforced, and metal sunshields placed above them meant a rocket's first impact caused detonation above head height, showering a wider area with added shrapnel. A wall of Hesco surround them, large wire-mesh and fabric baskets filled with desert sand and rubble, stacked two high, providing protection from any other threat. I was sharing with Kat, and it was the same layout as the one I had used in Bosnia, though dustier. They offered more privacy than the tents, and beds instead of camp-cots, along with a chair and single wardrobe. We provided our own bed linen; a small on-base 'convenience store' was a popular source. Unfortunately, our Corimec was the furthest one away from the ablutions, again, which meant a walk past everyone else, and the need to wear body armour and helmet. Our body armour was the same version I had worn during the war in Bosnia, but this time I had Kevlar plates in place, so at least it provided some protection. The jacket I wore for flying felt more substantial and protective.

One day we were tasked to deploy our MIRT into the desert, so we collected a FOB kit. It included camp-cots and mosquito nets, and a metal trunk containing enough ration packs, cooking materials and bottles of water to last six people forty-eight hours. I didn't mind living in the open desert at all – it went with the job – though I did worry how successfully I would be able to shield my daily routine. Living in austere conditions didn't mean I shouldn't find a way to protect myself from possible humiliation.

After an early morning start, we found the temporary encampment as expected, on the edge of a disused Iraqi runway in the flat, open desert of the Maysan district. Narrow green lines of squat, rugged bushes breaking up the desert beige hinted at moisture, though we were far from the River Tigris to the west. As we circled to land, we scoured the outer perimeter for signs of enemy activity. Andy and Alex crouched alert behind the guns, watching for signs of threat, just like the protective screen of troops in their armed vehicles below. Our two combat medics joined in our scan of the desert landscape, their life-saving equipment secured but at hand. Half a dozen light-armoured Scimitar reconnaissance tanks and armed Land Rovers of the Queen's Royal Lancers formed the fighting force below us. Tucked in behind camouflage netting, they blended into the undulating

6–8-foot-high sand berms surrounding them. The berms were man-made walls of defence, residues of the 1980s Iran–Iraq War ramparts, bulldozed into place to form a protective perimeter around the runway. The Iranian border was close to the east, and the surrounding desert was deformed with such ramparts, the debris of war strewn amongst them, rusting wreckage slowly decaying back into the ground.

We were here to provide an emergency evacuation measure for potential casualties, a combat air ambulance. To have the best possible chance of survival, seriously injured casualties needed to be evacuated off the battlefield and received at a medical trauma centre as soon as possible, and certainly within one hour of injury, a period known as the Golden Hour. There weren't enough helicopters in Iraq to base one with each patrol, so one operating base would cover many different ground units, and not just UK ones. This patrol group was on a mission out of range for a helicopter on standby to recover casualties to the closest combat trauma centre within the hour. The reaction time and flying involved for the round trip would take considerably longer, degrading survival chances. Forward deploying a helicopter and medical team with the patrol meant cutting out the time to get there. It also meant the patrol could operate further out into the desert, if the trauma centre was still reachable inside the Golden Hour. In a couple of days, this patrol would be back inside the range for home-base emergency cover, but we would remain with them until that happened.

We chose our landing position carefully. The powerful rotor downwash of a Merlin helicopter would easily damage the patrol's camouflage netting, communications equipment and low-profile tents. Kat closed the aircraft down and we were greeted outside by a young Lieutenant. His warm welcome extended to a warning.

'Stay alert, we have indications of a possible attack...' – he paused,

seemingly as he realised the cockpit crew were women – '…so weapons and armour at all times. You'll best help cover from the berm.'
He pointed at one of the desert mounds adjacent to our aircraft. Our
helicopter was a sitting duck on the ground, especially being outside
the berms. We had already been rocketed twice today. The first attack
had been at 3 a.m. at Basra, the attack siren waking us out of bed to lie
on the dusty floor. The second attack came just a couple of hours later,
as we were taxiing our aircraft.

'Incoming rockets… Red! Red! Red!' the air traffic controller shouted over the radio.

In the background of his warning we could hear the distinctive
cyclic warble of the attack siren. We had just seconds to move: with
flight-speed on the rotors, it was safer to go than to shut her down and
seek hardened shelter – the big sky and small moving target theory.

'Are you happy if we bring the aircraft inside your perimeter?' I
asked the Lieutenant, assessing the gap where the old broken runway
cut narrowly through the berms. 'It's a bit of an easy target out there…
and gives your position away.' He agreed, though he clearly wasn't anticipating the whirling dust storm that followed. The only way to move
our fifteen tons of helicopter was to start her up and taxi. Pulling in
power lightened the aircraft on its wheels, making it possible to move
forward, but doing so was always a trade-off, with the rotor downforce
stirring up anything loose. The only consolation was that their vehicles
and tents were already full of sand. The smiles returned when they saw
that the first items offloaded were the bulging grey-fibre mail bags we
had brought them. I walked a short distance outside the berms to see
if the aircraft was hidden any better now. 'Well, better than before!' I
reassured myself. The main lower fuselage couldn't be seen, but there
was no escaping the topside, the tail rotor, or the main rotor head,
doing a great impression of a giant, five-frond palm tree.

Around us, off-duty troops were resting beneath camouflage nets draped from their vehicles' sides. Throughout the scorching heat of the day I kept abreast of the intelligence scenario and attended various command briefings with the troop commanders. Kat had developed a throat infection and took shelter in the shade of the aircraft. The crewmen made sure the aircraft received her post-flight and pre-flight maintenance checks. Eventually the declining sun began to dull the day and our thoughts turned to food. We broke out the ration packs and small disposable hexamine-block burners.

'Chicken and mushroom boil-in-the-bag pasta tonight!' teased Tim.

The medics didn't have additional duties to perform here, unless someone became ill or hurt, so Tim had kindly appointed himself chief cook. It didn't smell much like chicken – mushroom, perhaps. Its bland 'one taste fits all' flavour was enhanced only when our chef pulled out his 'secret ingredient', a packet of curry powder. There wasn't much out here to test the sensitivity of the nose, just machine oil, or the smell of coconut from liberal use of sun cream.

As darkness fell, I watched in awe as the sky came alive. The night skies were so clear out here, void of pollution or weather; the whole universe opened out above us. So many brilliant shooting stars, so many wishes, all of mine the same. The pitch-black darkness offered me a safety cloak when combined with the essential 'no visible light' policy. To have a wee meant a blind stagger to find a suitable place out of sight of inquisitive eyes. To pull down my desert-beige flying suit meant removing my armour, camouflage jacket and weapons belt first. The guys didn't have to go through such a cabaret! A depression in the desert just on the blind corner of a berm was suitable. I was out here for a different reason, though – the reason I had felt anxious when told we'd be deploying into the desert. I loved being a natural red-head, but it hurt. Each try of 'the latest development in laser hair removal' wasted my money, and my work routine prevented the preparation time needed for electrolysis. I had a small tube of cream, a balm that would hopefully prevent tell-tale nicks from the razor, specially sourced because its contents dried clear, unrecognisable if I left any residue on my skin. I hated having to shave. It was worse than the threat of danger. I hated it so much. My shooting star wishes would help: my childhood dream come true, to wake up perfect. As I returned to the aircraft, I wiped my face with a gloved hand, once, twice to be sure, again just in case. Now I would be human for another fifteen hours or so. I wondered if the sentries had noticed, their night-vision devices removing the privacy of the dark.

The spacious cabin floor of the aircraft provided enough room to spread out six sleeping bags in pairs abreast. The side doors weren't fitted, allowing the machine guns to be mounted, so the warmth of our winter-weight sleeping bags was much appreciated. At least the rear ramp could be raised enough, even with its gun in place, to keep out the creepy crawlies and creatures of the night; it was like a drawbridge. It wasn't the most comfortable place to sleep, but it was a familiar home, for a while.

After two days, the patrol group was preparing to move and we were stood down from the MIRT. Clearing away the cabin and working silently in the dark, aided by the dimmest of glows from our night-vision-compatible torches, we prepared the aircraft for flight. It always felt reassuring somehow to sit back in the cockpit and begin strapping into my seat, the tightened shoulder-straps providing a false sense of security from the threats outside. The helmet was cold to put on, heavy too from the night-vision goggles and their counterbalancing weight. Once we were all in position and ready for start, the noise began, first the auxiliary power unit, charging into life all the avionics and their incredibly noisy cooling fans, then the engines and rotors.

The quiet peace of the desert was now shattered for miles around. Climbing away into the dawn sky, I wished the troops well, with one final radio call, before switching to the area operations frequency.

Back at Basra, Kat had a parcel waiting: a couple of rolls of wallpaper and some glue. We had already acquired a piece of carpet for the floor of our Corimec, now it was time to add a pink flower damask pattern to the plain white gloss walls. Although there was only enough for part of one wall, it made a definite improvement and attracted inquisitive visitors. We laughed at the idea that the occupants after us were likely to be male and it would open them up to banter.

In the UK, a factory accident had affected the resupply of countermeasure stocks, used for defence against guided-missile attacks. If we ran out, the risk of losing an aircraft would prevent all but the most critical life-or-death MIRT missions, and even then, that risk would have to be measured and authorised from the very top, so a closely monitored audit was introduced. Against missiles, the defence system had to respond automatically: if it just provided warning then by the time the crew interpreted that warning and reacted, it would likely already be too late. Split seconds counted. In automatic mode, the system would take no chances: if it thought it had seen a missile approaching, it would trigger countermeasures. Countermeasures against heat-seeking missiles included a small arsenal of flares mounted in dispensers, front and aft on the aircraft. These would be fired as a sequence of intensely hot pellets, to confuse the missile's tracking of its target and lure it away. Usually the warning was a false alarm, but not responding had proven fatal on far too many occasions, and too recently. The warning came from a visual display and a loud audio tone over the crew intercom, and it was never assumed to be a false alarm until a certain period after the attack, if no signs of a missile or explosion had been seen. Sometimes the visual background meant the missile couldn't be seen anyway; crew reactions were therefore the same for every alert. One morning at 4.30 a.m., as Kat and I checked with operations for our day's tasking programme, a Post-it on the aircrew information board was pointed out to us. It said 'Fly DAS in Manual', DAS being our defensive aids system. This instruction was crazy – it went against everything I knew, everything I taught – but it was too early in the morning to find someone to discuss it with. As the tactics expert, I told Kat to ignore it; we should remain in auto. She was the aircraft captain, so it was ultimately her choice, but she trusted me. Later in the afternoon we returned to Basra, and I went in to complete the audit document. The boss was waiting there, his hand pointed me out: 'Ah, here Caz is now, we'll see how well my plan worked… Caz, how many flares did you release today?' We'd had a few false alarms, where no missiles had been observed. Because we hadn't selected 'manual', the system had released flares automatically. I revealed our flare stock; several had been fired. A look of shock came over his face. 'But did you not get my order?!'

'Yes, sir, but I advised it would be foolish to comply.' I answered, waiting for the reprimand. I wasn't in the habit of ignoring orders, but I knew I had more expertise in this subject than the boss did; after all it was my job, as a tactics instructor and platform protection specialist. Kat walked in behind me. We had been stood down from further tasking for the day. 'My office, Kat,' he beckoned. It was my advice she had acted on, so I followed her. He sat down, while we stood together in front of his desk.

'You do realise the gravity of the current situation? Why did you not follow my instruction?'

I jumped in and explained why it was a bad idea. He listened and asked what alternative there could be. Had I known the decision before we had arrived for our first mission of the day, I could have pre-empted this. I offered an alternative solution.

'But is that possible?'

'Yes, sir. I will need to confirm with the relevant agencies in the UK but if they agree with my proposal, it could be done in days.'

'OK. I want a written brief on my desk as soon as possible, high-lighting the options, advantages and disadvantages.'

I went straight to Operations. There was a computer in there with a classified connection to the UK. Within hours I had my reply: they liked the idea, a lot, and would put it in action. My solution would reduce the amount of flare usage, but without reducing the aircraft's protection. It meant we could still fly in 'auto', but it required soft-ware changes to systems that would usually take several weeks, if not more, to bid, write, test, tweak, test, and test again, and then authorise. Within three days the data was couriered out to Basra by Mikey Kay, on his way to Baghdad as the Puma Detachment Commander.

I briefed the crews on the new procedures; everyone was happy. I was pleased I had talked my way into joining this detachment: my knowledge had become crucial, and I felt I was in the right place at the right time. I was incredibly impressed with the team in the UK: they had turned the requirement around at unprecedented speed. It worked, and it carried us through until the supply chain was restored. I had directly influenced the continued operational capability and safety of Merlin missions in Iraq. But just as importantly for me, and my self-confidence as a person, I had gained tremendous respect from my colleagues, the very people I was here to support. I had their backs, and they had mine. Now the bullies had no valid argument about my ability and value to military operations.

Ten days later I was swapped with a pilot onto the IRT crew, so I would be available for a tri-service meeting regarding tactics later in the af-ternoon. Not long after taking over the duty, we briefed for a medevac to fly a patient with stomach pains to the hospital at Shaibah. As we waited for the ambulance to arrive, people around us began running. Air traffic control shouted a warning over the radio: 'Rockets inbound!' The ambulance wouldn't come now. We scrambled airborne, just behind my own crew, off on a task to Kuwait. After orbiting for an hour, we were cleared back in and met with the ambulance. The medical transfer went without further incident, but walking back in for a cup of tea, we were scrambled for a casevac. Medevac was a premeditated pick-up or transfer of a patient under care; casevac meant an unplanned urgent response to battlefield injuries, or medical emergencies. I ran to the ops room to collect the details, while Colin ran to the aircraft with Winnie, the No. 2 crewman, to get it restarted. The aircraft was rotors-running as I scrambled up the ramp along with the No. 1 crewman, Dave. 'Basra Palace!' I shouted at Colin as I climbed into the cockpit. He was already taxiing forward as I strapped in. As soon as he had turned into wind, we lunged airborne, straight from the parking space. Our 'Rescue 21' call sign gave us priority and direct routing, maximum speed at roof-top height over the city. The casualty had a life-threatening gunshot wound to the stomach. Leaving the Palace, the Merlin's anti-vibration system was making the flight as smooth as an airliner, even at the maximum possible speed, as the medical team in the cabin worked hard to keep him alive until we reached the hospital at Shaibah.

On return to Basra, we taxied over to the refuel point. A Lynx, call sign 'Skunk 34', cut in front of us: he was on a priority mission and needed refuelling urgently. As we waited our turn, we were warned to standby for a further rescue mission. A second refuel point came available, and as we took on fuel the grid reference came in; it was only four miles away, just on the edge of the city. We unplugged from the bowser and scrambled airborne behind the Lynx. He was going the same way, flying extremely low, with erratic manoeuvres. It turned out he was our escort, but nobody had told us that. Later, he explained the erratic manoeuvres were because he believed he was being shot at. Nobody told us that either, although we were just behind him!

The casualties were Danish soldiers and the pick-up point was on a street in a built-up area. Danish armoured vehicles and troops formed a protective cordon as we offloaded the medics. Crowds began to gather. Just above us, the Lynx, armed with its heavy machine gun, continued its wild aggressive gyrations in a protective orbit. An armoured ambulance backed up to our front and a stretcher came out, its bearers ducking down low as they ran under our rotor blades, carrying a soldier with a gunshot wound to the neck. A second stretcher followed – gunshot wounds to the shoulder. It wasn't a safe part of town to be in. People now filled the flat roofs surrounding us; we were vulnerable to sniper fire or worse, RPG. A rocket-propelled grenade would be catastrophic, and a static helicopter, or the armoured ambulance, was such an easy target.

With everyone on board, we lifted and departed, the nose burying as we accelerated as fast as we could. Flare countermeasures were triggered as we raced away over the open ground to the west of the city, and the Lynx took up station behind, watching our back, our 'six'. I radioed ahead with an estimated arrival time at the hospital and outline details of the casualties. It had seemed a lifetime, but from scramble to landing at the hospital site was under twenty minutes. I got to attend my tri-service tactics meeting, but our day paled when I learned that our earlier casualty had succumbed to his wounds at Shaibah Hospital. Back at my Corimec, a large furry camel waited on my bed; he came from Kuwait and wore USAF DPM uniform, and he carried a message. 'To Caz, from your crew. I am Colin, I am here to look after you when your crew go home.'

As Kat returned to the UK, we mixed the crews around; now I would be flying with Michelle Goodman, another good friend, and Dino and Chris as the crewmen. We got on very well together as a crew. One of our first missions was a difficult night-approach into the Old State Building, a place with traumatic connections. Five months later Michelle would become the first female pilot to win a Distinguished Flying Cross for bravery, evacuating a critically ill soldier from near here during a determined mortar and rocket attack.

On Christmas Eve, we inserted a 'Black Dagger' patrol of troops on the outskirts of Basra. 'Black Dagger' was the operational name given to the early morning counter-insurgency patrols conducted by the RAF regiment, aimed at preventing the rocket attacks on our base. The insert was made under the cover of darkness and we would extract them just before dawn. It was a long wait trying to rest in the crew room but stay alert to any call for immediate extraction. At the agreed time, we landed at their pre-briefed extraction point. In the dark we waited, and waited. Eventually I raised them on the radio. They were making difficult headway through muddy terrain and still had a way to go. We asked for a position and went in search. As we got close enough, they switched on their firefly, a covered infra-red strobe that could only be seen using night-vision aids. Cross-checking the map showed they were close to several tall electrical pylons and wires; they switched off the firefly and we approached with caution. It was a dark night for night-vision goggles and the wires blended into the darkness. The pylons were slightly easier to see, so we followed them in, carefully. The pylons were either side of us now; there wasn't much room for error. We found the patrol grouped in a defensive formation, just below the wires – not good. The ground wasn't good either, a lake and mud basin. We landed as close as we could, but it was still over 100 metres away. When they finally got on board, daylight was breaking. They were fatigued, cold and soaking wet; the mud had been deep and viscous. I looked back and saw smiling faces. Of course, they could relax now, and be warmer, but that wasn't it – the crewmen were handing out chocolate bars from our crew room ration box. It was Christmas Day, after all. I looked over my left shoulder; a pair of US Army Apaches were following us. This was particularly comforting as our own expected escort had landed at Basra as we took off.

Back at my Corimec, I was spoilt with Christmas presents from home, mostly chocolates, Christmas cake and sweets, though Auntie Val had contravened instructions by sending a 37cl bottle of wine, and Kat had sent a small bottle of Prosecco. Alcohol wasn't permitted; usually it was detected and confiscated in the post. I would have to delay drinking any until I could guarantee being off duty the next day, and I would have to be careful when disposing of the bottles. As I lay back to get some sleep, a whistling shriek passed low overhead, followed by two loud explosions, shaking the room. The enemy had brought out their bigger rockets, no doubt especially for Christmas. I was prone on the floor before the IDF attack alarm sounded. There might be more inbound. I fell asleep wearing body armour, not for the first time. At 5.30 p.m. we all congregated in the mess tent for Christmas dinner, wearing uniform and body armour with Christmas party hats. There was more turkey than I had ever seen. The ban on alcohol was relaxed for Christmas night and we were given two cans of lager each to celebrate.

My time with 1419 Flight was going well. I had their respect and I wasn't treated any differently to the rest of the Flight. But away from their company, life was still unsettling. I still couldn't go to the gym tent without people staring and gossiping, and it was the same in the dining tent. Women still made up only a small percentage of the military, less than 9 per cent as an average, and this was reflected on operations. All the girls had to put up with staring from males, which was predictable, but I knew the attention directed at me wasn't one of 'eye candy'. It was puzzlement, reservation and sometimes unsubtle disrespect. Some groups, sat at their wooden trestle dining tables, would raise conversations as I passed by, just loud enough to reach my ears. Comments, thoughtless sniggers and hand-over-mouth muttering made it clear they knew my background. Stares were thrown that I could only answer back with a smile, the only defence in my armoury. My smile was sometimes enough to catch them off guard, though sometimes it appeared to insult their masculinity. I was disappointed my colleagues never showed any awareness; perhaps my ears were tuned in better, or perhaps they just weren't listening for such 'banter'. Whatever the reason, I wasn't going to mention it myself. I'd be 'worrying about something that was nothing'. 'Just ignore them, don't let them get to you, they're not worth it.' I defy anyone to not be bothered when people are talking about them negatively in proximity. I didn't want anyone to intervene aggressively, but a clear display of support sends a powerful message. It wasn't about personal security – that wasn't at risk – it was about how I felt. Why did I deserve such comments? After all, weren't we all there to do the same job, risking our lives together, facing a common enemy?

I knew the malicious comments came from a weak minority, and I had no doubt the majority shared impartial, perhaps even positive, opinions, but they remained silent, and when negative comments aren't being balanced out or redressed, they hit harder. I wasn't expecting praise, but I didn't deserve disrespect either. Those who relish the assumed power gained by exploiting someone's difference are usually blind to the contempt in which colleagues may hold them, and not being challenged helps to foster that ignorance. The military thrives on banter. Appropriate banter is invaluable: it cheers, it raises morale, it ties people together in moments of stress, it calms tension – but there's a fine line between banter and intimidation, and some people don't know the boundaries; these are the bullies. A negative reaction, or obvious distress, is laughed off with 'It's only banter!' I decided I should rise above any disrespect. I would go about my daily business with my head high. I would show them that I was a stronger person than they were. That wasn't as easy as it sounded.

15

HEY DOWN THERE!

2007–2009

Back in the UK, it was business as usual. Andy Ouellette had joined the Merlin desk prior to my second Iraq tour. I had instructed him on the tactics instructors course back in August 2005. He was very proactive and focused – just what was needed. Rob Bray was the third member of our team, an experienced helicopter crewman who was eager to share responsibility and be the first to spread 'interesting news', and he was always happy to confront anyone he thought may have shown me any disrespect. I counted them both as friends and it was a great working environment, but we were about to have our hands full. The press had exposed the Army's desperate need for more tactical trooping helicopters on the battlefield.

I was summoned into Mikey's office, where he greeted me with a handshake. 'Congratulations, Caz. Commander Joint Helicopter Command (JHC) is awarding you his commendation for the exceptional work you have done regarding the Merlin DAS and in particular your efforts out in Iraq!' I knew Mikey would have written me up for that, and I appreciated that he had done so; the fact that Commander JHC, a two-star Army General, had put his name to it, was incredibly uplifting. Sadly, none of my family could be there to witness the award ceremony, but I did get the most beautiful bunch of pink carnations and lilies from Sandra, and I was delighted when Val and Andy agreed to be there, hosted by Mikey.

My work life was going better than my personal life. I had been trying online dating agencies with no success at all. As reluctant as I was to go down that route, I could see no other way to meet people. If I wasn't transgender, I know I would at least have been chatted up by now, but the military was a macho environment and what man would want to risk the banter fired up by dating someone like me? It would take someone who was so secure within himself that the opinions of others didn't matter. I was well liked, just not in one important way. It made me value myself less: if I was invisible as a potential partner, what was the point of living? I had mentored a couple of individuals who had transitioned, following my exposure in the media, and one of them had found a partner already and in fact was engaged. So there were rare examples of civilian men who didn't see difference as an obstacle, but no one in my experience, and certainly not military men.

There had been a glimmer of hope in Iraq, from an American radar technician. I had seen him a few times, as I walked past his radar post between the operations room and the aircraft. I always said hello to anyone I passed, even with the risk of my voice causing a demoralising response. It would be rude not to acknowledge someone else. Then one day, as Kat and I were walking in from an aircraft, he walked over to meet us. He looked at me, 'Would you like to meet for coffee later this evening?' I couldn't, it had been a long day, and we didn't have much time in the evening for sleep before the next day's task. I explained politely, adding, 'Perhaps another day!' I was surprised and nervous about the idea, and I discussed it with Kat back at the Corimec. 'It's only coffee!' she'd advised.

The next day, he asked again. 'OK! When and where?' We met in a dining tent with an all-day tea urn. We had to make do, as the coffee was an unknown 'best value' instant powder, left out in a small dish next to a hot-water boiler; stewed tea was the better option. We had a nice chat for about an hour, and a few days later we met for the same. It quickly became clear he wasn't interested in anything other than 'talking to me over coffee', or tea in our case, but I couldn't understand his motive. Did he just never realise I was transgender? Was he just enjoying some female company? I didn't want to ask. He did all the talking anyway; I learned all about his large family in the USA and his devotion to them. In many ways, I was relieved: I wanted to meet someone, but I was genuinely nervous about the whole idea. I think shortly afterwards he returned to his main unit base, and I never heard from him again. But in nine years of openly being Caroline, that was the sum of my 'companionship experience': a cup of tea. Although I was surprised by how nervous I was about just meeting for a chat, I was also depressed that no one seemed the slightest bit interested in getting to know me.

Then I saw a newspaper article that was similarly disappointing: a reservist Army captain called Jan was being announced as 'the first officer in the history of the Armed Forces to undergo a sex-change operation'. It was 2007; the newspapers had revealed my story seven years ago, and one reporter even contradicted her own report by mentioning my name in passing. It was pointless getting bothered about it, but there was more to come. Next, the claim became a marketing statement for a *Cutting Edge* television documentary. It bothered me that they were dismissing the history of transgender service in the military. I wrote to Channel 4, who had shown the documentary; they explained that it was made by an independent TV company, and provided their address. Writing to the producers, I politely pointed out

their viewer-guidance summary misled audiences. I received an acknowledgement, saying they would be in touch, but they never were.

Andy, Rob and I had been spending a lot of time on UK ranges in
Lincolnshire and Pembrokeshire testing new defensive systems, including a large aircraft infra-red countermeasure (LAIRCM) for
Merlin, a laser-based improvement of the DIRCM system. Its amazing technology would fit into a *Star Wars* movie: an aircraft-mounted
system that detects a missile launch and then points a narrow laser
beam of infra-red energy into the missile's optics, to overload its
guidance, such that the missile manoeuvres away violently, sometimes
causing it to break up. Now it needed to be tested in an operational theatre – Iraq. A specialist team from the APP OEU and DSTL
would lead the assessment. They had no helicopter operator experts
of their own, which meant I would need to be one of the in-theatre
crews, operating the system and providing informed assessments on
its performance during operational missions. The most appropriate
timing for the tests fell when No. 78 Squadron crews were in theatre,
and they were happy for me to join them.

Checking in for my flight from RAF Brize Norton, I was shocked
when the Corporal on the desk exclaimed, rather too loudly: 'Oh no,
sir! You've made a mistake… You've brought your wife's passport, not
yours!' It went quiet around us. Bemused looks betrayed the fact that
he had been heard from several yards away. I looked at the passport.
'Nope… it's definitely mine!' I didn't know whether to be upset that he
had identified me as male, or pleased that my passport clearly didn't. I
took the positive: in my passport I looked like someone's wife! Maybe
one day.

There had been a big increase in US personnel in Basra Contin-
gency Operating Base (COB), and the protective infrastructure had

been considerably upgraded. At my accommodation, I was introduced to the 'Stonehenge', colloquially known as a 'Coffin' – I could see why. Beds had gone: in their place, mattresses set on the floor were surrounded by breeze-blocks, four high, like those we had placed around our tents, now giving more individual protection. A small entrance and a metal plate for a roof, covered with a heavy anti-fragmentation mattress, gave each sleeper protection from blast and shrapnel damage. The idea was to crawl into this brick 'den' head-first, so that only the feet were exposed at the narrow entrance, but that did make it feel like a coffin, so I risked sleeping the wrong way round, leaving my head exposed. It was dark inside, and when I slept the right way round, I frequently bashed my head, forgetting where I was. I worried that the camel spiders and wolf spiders liked Stonehenges too, but I had to trust in 'What you can't see can't bite you'. As well as offering personal protection, the base had grown a significant system of perimeter defences, including rocket detection radars and weapons that shot back or engaged incoming rockets.

However, even with the extra protection, the increased frequency of attacks meant the aircraft were in danger of being destroyed on the ground. Helicopters remained in short supply and high demand, and the risk of loss was considered too great; so a decision was made to base them over the border in Kuwait, for maintenance and repair. Tasking would still be carried out from Basra, but it meant flying there from Kuwait, before the first mission of the day or night, and returning there after the final one.

Crews and a small engineering and ground support team still worked out of Basra, on a shift-cycle for tasking, but the main engineering and support base was now in Udairi, in the Kuwaiti desert, just twenty-five miles south of the Iraqi border. It was a US Army base known as Camp Buehring, and it was far more relaxed, with a US Army 'Px' (Post Exchange) – a large supermarket, along with commercial fast-food outlets, and even a cinema. Nobody could argue with how the Americans looked after their troops abroad, though they deployed in much bigger units, and seemingly with far bigger budgets.

After a couple of weeks, Merlin 'Echo' arrived, wearing her new defensive outfit. 'Echo' was the fifth aircraft of the twenty-two Merlin HC Mk3's registered; all the aircraft were known affectionately, by the crews and engineers, by their own individual letter of the phonetic alphabet. The four letters omitted from the list were India, Victor, Yankee and Zulu. The AWC and DSTL team arrived the following day. They would operate the data acquisition unit, and I was looking forward to seeing it in action. After a few 'breaking-in flights' within the safety of the Kuwaiti desert, we moved over the border, into the far more demanding environment that was Iraq, and in particular around Basra City.

Tasking included a night mission as part of 'Operation Charge of the Knights', an Iraqi Forces-led mission that had begun with Basra but now targeted Al Qurnah, a small town on the junction of the Tigris and Euphrates rivers, near the Garden of Eden; ironic that it had become a haven for violent criminal gangs and insurgents. Our mission was to insert Iraqi troops, using two Merlins and two US Army Chinooks, with two US Army Apache attack helicopters as our escort. We also had top-cover from fast-jets, and over-watch from intelligence and surveillance platforms, far more protective support than we had ever had before. It was a good test for our new system, and a successful one. The routine tasking was much along the lines of my previous tours and the busy days meant time passed quickly. I had identified issues with the ergonomic placement and lack of associated crew warning regarding 'safety switches' in the cockpit, where the non-handling pilot/navigator was having to overstretch to operate them, which usually meant having to remove their shoulder harness to do so; because the switch was ordinarily moved during take-off and landing, that wasn't safe practice. It was also then difficult to see or feel if the switch had been selected to the right position, especially in an unlit cockpit at night. It meant a simple mistake would leave the aircraft vulnerable. But I would need to prove the risk before people would spend any time and money on fixing this, so I introduced an experience feedback procedure to gather evidence and drew up plans for a solution, in anticipation.

The UK's involvement in Iraq was winding down, and Merlin would soon come home, but not for long – there was a need for more helicopters in Afghanistan, and the threat there was better funded, better equipped, more abundant and just as determined to kill people. Merlin needed additional equipment to remain safe there, and that meant plenty more trials for us.

Simon was now the 'B' Flight Commander, on 28 (AC) Squadron, and our friendship had grown strong over the years. When I offered my expertise for my fourth and final tour in Iraq, he gladly accepted. Once again, the hardest part was convincing my chain of command that I needed to return. Fortunately, my Flight Commander was now Si Kovach, known as 'Siko'. The nickname was ironic; had he been any further relaxed, he would have been sleeping. Siko was another friend I had instructed on the Helicopter Tactics Instructor Course, and we had worked together on the Merlin desk, before Andy had taken over from him. He understood my reasoning.

The aircraft had moved back to Basra COB permanently now, but as UK forces relocated there, allowing Iraqi Army and police units to assume wider control, the rocket and mortar attacks became more focused, and their chosen target had grown bigger. One day a truck arrived at our Corimecs and unloaded heavy anti-fragmentation mats: our roof-top protection had finally arrived. It took a lot of team effort to lift the heavy mats into place, but with the Stonehenges, Hesco walls and protective roof, the Corimecs were much safer places to sleep – though the loss of eye-contact with anyone else when sheltering in a Stonehenge did make it a very lonely place to be during the moments of attack.

To prevent the attacks in the first place, the perimeter patrolling was stepped up, and that meant more missions for us, inserting more Black Dagger patrols into the darkness and collecting them before dawn. During one such extraction mission, an American drawl came over the radio: 'Hey down there, do you guys need any support?' I looked around and saw two US Army Apaches approaching from behind.

'Thank you kindly, but we're just about done here!' I replied.

'Roger that! Have a good day!' They moved away, though not far, until we had lifted safely and set off for base. It was nice to have the offer, and a comfort knowing we now had more of this kind of asset in the area. The RAF regiment's roving patrols added a key deterrent, and marine patrols on the adjacent waterways added to that, yet still the rockets came, from all directions.

We also had new desert DPM (camouflage) flight vests with bulkier, heavier armour plates, though the aircraft was still lacking armour; options were being investigated. We were also issued with fire-resistant two-piece desert camouflage flying uniform, identical in appearance to the soldier's version. It meant we didn't have to wear the one-piece flying suits any more, and that was so much better for girls; we didn't have to take our body armour off to go to the loo.

Our few old and battered Land Rovers had either fallen apart or been 'reallocated', but now locally employed civilians (LECs) were hired to drive small buses around pre-planned routes, around the key base areas, during daylight hours. To get to or from work, I could wait beside a concrete IDF shelter, looking for a dusty bus with JHF(I) scribbled on a card placed in the windscreen and an always widely grinning LEC driver. Often it was quicker to walk, though on occasion I had seen three buses arrive together! For security reasons, we remained armed at all times. The dining tents had gone now too, replaced with DFACS (dining facilities), huge concrete warehouse-type buildings, designed to withstand a direct hit from the largest of rockets. It was a shame such protection came too late for too many, and just before we withdrew; the secret was always in the timing.

Tasking was as busy as always, though there were far more VIP moves into and out of Basra City, as UK and US commanders handed further responsibilities over to Iraqi forces. Once such sortie saw us move Michael Portillo, the former British Cabinet minister turned journalist and TV presenter, down to Kuwait to catch an onward international flight. Under his civilian body armour and helmet, he still wore his characteristic bright pastel-coloured jacket and 'typical male Army officer'-style trousers.

As my tour ended, I was invited to join a group of girls meeting in the unit medical centre for a rare opportunity to enjoy a social gathering and try some spa and makeup products, sourced specially for the evening. I was running late, and I was in two minds whether to go or not, as it had been a busy day's flying and I was tired. I delayed for a few minutes, then decided to go. As I picked up my armour and helmet and stepped outside my Corimec, the attack alarm sounded. I dashed back inside and took cover in my Stonehenge. An unpleasantly familiar noise whistled through the air above me, followed quickly by a loud explosion nearby; now I would be even later. After the all-clear siren sounded, I set off to the meeting.

Just after I'd arrived, a messenger warned us not to go outside, and to remain wearing body armour and helmets. A rocket had landed in the compound just a few metres away, and the medical centre had been hit by some shrapnel. There were casualties, including a fatality; a group of LECs had been caught in the open. Inside our room, the military spirit remained intact, but the news had curbed any wish to indulge ourselves and, as soon as we were able, we dispersed. I didn't get to enjoy a social, though I did get to meet some great military ladies. My delay had been fortunate; arriving there any earlier would have put me at the right place at the wrong time. It was time to go home. And I had someone to meet.

16

THE GREEN ZONE

2009–2010

Just before I had deployed to Iraq, I had been contacted by someone on the internet dating site I had been a member of for nine years. The content of my profile had always been a dilemma for me. Should I be upfront and tell potential dates my background? Knowing I was a transgender woman would prejudice how a heterosexual man thought of me – how could it not? If I didn't reveal that straight away, then when did I? It would probably be obvious on our first meeting anyway, but they might feel that I had misled them. If we had more than one date before they knew, they might consider I had deceived them, possibly even get violent, or humiliatingly abusive in public. They might not want to know, they might be happy believing I was who I was, never asking. But how could I possibly judge that? It was such a difficult position, and not one any friends could answer. It was my decision, and it was another incredibly difficult one.

I felt I couldn't let a relationship develop without being open and honest. I knew that being exposed on the website meant the rare opportunities of someone getting in touch would become even rarer, that I was effectively writing myself off. I didn't expect anyone to date me anyway, but open honesty was a vital foundation of any relationship.

Consequently, I declared my background, with a brief explanation, and then I waited, and waited. In nine years, my profile had been visited over 3,000 times; in that period, I had been contacted four times. When I asked those four if they had read my profile, I never heard from them again.

This contact was therefore new territory for me, and when he confirmed he had read my full profile but still 'wanted to get to know me', I expected a catch. I had warned him we wouldn't be able to meet for quite a while, but he emailed and wrote letters and cards while I was in Iraq. His letters were nice, positive and funny. He acknowledged my past, and couldn't understand why people had a problem with it, but he was happy to not discuss it further unless I wanted to. It was fun having this contact; it was enriching having someone who saw me as a woman. He kept sending me cartoons that made me laugh. He was a six-foot-two, divorced, semi-retired company executive, his name was Jon, and he was looking forward to meeting me. For the first time ever, I was looking forward to getting home to meet someone. I offered to meet halfway between our locations, but he decided to book into a bed and breakfast near me. We met in my local town, at a restaurant of my choice. I was nervous, but we had a nice talk over a meal, then his mobile phone rang. He 'had to call someone back', 'it was an emergency', he stepped outside. Five minutes later he returned to the table, his coat in hand. He had to go, but he would be in touch. I never heard from him again.

A week later I took Merlin 'Oscar' up to RAF Leuchars, to instruct on my eleventh UK Qualified Helicopter Tactics Instructor Course (QHTIC); it was business as usual. I was entitled to time off after Iraq, but I wasn't going to miss this. Andy had been promoted now and posted to JHC, and my trainee from last year's Tactics Course was now the RWOETU Merlin pilot. 'Shug' McCulloch was the only trainee to have ever bought me flowers as a thank-you.

It was good to be back at Leuchars, but it was a ghost town of a base, in comparison to its heyday as a fighter base. We were based out of the HAS site formerly used by No. 43 Squadron. In the centre of the site was a tumbledown listed cottage, surrounded by wild grass and a small copse. The voices of aircrew broke the silence, sitting outside in the sun, having a rest between briefings and missions. They didn't pay any attention to the sad-looking tree, planted in memory, or the short wooden stake holding a weathered grey wood panel, bearing an oxidised brass plaque, all glowing in the direct sunlight. I stood staring at it for a while, head down, deep in thought, names and faces, reminders of how dangerous military flying could be, even in peace. Training for 'times of tension' had to be realistic, and that realism came only with real-life action. 'Train as you fight', it was called, and it brought risk. Sometimes, the training came too late. If they could see the plaque, my colleagues wouldn't know the names etched in it, but I remembered that day vividly, 20 April 1988. Every year on that date I toasted 'absent friends'. Had it been twenty years? I wondered what they would think if they were watching me now.

The QHTI course was as challenging as it could get in operating a battlefield helicopter without being on operations. It was demanding for the crew and the aircraft, not forgetting the support teams and the engineers, keeping the aircraft on top form for four weeks of intensive flying. The trainees had already learned all the techniques, procedures and essential knowledge in four weeks of ground school and mission simulators at RAF Benson. Now they would hone those skills evading radars and anti-aircraft weapons, fighter aircraft and attack helicopters, conducting troop assaults, or evacuating civilian nationals from various scenarios, then surviving the return journey. As annoyed as I was that my promotion was being denied to me, I was still eternally grateful that it meant I stayed in a flying job. This was what I was born for, not flying a desk. Not one person I flew with, in any sortie of turning and fighting a helicopter against a fast-jet, came off the aircraft without the world's biggest grin. It was a crew fight, a formation fight, and it was extremely demanding, but what fun! This was the joy of what I taught: teaching people skills that one day could save their lives.

When the course finished, we set off home in 'Oscar'. Shug was flying, with Rob and Richie as rear-crew, and we carried twelve passengers, mostly Merlin aircrew, with a couple of engineers and our boss. As we approached the Cheviot Mountains, the weather worsened. We needed to cut through Newcastle Airport's airspace, so I called them on the radio for permission. We were down at fifty feet above the ground now, and nobody else should be down here in this weather, only other military helicopters. Newcastle Radar called us: 'We have a Robinson 22 to the west of you, he's reporting VFR.' Visual flight rules meant he was in much better weather: a Robinson R22 is a tiny two-seat helicopter with only basic flight instruments, and he needed better weather for his flight to be legal.

I directed Shug into a shallow valley, giving us a slightly better clearance from the cloud base, and he accelerated us back up to a comfortable speed. I was looking for hazards, assessing the weather, looking for better options, seeking the safest route. It hadn't been forecast to be this bad. Without warning, Oscar pitched nose high and banked hard to the left. Several cockpit warning lights illuminated. I glimpsed a dark shape before it passed down our right side. Audio warnings drowned out our voices.

'What was that?!' someone shouted.

'That Robinson!' Shug answered, swinging Oscar around and putting her into a hover now. Newcastle Radar came on the radio. 'Vortex, be aware the Robinson may be close to you.'

'I know... we just gave each other a scare...' I replied. 'Standby!'

'You sure did!' came the voice of the other pilot. Richie had seen them briefly as they passed down our starboard side, also evading hard. We did a quick search and found them on the ground in one piece. After circling above to make sure they were OK, we continued our journey south. In the back, our twelve passengers were well awake now, but very silent. What on earth was the Robinson doing here in this weather? He wasn't permitted to fly in these conditions in that aircraft, in controlled airspace. We had been metres away from a fatal mid-air collision. Eighteen people, including the two in the Robinson, would have lost their lives if Shug hadn't seen the aircraft in the last second. His violent evasive action exceeded Oscar's normal limits, setting off all our warning captions and alarms. Oscar was OK for now, but she would get a full check over once we were home. It was an incident that would motivate me when asked to investigate collision warning systems, but for now my focus was on Afghanistan.

• • •

I had wonderful friends, and Val, Sarah and I met annually for a holiday somewhere nice – this year's was to Slovenia, and we had a fabulous time – but without a partner, or other distraction, my main focus was work. Merlin was off to Afghanistan, and I was determined to go with it, for all the same reasons I'd pushed hard to go to Iraq. There was much to do: it was a new mission, with a new enemy, for Merlin at least, and that meant different threats and enemy tactics, as well as a totally new operating environment.

History had taught the world never to underestimate the low-tech adversary that existed in Afghanistan. The Soviet Union had lost over 300 helicopters there in nine years, following their invasion in 1979. It was an extremely dangerous part of the world to fly around. The operating environment was a factor too: the weather, the dust, the terrain. We knew much from the Chinook experience; they had been there several years already. It was demanding on the aircraft, equipment and people – everything would need to work harder. The aircraft was to gain a Kevlar-armoured floor, protecting the troops and rear-crew from small-arms fire from below, and armour plate replaced one of the direct-view windows beside the pilot's/navigator's feet, adding to the protection provided by the standard cockpit-seat wing armour and the armour plate in the aircrew flight vest.

We had also gained LAIRCM, to protect the aircraft from the heat-seeking missiles known to be in this region. The trials we had flown in the deserts of Iraq in 2008 had proven their invaluable worth now. However, Afghanistan was different in so many ways, and I needed to be there as early as possible – but there was a problem. The squadrons wanted to get their own crews experienced there, and there were only so many authorised places available. It was a war zone: putting additional people at risk without good reason wasn't permitted. The squadron had its own tactics instructors too; I had helped to train them. They were happy that they were given priority places, but I wasn't. I asked my boss to argue my reasons, but the squadrons dug their heels in. They believed their experience in Iraq was good enough to prepare them for Afghanistan without my help, but I wasn't arguing to go to a war zone for the fun of it.

Was I being foolish? I was approaching fifty soon. Few people went on operations in their fifties in the military; even fewer went there in frontline roles. Most military people of my age had jobs in staff appointments, or were perhaps winding down for their upcoming retirement. They had played their own part already, now it was someone else's turn in the desert. But I didn't see it that way. My age wasn't going to jeopardise my ability – in fact, my experience and knowledge enhanced my ability. I had been in this position before, with Iraq, but I had got there, and I had helped fix things that were broken. But I couldn't persuade them to include me in the first tour. 'Maybe a later one!' That wasn't acceptable to me.

The work-ups began immediately. No. 78 Squadron would be providing the first crews, but they were to retain the 1419 Flight identity created for Iraq. The squadron as a whole wasn't deployed on operations; it sent a detachment of engineers and four or five crews at a time, in rotation with 28 (AC) Squadron, to fly the aircraft both units shared at RAF Benson. I still had a great relationship with the AWC's platform protection team at RAF Waddington, and I knew they felt the same way I did: they were also keen to get out to Afghanistan and evaluate equipment in operation. Their work in the UK was conclusive, but there was nothing like making sure, especially when it came to keeping people safe. They intended to visit theatre at the same time Merlin arrived, and my experience was a welcome addition to what they had in mind.

I had a sponsor, but I still needed my boss, the Joint Helicopter Command (JHC) and the Primary Joint Headquarters (PJHQ) to authorise my visit. If I was deploying with a 'formed unit' it would have been so much easier. There was also the question of who would provide the appropriate training for me to deploy. I couldn't just jump on an aircraft to go. I had to have paperwork saying I had completed the mandated training – weapons skills, medical and dental prep, mine awareness, rules of engagement, biological and chemical attack drills – and that I had the right equipment and clothing issued. There were more rules for personnel going off-base. If I was remaining inside the main base's perimeter walls, the training requirement would have been less strict, but flying meant there was the risk of being forced down, away from a secure base. That required downed-aircraft drills,

and convoy attack drills, including IED awareness training. Fortunately, we got permission from PJHQ and JHC, and I persuaded the
Second-in-Command of No. 78 Squadron to let me join their aircrew
pre-deployment training and crew work-up.

It was a lot of effort to get out to a war zone, and occasionally I sat
down and wondered what possessed me to do this. It was going to
be hard for me, and not just for any risk I was accepting, but for the
personal issues that came from being there. My experiences of sharing rooms and communal areas were fresh in my mind from Iraq, just
eight months previously. If I stayed at home I would have none of
these worries. Could I not just let the AWC team do their work, then
meet them when they got home for a debrief? No – and besides, they
were only a small team and their focus was on embedding Merlin
safely into theatre. They valued my expertise as a Merlin operator and
my familiarity with the systems they would be evaluating. A month
later I was on my way to Camp Bastion, in the Helmand province of
Afghanistan.

It was quite rare to be able to stand alongside a Merlin and pat her
on the nose while she was flying, at the highest she had ever been, and
the fastest too. Even more so as the aircraft had no rotor blades fitted
and there was no crew on board. I was back with Merlin Oscar, and
we were on our way to Afghanistan together, inside an RAF C-17A
Globemaster III transport – a 170-foot-long, four-engine heavy-lift
aircraft that carried its cargo snugly along at 30,000 feet. Spread
around Oscar, in an organised and secure fashion, were aircraft sections and boxes of engineering equipment. In amongst all this lay a
dozen or so people trying to get comfortable, stretched out on the
floor where they could, multi-coloured sleeping bags breaking up the
military green, grey, black or white that dominated the cargo area.
Others, in the sideways-facing seats lining the left side of the cabin,

sprawled awkwardly across several seats, or sat upright reading books, earphones in. Oscar was the second Merlin to be sent to Afghanistan.

Eighteen hours after leaving the UK, including a short stop at Al Udeid, we approached the descent point for Camp Bastion runway. We were woken up and instructed to don our Osprey body armour and helmets. The lights in the C-17's cargo hold flickered then went out, followed by a slight bump and a rumble as the aircraft touched down. It was dark, in the early hours of a Friday morning in December, and it was already warm. We were met by the Senior Engineering Officer for the Merlin Detachment, and we were astonished to discover the first aircraft was due to go tasking, without our evaluation equipment and team. It wasn't our place to say, but we would have waited the one extra day it would take to set up. It soon became clear people didn't understand our mission, as the specialist analysts were frequently removed from flight manifests.

My accommodation was Tier 2, in a stone-coloured two-storey prefabricated metal-clad building, with rooms on each side of a central corridor. Each room slept two in narrow metal-framed beds, or four in bunkbeds. I was sharing with a young airwoman called Helen. The rooms were better than being in tents, or in more austere conditions, though they were noisy, even with sleeping shifts.

With only one Merlin available until Oscar was prepped, it was difficult to get any priority to fly, but when we did it was extremely worthwhile. Rob and Stu from the APP OEU operated the DAU, with John, a DSTL specialist, analysing the data on the ground. I would fly whenever I could, to observe the in-flight results and to see the kind of area Merlin was operating in, to understand the operating procedures and tactics used, identifying those we needed to adapt, or adopt, and took these back to my own unit for consideration and action where need be.

Everything was a step up from Iraq: there were far more rules and regulations, and the briefings took longer. It was a very different way of operating, and that made it more important for me that I was there. Everything was bigger and better – armour, radios, weapons, vehicles, even procedures. There had been a lot of investment, and for good reason: the casualty list was already in the hundreds. The landing sites had varied threat levels, depending on the level of risk. 'Green' meant, as a minimum, two helicopters could support each other with their own weapons, 'Amber' meant at least one Lynx went as escort to a troop carrier, and 'Red' usually meant a pair of Apaches in escort, if they were available. Camp Bastion had a detachment of UK Apache attack helicopters, on their first operational deployment, highly regarded and respected by everyone, including the enemy.

In Iraq, I had captured the evidence needed to justify the repositioning of the essential protection system safeguard. I was delighted when I saw the new system preventing a potentially disastrous mistake, and the reassuringly straightforward way the crew used it, witnessing evidence that I was making a difference. It was only a short tour, but it had given me and the AWC team a lot to think about. They were 'over-the-moon' with what they had seen, captured and learned. We had much work to do.

17

ABOVE AND BEYOND

2010–2012

My time in Iraq and Afghanistan had taught me several things.
The first was that my self-confidence was only being held back
by myself. I was always confident in other people's company, but they
never saw the other side of me. I didn't allow them to because they
were my friends, and I didn't want to let them down. But it was always
disappointing when one thoughtless act had the power to ruin so
many good ones. When I was in town shopping, thousands of people
would walk by me without registering my presence, yet I could always
be sure of somebody doing a double-take, then following me and
sneering, pointing me out to a companion, making me feel uncomfortable. Goodness knows why! Shopping with a friend seemed to
ward off such rude people, though not always. But the soldiers' attitudes in Bosnia and Iraq, and now in Afghanistan, replicated those of
the general public in many ways. It could only be because they didn't
understand. They didn't know what it meant to be transgender, so they
happily mocked it.

The key to understanding anything was education, so I decided to
do something about it. I was already advising on policy, but I needed
to do more. I got in touch with Squadron Leader Michelle Randall

at the Joint Equality and Diversity Training Centre (JEDTC). Positioned within the Leadership and Management Division at the Defence Academy of the UK, JEDTC was the 'Centre of Excellence for Equality and Diversity training across the MoD'. Michelle understood, and invited me to talk to one of the tri-service courses she ran; it was the perfect starting place. We got on well, and became good friends. Michelle was from Orkney and, apart from being a very caring lady, she was devoted to her three terriers and her horse, Dexter – and her husband Chris, of course, a Major in the Royal Logistic Corps. Over supper and a glass or two of wine, we discussed a series of 'E&D roadshows' she was planning, to visit RAF units. I happily accepted her offer to participate, and they proved to be a runaway hit.

I had also been invited to be the 'trans member' on the RAF's LGBT Forum. This was a group of amazing LGB servicemen and women who, in their own spare time, offered support and advice to LGBT personnel, or their non-LGBT peers and commanders. I had been mentoring transgender individuals for some time now, and not just in the RAF, and with my long experience on working with policy holders, I was more than happy to get involved. The leader of this group was a Wing Commander called Mark Abrahams. I knew him as 'Abbo', and he was the most senior openly gay officer in the RAF. He had been a Chinook crewman friend on RWOETU, before I had left to transition twelve years previously. Had I known then, of the secret he had also been forced to keep, I may have confided in him.

There were undoubtedly several people I had served with who were also withholding their true sexuality or gender identity in fear, but none of us could know that. The ban, on LGBT personnel serving in the UK Armed Forces, had created an environment of enforced secrecy, fear and peer-reporting. How could that possibly be a good thing, for a force that had long relied on its people being a team, a force that had been led and championed by some of the very people it tormented? And people wrongly assumed to be gay, or rumoured to be gay (perhaps maliciously, to cause trouble for them), had suffered alongside those who were. Even though the MoD had finally repealed its ban in January 2000, there was still a way to go to enlighten those members of the military who showed no understanding at all of the value of diversity and inclusion. Sadly, these dinosaurs still existed, and while they did, there would always be a need for campaigns, to educate, support and challenge where need be.

After a talk at RAF Halton, I was approached by a Squadron Leader who identified herself as Catherine Armstrong. She admitted having been one of those voices that didn't understand why someone like me should be allowed to serve in the military. Her sister had encouraged her to attend this event and to listen, and now she regretted expressing that opinion. She had enjoyed my talk, and learned so much, and there were others who said the same. This was what I was here for; having this impact on just one person made it all worthwhile. Cathy, her sister Julia and I became good friends. Julia was proud of her sister and delighted that I had encouraged the understanding she'd been striving to inspire for years.

It always comes down to understanding: if people don't have that, they are more susceptible to being influenced by fabrication or rumour. Most people feel enriched by knowledge and compassion. Of course, there were always going to be bullies, those who didn't want to listen, who were frightened they might lose some of their power if they could no longer look down on those they perceived as weaker. The victims of bullying weren't weaker, though. Anyone who has had to live with difference, with any diversity that brings unwarranted intimidation, harassment or mocking, is already a far stronger person than any bully, anywhere.

The roadshows were a success and Michelle suggested I talk at the annual tri-service LGBT conference in July 2010. It was to be amalgamated with the civil service LGBT summer forum and held at the Ministry of Defence Main Building in London, for the first time. At the conference, I spoke of my personal journey, my experiences of transitioning in the military, the positive and the negative aspects, and how peers and managers could help to be supportive, even if not openly. Some people weren't sure how they could help, and others feared being supportive might expose them to ill-placed banter or rumour. In the first case, it is easy: just respect a transgender person as you would any other person. The simple act of saying hello, with a smile, means more than most people realise. I knew that ill-informed people sometimes spoke negatively about me, or about transgender people, when I left a room, but I also knew that friends or supportive colleagues who were present stood up to that, and rational argument usually trumped rumour. They would never tell me, but I sometimes overheard follow-on discussions. Talking is healthy; harassment is not. In the second case, if anyone worries that it's going to be awkward supporting someone who is transgender, then realise how much more difficult it must be for that person, and take strength from how they are standing up to it.

Then something else nice happened. Siko called me in to his office. 'Caz, many congratulations – Commander JHC has awarded you his personal commendation for exceptional service!' I was honoured; few people received two of these. I thanked Siko, as I knew he would have made the recommendation in the first place. But again, a two-star officer, an Admiral this time, had endorsed my contribution. The citation was for my 'dedication, drive and real desire to ensure the Merlin Force aircraft and crews were protected as best as possible', for being a 'significant driving force, operating at a level normally expected of individuals of considerably higher rank', for 'enabling the delivery of operational capability', and for 'single-handedly writing tactical advice and crew training, and standing firm against intransigence and operational pressure to ensure the best possible protection'. I wished I could have shown this to those loudly outspoken denigrators who predicted that, as a transgender person, I would be a liability in the military and not fit for operational service. I hoped Dad would have finally been proud too.

The results from the first evaluations in Afghanistan led the specialists into some very interesting areas that needed further detailed evaluation, so we were going back. This time, we had two DAUs: I was to take one myself and operate it on Merlin, and the rest of the 'Tiger Team' were going to Kandahar, to focus on the large fixed-wing assets operating in theatre, the C-130s and C-17s. The team split was a decision made on the flight out there; originally, some of them were due to come with me, but they trusted me as the Merlin expert to look after that part of the evaluation.

I knew how to operate the Fieldworks DAU but they normally set it up in the first place. In the dark cargo hold of a noisy, bouncy C-130, John, the DSTL analyst, sat next to me shouting instructions in my ear as I scribbled the details on a folded-up piece of paper I'd found in a pocket. The laptop had to be plugged in to key parts of the aircraft systems and sensors to know what the aircraft was doing in terms of speed, height, attitude and position, which required a wiring loom to be installed by Merlin engineers.

The missions I flew in Afghanistan all averaged over eight hours of flying, and when each was completed I had to go through the data so I could brief Rob, the AWC team leader, and the rest of the Tiger Team. It made for incredibly long days, and I always attended the briefs with the crews too. I had to know the mission, and not just for evaluation purposes; should anything go wrong, survival could depend on the situational awareness I had. Each crew had their own brief on actions in the event of coming down in a hostile area, though the aim was always in accordance with standard procedures – evacuate the aircraft, account for everyone, establish a defensive perimeter – before a head count if need be, and assess the situation – and there were additional responsibilities that needed to be briefed. As the detachment came to an end the Kandahar/Kabul team joined me at Bastion to review them. It was so rewarding to be a key part of this important assignment.

On my return, I became aware of a request from Esquadra No. 751, Portuguese Air Force, for help with tactical training. They flew Merlin in a peacetime search and rescue role, but the aircraft was also fitted to a similar specification to the UK's Merlin Mk3A for trooping. They wanted to combine these capabilities to provide combat search and rescue for European defence forces. Although the request had already been turned down by JHC, I presented a case to help, and volunteered my own support. In March 2011, I jetted off to Montijo Airbase, located south of the Tagus estuary on the south side of Lisbon.

From the moment I arrived, the welcome and hosting were exceptional. They were very proud of their squadron's achievements and its motto: 'Para que outros vivam' (That others may live). At an evening social event, they marked the 2,500th life rescued since the squadron began SAR in 1978. Their aircraft all proudly wore a St George's Cross, a sign introduced by English Crusaders in 1147 when they diverted, en route to the Holy Land, to help King Afonso Henriques recover Lisbon from the Moors. The Anglo-Portuguese alliance of 1386 remains the oldest alliance in the world still in force today.

I arranged a bespoke three-day training package, after which we took two aircraft and crews ninety miles north to Monte Real Airbase to put it all into practice during Exercise Real Thaw 11, an annual military exercise hosted by the Portuguese Air Force, including Army and Navy assets, as well as foreign forces. I knew they were aware of my background – Portuguese Merlin aircrew frequently visited RAF Benson, to practise aircraft emergencies and other skills in the simulator – but it was never mentioned; there was no need. They were totally at ease with being taught by me, and I rarely met a group of individuals who collectively paid so much attention to detail and asked so many relevant questions. After one of the missions, a female officer approached me and said how proud she was that a female aviator could teach all the things I did. I told her I wasn't the only one! When it came time to leave I was presented with a signed print, several badges and honorary membership of No. 751 Squadron. And I returned home with new-found friends.

In September 2011, my Desk Officer decided it was time for me to move from RWOETU. The average posting length was three years, and I had been there six. Moving people around spread experience and enabled different experiences to be gained. It made sense I had been there for so long, to give continuity to the projects I was working on, but where did I go from here? I only had three years left before I reached my maximum age for service, so a promotion was unlikely. I could easily have asked for a 'restful job', somewhere I could put my feet up and get ready for retirement, near an area that I wanted to settle into. I wanted to use my skill, experience and knowledge, though, and the only way to do that was to remain in a frontline role, on a squadron. The only problem was that I would be fifty-two soon, and the operational pace was hard for young aviators, let alone someone twice their age. But I had coped on recent operational tours, and I knew I wanted to leave the RAF from a flying job, and, most importantly, my colleagues and friends were still in Afghanistan and could benefit from my experience. So I asked to go back to No. 28 (AC) Squadron. I had seen Merlin into service with 28 Squadron; it would be nice to leave from there.

Given all my experience and my current Combat-Ready status, I was upset when the Squadron Commander reduced my status to Non-Combat-Ready on arrival, raising it to Limited-Combat-Ready (LCR) after I had flown a 'squadron acceptance check'. There was no good reason to do this. He said it was because I came from a unit that had 'less flying currency' than his, yet I had flown forty-two hours in the previous three weeks on RWOETU compared to only sixteen hours in the first seven weeks on his squadron. Most of my flying so far was on operations, teaching people tactics in the UK to fly on operations or evaluating systems that kept them alive on operations. It was unjustifiable to equate that to someone who had just joined the squadron from training.

I had been nominated, and shortlisted, for an award at a tri-service ceremony organised by the Ministry of Defence, 'for people who had significantly contributed to diversity and equality'. When I learned the press might be involved, I informed the boss, as a courtesy, but sadly he wasn't interested. I was confused, though, when my annual report said I was 'resting on my laurels'. I was contributing to diversity and inclusion in my own time, because I was busy at work, teaching crews vital skills, mentoring the inexperienced tactics instructors, writing a training manual, and helping RWOETU with some of their tactics programmes, courses and conferences.

The MoD People Awards 'recognise the endeavours and exploits of those in Defence who go above and beyond their day job, to promote the core values of inclusion, tolerance and diversity, while inspiring others'. The ceremony was held in London, in the MoD Main Building. There were four categories: Leadership, Inspiration, Community Involvement and Inclusivity. I was nominated in the Inclusivity category. The winners had been decided by a panel of six judges, all heads of key government and defence organisations or departments.

I could only take one guest, so, as a thank you, I had invited Squadron Leader Janet Adams, the RAF Equality and Diversity officer who had nominated me, with a contribution from Abbo. Sat beside her, I listened excitedly as the top three shortlisted nominees in my category were announced. Everyone applauded as I was invited forward to receive a certificate and a medal token as runner-up. The competition was astonishing, and hearing all the citations was humbling. Then the presenter announced one final award, a 'Special MoD People Award', from the Permanent-Under-Secretary of State (PUS) for Defence, Ursula Brennan. She held the civil service equivalence in seniority to the highest rank in the military. The citation suddenly started sounding familiar, and people were looking towards me. I looked at Janet, who had a big smile on her face, as the presenter read out the words:

for being a trailblazer in the field of inclusivity, for determination to succeed in changing attitudes, breaking down barriers and tackling ignorance, for being an inspirational role model to all transgender personnel in the Armed Forces, to those currently serving, and those considering a military career, the PUS Special Award goes to... Flight Lieutenant Caroline Paige.

The applause seemed even louder now. Janet congratulated me and I went forward to collect my award, from Mr Paul Jenkins QC, the civil service diversity champion, Queen's Proctor, and head of the government legal service. It was a total shock, and amazing to realise that people were interested in what I was doing. A microphone was handed to me; I had to think of some words on the spot, some thank-yous. Later I felt bad when I realised I had forgotten to thank Janet, of all people.

Afterwards there was a group photo, a buffet lunch and a chance to chat with those present before I set off back to Benson. My boss still wasn't interested, but then there had been no press interest anyway. Nothing was mentioned in the squadron daily brief, where all awards received by squadron personnel would be proudly announced to those in attendance, but the honour of receiving it was far more than I had expected anyway.

Just after Christmas 2011, I set off to Afghanistan for my third time. Part of the lengthy arrival process involved learning all the 'routine' things again: rules of engagement, combat First Aid, mine clearing, rifle and pistol zeroing, personal health and more. I was stood in a long queue, anticipating a mug of stewed tea and a snack of some kind, when my Flight Commander approached and motioned for me to join him to one side. 'Caz, as it is near midnight New Year's Eve, I can now tell you that you have been awarded a Commander-in-Chief Air Command Commendation, in the Queen's New Year's Honours List!' I didn't know what to say. Apparently, I wasn't allowed to know until now, but what a place to be told. He walked away, and I lost my place in the queue. It was a bit odd to be told like that: there was no announcement, in fact no further mention of it to anyone, so we were the only people on our unit who knew. I didn't want to sound egotistical by going around telling everyone, but at the same time it was an amazing award and I was desperate to share the news. Then he returned. 'Caz, I'm ever so sorry, did I say Commander-in-Chief Air?

I meant Air Officer Commanding No. 1 Group, sorry!' Well, it was a lower award, but it was still a really good one.

'What did I get it for?'

'Err, not sure!'

Back in my room, I found the honours list had been released on the internet. My Flight Commander had been right first time: it was a Commander-in-Chief Air Command's Award!' It was exciting, but I would still have to wait until I got home to find out what it was awarded for.

I was sharing a room with Steph, one of 'A' Flight's Sergeant rear-crew, and when I wasn't on nights we would sit chatting into the early hours about anything. She was great fun to be with, and a real sanity check in such a male-dominated environment. We tended to be forgotten by the guys, because we lived in a different corridor. Information was rarely pushed our way when off-duty; we had to find it out ourselves. When she returned to the UK, off-duty time became lonelier, though having the room to myself for a short while made sorting my face out less stressful. Even in the UK, I didn't have the time needed for visiting electrolysis clinics, and by now I had spent thousands of pounds on different types of 'new laser hair-removal techniques', each one promising it could now treat white or red hair, but it couldn't. They were all useless, even the versions that had me paying for additional lotions, 'to be applied several hours before each treatment'. Home electrolysis kits were no better, so my major source of embarrassment followed me continually.

On Thursday 19 January, my crew – Chris, me, Dave and Lee – spent the night moving troops, between patrol bases and FOBs, when suddenly the radio chatter went mad. Irontail 06, a CH-53D Sea Stallion, had pulled out of formation on fire, releasing infra-red coun-termeasure flares. There was an explosion; she now lay burning on the open desert floor. Immediately a rescue operation was put into action and we were recalled to pick up troops to put in place as a protective screen for rescue teams on the ground. At Bastion, we refuelled and listened on the radios, our thoughts with the crew and all on board. We sat rotors-running, two Merlins, waiting and waiting. An hour went by, more; the delay wasn't a good sign. Then we began to smell smoke, an acrid smell. In the dark, no evidence could be seen, but the smell was getting worse. The crewmen looked for visible signs of fire, while Chris and I checked through the hundreds of electrical circuit breakers behind our seats and in the roof panel. Perhaps it was coming from outside; some of the nearby rubbish tips contaminated the wind with all sorts of horrible smells. Instinct pointed to an electrical fault, but as we closed the engines down, our standby posture was cancelled; that was definitely a bad sign. A military ambulance appeared, its blue lights flashing. 'Who's that for?' we asked. It was for us; the duty authoriser had called it as standard procedure, for the inhalation of fumes.

As we entered the hospital trauma unit, we were each met by a team of medics and led to separate areas. It was clear the staff had geared up to receive casualties from the crash: the room was full of surgeons, specialists, nurses, all waiting, forlornly, unable to help; the crash wasn't survivable. The focus was now on us. I felt embarrassed; I was here for inhaling smoke, but far worse had just happened to others. I was asked to lie on a trolley-bed for tests, questions and blood samples. We were discharged as 'not fit flying duties for twenty-four hours', and instructed not to be alone for at least twelve hours, but I was in a different corridor, in a room on my own. Nobody knew the exact cause of the crash yet. The crew of six were all lost, and the CH-53s were grounded until a cause could be identified. Provisionally it looked like the result of a catastrophic mechanical failure, not enemy action. It was a sad day: being allocated that aircraft to fly was just the luck of the draw, but it could have been full with troops too.

Not being able to fly for a short while freed me up to pay my respects to the crew of Irontail 06 the next day. Their bodies had been recovered and were going home via Bastion for a Vigil ceremony and repatriation. Vigils came far too often: they were ceremonies of respect for fallen comrades before they were returned to their loved ones. It was a formal occasion, with a standard uniform dress code, including berets. Five of us could attend from 1419 Flight: crewmen Rob, Dave and Ade, together with me and Søren, our Danish-exchange pilot. The turnout was heart-warming: hundreds of US and UK personnel, with other nations mixed in. It was difficult comprehending that this crew had been tasking last night just like us, and now I was watching their coffins being paraded from a container, one at a time, each draped with a US flag. Slowly, and with great dignity, they were carried on shoulders held high, gentle sways as they moved to the beat of a slow march, towards the waiting C-130 Hercules, each one being saluted by personnel, stood in rows behind rows, in groups of twenty-five, each side of the approach to the Hercules' ramp. The salute was led in the American way, slow and deliberate movement, turning to face them as they were boarded, only turning back for the next, six times, six long salutes. All conducted with the finesse of military accuracy, without rehearsal. After ninety minutes of silent respect, as the sun began to set, we dismissed back to our day's duties, leaving their comrades to pay individual respects.

Personnel had to route home from Afghanistan via a mandatory delay process called decompression. It involved stopping overnight in an isolated compound in Cyprus, to 'wind down' from the pressures and stresses of being on active duty, before being 'let loose' back in the

UK. It included compulsory briefings on mental and physical health, and how to readjust to 'life', as well as some evening entertainment, usually a comedian and a band. A few pre-purchased tokens could be exchanged for beer or wine. In the daytime, there would be a pre-arranged leisure activity: water-sports on an isolated beach, or a day by the swimming pool at RAF Akrotiri. It was decided we would go to the beach, but it proved too windy to allow people in the water. The waves were too big to launch boats, and the wind-chill factor had everyone sitting on the beach wrapped in service-issue sleeping bags, waiting for the coach to come back. I ended up talking to two Army Majors. Out of the blue, they began talking about a transgender SNCO I knew serving in the British Army, someone they had seen at a headquarters unit in Afghanistan. I listened in, not wanting to interrupt; I wanted their conversation to flow openly. It seemed to me they hadn't realised I was transgender, or perhaps they had. I didn't want to prejudice their thought processes, because it would help me to understand what other people genuinely thought. They couldn't understand why she was in a relationship with another woman: 'Why would someone go through all the mess of "changing sex", then be with another woman?' It was the classic misconception of confusing sex and gender.

The easiest way to consider this is by completely ignoring the fact that a transgender person was born with genitals that someone de-cided made them male or female. Genitals don't control who you are attracted to; the brain does! My brain identity is very much female: I am, and I have always known myself to be, female, just with a mismatched body. As a female I may, just as with any other human female, be attracted to a man, or a woman, or both, or neither. My sexual preference is not dictated by my gender identity. I don't 'want to be a woman to be able to sleep with a man', I am a woman first, and

the rest depends on where my sexual attraction happens to lie, if anywhere. The lady in question was a girl who happened to like girls, but
was born transgender. It's simple if people realise that sex and gender
are two completely different things.

Eventually I got home, after being depressed by the decompression
directives: 'Don't be on your own for a while', 'Understand your partner's needs', 'Don't rush into sex', 'Understand your new place in your
family', 'Go easy on the alcohol', 'Let someone else drive for the first
week or so' – all the 'useful' things that are impossible as an unattached
single person, driven in with video examples as well as aural harrying.
I wondered how many other people felt worse after the mandatory
patronising.

A couple of weeks later, I found out what my award was for, and that
it had been submitted as a recommendation for an MBE, an honour
granted by the Queen. That recommendation had apparently been
vetoed because other RAF Benson personnel had received MBEs in
the past year, and 'such rare awards needed to be shared amongst other
units'. But I was unbelievably proud of the award I did get: it was amazing someone had kindly thought to make such a nomination. It was
unique to receive two awards for 'exceptional service'; I had been given
four, from a Major-General, a Rear-Admiral, a Permanent-Under-
Secretary, and now an Air Marshal, truly Quad-service! Not bad for
someone once labelled 'a liability', for being transgender.

2012 was the Queen's diamond jubilee year, and my award entitled
me, and a guest, to watch the diamond jubilee muster of troops in
front of Her Majesty the Queen, then join a royal party for lunch.
Sandra had never been able to come to any of my social or ceremonial events, so I was delighted when she said she could come. Stuart
travelled down too, so we had a lovely catch-up the evening before.

Sandra looked fabulous in a dark navy single-breasted jacket and skirt with white piping, and I was in my RAF No. 1 Ceremonial uniform, with eight of my medals and their ribbons adding colour. We were seated in the same stand as the Queen, separated in a group just twenty yards away, watching as nearly 2,500 personnel, from all three services of the Armed Forces, marched on, accompanied by the music of six marching bands. After the Queen's speech, a Drumhead ceremony and an RAF fly-past, the parade marched off and we all retired for lunch in the large pavilions behind us. It was a lovely day out, and I got to enjoy the company of Sandra and Stuart for the rest of the weekend, with my nephew Iain visiting too.

On 3 June, I met Val in London to watch the Queen's diamond jubilee regatta, a flotilla of 1,000 boats of all shapes and sizes, old and new, powered and rowed, assembled from across the UK, the Commonwealth and around the world, sailing the seven miles from Chelsea to Tower Bridge, the largest such celebration on the River Thames since the reign of Charles II, 350 years previously. It was an incredibly cold and damp day for June, and we worried for the health of the Queen and Prince Phillip, exposed to the bitter cold on top of their royal barge, but hundreds of thousands of people cheered them the length of the riverside route. We had reserved a table in a riverside restaurant beside Tower Bridge, unknowingly exactly opposite where the barge moored to acknowledge the flotilla as it passed by, a perfect ring-side seat, with the welcome luxury to step inside for a warm-up. It was an amazing event to witness.

Three weeks later, I saw a smaller royal river pageant from a different angle, looking down from the cockpit of a Merlin, in formation with a Puma, as we provided a fly-past salute over the Queen and the Duke of Edinburgh, and 4,000 guests, at a summer jubilee garden party, on the lawns of the historic Greenlands country house and estate, just outside Henley-on-Thames. It was such a pleasant contrast to the flying I had just returned from in Afghanistan, but my reintroduction to UK flying hadn't begun well. On 31 May, in my first week of flying back in the UK, Chris and I were programmed for a day currency check with a squadron helicopter instructor, Jonny. Two of our crewmen, Nick and Dave, being checked by a third, Tom, made up the rest of what was a very experienced crew. We were in a Merlin Mk3A, 'Alpha Charlie', and to save hours I flew the first hour-and-a-half of our plan in the left-hand seat, with Chris in the centre seat, then we swapped over halfway, at an Army base near Blandford Forum, in Dorset.

Three miles after departing the camp, Chris was settling in to some low-level flying and we were moving along, eighty feet above the ground at 150 mph. Jonny looked inside to select a radio frequency, so I focused my lookout forward, to cover any gaps. At 3.42 p.m., as we approached the crest of a shallow ridgeline, the dark shape of an Apache helicopter suddenly filled the left side of the windscreen, its nose stretching skywards, exposing its belly as it banked and pulled, twisting right, as hard as it possibly could, desperately trying to avoid hitting us. I could see no way for it to miss; I shouted out, but there was no time for a warning. 'Woah…' was all I could say, as it disappeared down our left-hand side, out of my view.

There was no time for Chris to even begin reacting, though he tried. I braced in my seat as I expected the Apache to collide with our main rotors. Jonny caught only a glimpse of something. 'What was that?!' he called. 'An Apache!' I replied, for the benefit of all the crew, not believing we were still in one piece. Jonny took over the controls and turned us right, everyone looking for the Apache. Where was it? Was it OK? How could it possibly have missed us, being so close? We found it hovering in a field, flashing his landing light at us. Thank goodness everyone seemed OK. We contacted them on a common radio frequency. Their hearts were racing, probably more than ours; we hadn't seen them until it was too late, whereas they must have had what seemed like an eternity of anticipated horror. Our camouflage greens had worked perfectly: the handling pilot of the Apache hadn't seen us either. The first he had known was when the front-seater grabbed his own controls and manoeuvred without warning; seeing us in the very last second he had to respond. A fraction of a second later would have been too late. The violent manoeuvre was what had caught my own attention. They were on a recce mission, focusing on the ground, when we suddenly appeared over the ridgeline. They couldn't believe they had missed us either. The lightning-quick reactions of the Apache front-seater had overstressed their aircraft, which would need a double engine change, but he had saved eight lives by doing so. He'd earned a lot of thank-yous, and more.

They began a transit back to Middle Wallop, while we continued the same way, a couple of miles apart. We intended to carry on our task, but we couldn't, nobody could focus. Our minds were replaying the fraction of a second that separated us from a fatal outcome. We climbed to a few thousand feet and flew in a straight line back to Benson. It was the quietest I'd ever heard the intercom of a crew aircraft. The formal process of reporting the incident began and the aircraft's accident data recorder was downloaded. For investigation purposes, the incident would be considered a 'fatal accident' and not a lucky escape, in order to learn as many lessons as possible. It was the closest we could be to having a fatal mid-air collision without the catastrophic consequences.

The shame of it was that 'Alpha Charlie' had joined us from Denmark with a working TCAS (Traffic Collision Avoidance System) fitted, but it wasn't maintained, because 'we didn't have them fitted on the Mk3 Merlins'. TCAS would have given us warning of the collision risk. Would this be the trigger for change, or would that still require a fatality first? Ironically, I had previously filed a report to Commander JHC at his request, considering TCAS and other safety system options, due to a rising concern about collision risk. My report had identified and compared in-use commercial equipment, listing their capabilities, advantages and disadvantages for use on military helicopters, and recommended options to integrate the systems. It had been highly praised by the Commander and was now in the hands of a follow-up team. In the spring of 2010, I had also evaluated, launched and trained aircrew on an encrypted online flight planning system that was intended to reduce the risk of collision by night, by enhancing aircrew and supervisor awareness on where helicopters and fixed-wing aircraft were planning to go. However, weather, diversions and delays during flight meant plans would change and aircraft would still have to see one another for avoidance, so an on-board collision warning was still a necessity. I contemplated the irony had I been killed in a mid-air collision!

Six weeks after this I received a phone call from Abbo. 'Caz, what are you doing tomorrow?' I was at home enjoying a short spell of leave; I had no plans.

'Can you get in to London for an afternoon reception at No. 10?' My invitation arrived attached to an email the following morning: 'The Prime Minister requests the pleasure of the company of Flight Lieutenant Caroline Paige at a reception for the LGBT community at 10 Downing Street.' Seven hours later I was knocking at the famed black door, my No. 1 ceremonial uniform getting another outing. The house didn't fit its frontage; it was so much bigger inside than I had imagined. I joined about fifty other guests in the garden, to mingle before our host arrived. Staff circulated amongst the gathered company, offering snacks from small silver platters. Over the garden wall I could see the seating constructed for viewing the forthcoming London Olympics volleyball matches, on Horse Guards Parade. The guests were all business figures and leaders of LGBT inclusion, but I found it difficult to break in to any of the large clusters that formed: they seemed more like private reunions. As far as I could tell, I was the only transgender person there, but I couldn't work out if that was the issue. I found two men who were happy to talk and ended up returning to their company each time I failed to 'circulate'. When David Cameron emerged, we were the first guests he met. I was more than a little disappointed when he ignored my greeting and spoke directly to the guys instead. This was the third time I had extended my hand to this Prime Minister, having met him twice before when he had visited Iraq, and on each occasion he ignored me but spoke to the guys either side. It was a lovely afternoon but it wasn't as social as I had expected.

Ten months after my award was announced, I finally got to receive it and see the citation. The protocol for it to be presented by an officer of the equivalent awarding rank had proven too difficult to arrange, so, at short notice, I was invited to join with an awards and medals ceremony being presented by the Air Officer Commanding No. 1 Group instead. At such short notice, the highest award of my career was presented with no family present, though Kat kindly came along. The citation was long, but it was written in recognition of 'exceptional professional contribution', 'for work to protect crews and aircraft in Iraq and Afghanistan', and 'for an inspirational commitment to equality and diversity'.

18

IF IT ISN'T LEAKING, IT'S EMPTY!

—

2012

It was the kind of bright sunny day that would have people in England wearing T-shirts and baring their legs, but I was back in Afghanistan and it was mid-December. Today we were in Merlin 'J' for Juliet, carrying twelve troops and a ton of essential supplies. Chris was piloting from the right-hand seat with me operating in the left; the No. 1 crewman was Dave; Rob was No. 2 crewman, on the aircraft ramp. This was our sixth sortie together as a crew and our first destination was Observation Post (OP) Sterga, a small UK military post perched on a cliff, with spectacular views over the River Helmand winding its course below. An escorting Lynx helicopter crew scanned the desert in front of us, looking for possible threats; their tactical surveillance camera system and heavy-calibre machine gun made welcome company.

Twenty miles to the north-west, in the Camp Bastion Air Mission Control Centre, a duty controller, call sign Overlord, was managing the skies above this region of Helmand province. He had no radar; it was all managed through radio calls. Crews reported altitude, position, what they were doing and where they were going next. In turn,

Overlord would provide information of what was happening in the region: where to avoid; what to watch out for; how to avoid a new fire-fight or potential mid-air collision. The skies above Helmand could be busy with many kinds of aircraft, from different nations, and not all of them were so informative, or even had crew on board. A collision with another helicopter or remotely piloted aircraft was as much a concern as being shot at, often more so – especially at night when no one had visible lights showing, just covert infra-red lights visible through our restricted-view night-vision devices.

OP Sterga had its own controller call sign too. 'Widow 30' pro-vided information about his own local area, such as where the closest known enemy were, whether the landing site was secure, which direc-tions were the safest to approach from or to egress through, whether any balloons in the vicinity were up. Above several UK bases, large white balloons hung in the skies like bright clouds, restrained at up to 2,000 feet off the ground; three stabilising tail-fins made them look like giant inflatable bombs. There were quite a few dotted around the area today, reminding me of pictures of barrage balloons of the Second World War. The balloons of Helmand held aloft vital sur-veillance equipment, ever watchful, day or night, for enemy activity beyond sight of the sentries in their various lookout towers. Balloons in the air meant cables keeping them in position, and cables were a real danger for low-flying aircraft; they were as difficult to see in the haze of day as there were in the dark of night.

Our call sign was heard, interrupting our crew talk.

'Molten One-Three, Overlord, Sitrep.'

'Molten One-Three, go ahead,' I replied.

Situation reports, abbreviated to Sitrep, contained information usually vital to aircraft safety. Noting the detail down as it came over the radio, I read back any key information for an accuracy check. Increased enemy activity had been observed to the north of our destination. I gave Chris a course change to fly, keeping us clear. It would require us to approach Sterga from the south, the desert side. The terrain there was relatively flat, and provided little in the way of cover for a low-flying aircraft.

Descending to low level for our final approach run, we hugged the desert at nearly 170 mph. Ultra-low-level flight ran a risk of hitting unseen obstructions or misjudging terrain clearance due to poor visual perception of how quickly the ground was rising in front of us. Flight at this height and speed required Chris to focus on flying, relying on me in the left-hand seat to keep us clear of known enemy positions and advise on obstructions. My lookout was vital, but I also needed to monitor cockpit displays, aircraft systems and performance data, navigation, self-defence equipment and maybe the FLIR display, if the weather was bad or it was night. If the pilot became incapacitated, perhaps through enemy action, I was prepared to take control and fly the aircraft to safety, though it wasn't a thought I relished. I probably wouldn't remain as low, but I had to be able to do it instantly.

OP Sterga was too small for a 72-foot-long helicopter to land inside its defensive perimeter; it was crammed with all kinds of radio antennas and masts, tents, vehicles and sheds. Landing outside wasn't ideal – it meant the troops would have to move outside to secure a pre-allocated landing area. Usually this would require a check of the landing site for IEDs. It could never be assumed that a landing site was safe because it had been cleared the day before. The enemy had proven they were very resourceful in such matters. The longer the troops were outside their post, the more they were at risk of attack, and a helicopter on the ground enticed rockets or mortars, endangering everyone. This meant our visit had to be expeditious; everything was about speed and unpredictability. I kept Chris orientated with where our landing point was.

'Four miles, on the nose.' We would begin our landing checks shortly.

Suddenly, five sharp cyclic metallic bangs rose above the sound of the engines and rotors. For a moment, there was no other evidence suggesting it was an attack, but it alarmed us. Even wearing a flying helmet fitted with basic hearing protection, helicopters were very noisy places to be; bullets passing close by couldn't be heard. Crews often return from missions not knowing they have been shot at, perhaps only learning from ground-based reports. Rob and Dave instinctively looked out for visible evidence of weapons fire. If a firing point was identified, and it was still shooting at us, the crewmen could shoot back. It was the international right of self-defence.

The role of our escort aircraft was to engage the enemy, allowing us to focus on escape. Sticking around to fight when flying a large, relatively slow-moving 'target', with the safety of up to twenty-four troops to think about, wasn't a good idea. The enemy often used smaller-calibre weapons to lure or run their prey into a far deadlier ambush.

For the moment, the Lynx remained oblivious to the attack, but I was convinced we had just been engaged by small-arms fire. It wasn't a normal noise: it was louder, and with a distinctive rhythm. An unusual noise is more often a sign something may be wrong, and when you couple that with flying in a place like Afghanistan, the safest thing to do is assume the worst: someone shooting at you. Shots were just as likely to be fired for disturbing someone's goat herd as they were for anything else. It could take just one bullet hitting in the wrong place to bring down an aircraft, regardless of how big or threatening it was.

I advised Chris to change direction. Flying an unpredictable flight path made it more difficult for a gunner to track the aircraft movement. There was no obvious evidence of aircraft damage; the engines, electrics, hydraulics and fuel systems all seemed normal. Dave and

Rob were still looking for a threat, while checking for signs of damage inside. The troops all looked healthy, though strapped into their four-point seat harness it would be difficult to see if they had slumped forward due to injury. There it was: the smell of aviation fuel. We all noticed it.

We were close enough to the OP now to prioritise landing safely; the remaining post-attack drills could be completed on the ground.

'Widow 30, smoke now, smoke now,' I radioed, a heads-up for the troops and the escorting Lynx, letting them know we were close to landing and for the troops to pop a smoke grenade.

A small cloud of green smoke rose gently from the ground, reveal-ing the precise landing point, and that the wind was blowing lightly from our left. We knew what colour smoke to expect, so we knew it wasn't an enemy ruse. Chris adjusted our approach path as I complet-ed our landing and safety checks. OP Sterga was a dangerous place to stop a helicopter; all our eyes were out on stalks now, looking for threats, ready to abort the landing if need be. Shutting down wasn't an option, unless damage to critical aircraft flight systems was evident. On the ground, Rob unclipped his harness line and took a cursory look around the outside of the aircraft.

'We're leaking fuel, it's covered underneath,' he reported.

Most aircraft leak some fluids. Aircrew and engineers often muse, 'If it isn't leaking, it's empty.' Today, the coverage told us a different story.

Seven troops and some supplies had already disembarked, and eight outbound troops had boarded.

'We can't shut down here,' Chris decided. 'It's too exposed, we'll have to go.'

I re-checked fuel contents and calculated how far we would have to go.

'Lash is the closest… It's ten minutes, we have enough fuel,' I replied.

There was a closer base, but we would have to route a longer way around to avoid the enemy activity reported earlier. 'Crucial Four-Four, Molten One-Three, we've taken damage, we're diverting to Lash.'

I reported the location where we believed we had been engaged; it was too late to do anything about any firer, but it meant other aircraft could avoid that location.

Accelerating away from OP Sterga, we considered our options and climbed to a safe height.

'There's a long white trail of fuel vapour out the back!' Rob exclaimed.

'What about fire risk?' someone said.

Chris began a rapid descent back to low level, without question. An emergency landing could be performed quicker from there, if need be.

'OK, let's start shutting off non-essential equipment, anything that could trigger fire or explosion,' said Chris, now showing increased concern.

I was trying to raise Lashkar Gar on the encrypted radio network, as well as the clear voice radio, but the low altitude wasn't helping us. The Lynx had gone quiet too.

'What about switching off the flares?' Dave asked.

'No!' I quickly replied.

The flares were protection against heat-seeking missile attacks. Everyone knows bad things come together, and switching off any critical defensive system was always a carefully considered last resort.

'I have an idea,' I said reassuringly.

I reconfigured what we had, reducing the risk of the system triggering a fire or explosion, but retaining as much self-defence capability as possible. As I briefed the guys, the radio finally crackled into life.

Lashkar Gar was a busy base with multi-national operators; stumbling blindly into it without radio contact would be where we ran the risk of mid-air collision. They would clear the local airspace now, giving us priority as an emergency. Thirteen minutes after being hit, we were safely on the ground. I smiled as I noticed the disembarking troops pausing just long enough for the obligatory selfies with Juliet. They would have something new to talk about now. It could have been much worse.

We will never know how many bullets were fired at us, but the main damage was caused by a 7.62mm round hitting part of the fuel system on the starboard side of the aircraft, halfway along the lower fuselage. Fortunately, it slowed as it went through the aircraft, and the armoured floor panelling beneath the troop seats prevented it reaching flesh and bone. The repetitive bangs were caused as it passed through various panels, narrowly missing an essential system. We would have to remain at Lash until a battle-damage assessment team had fully checked Juliet over and the damage was repaired enough to permit flight back to Camp Bastion. There would be several debriefs and reports to file when we returned, but tonight we would be put up here.

The following day, Juliet was repaired and cleared to fly for one trip only, back to Bastion, where she would get a more intimate check-over. We were instructed to fly back alone, even though we argued that the rules were to have an airborne escort, in case hidden damage – or further attack – brought us down on the way. As we landed at Bastion, two Apache helicopters were departing for Lashkar Gar. It became apparent over radio chatter that they had been tasked to be our escort. We shouldn't have returned alone; someone in Operations needed a good talking-to: this was no place for such errors. After several debriefs, we were met by the Padre who, with the decoy of bags of jelly babies, subtly set about finding out if we needed counselling.

Any battlefield helicopter crew asked about the risks in Afghanistan would usually tell you that the real danger is for the soldiers out on the ground, in direct contact with the enemy. While this was absolutely true, a helicopter was a high-value target for the enemy, especially one carrying twenty-four troops or more, all conveniently packaged in one target – a target that moved slow and low when it was dropping them off or picking them up, one that didn't fly too well when the moving parts stopped working. The risk was always accepted without question, but it's undeniably healthier to respect the threat, the danger: that's what keeps people alive – that and luck. I tried to reinforce that message where I could; that was why I had pushed so hard to be here, to keep the crews and aircraft safe, and by doing that it would keep on-board troops safe too.

Prince Harry was here too, flying Apaches. Captain Wales had escorted my aircraft on some trooping and resupply missions into the more exposed FOBs or patrol bases. It wasn't an exciting role for the Apaches, but troop-carrying helicopters were unquestionably a more accessible target when they weren't accompanied by their deterrent. We knew the enemy were often briefed 'Wait until the big helicopters are close.' So it was comforting for us, and for the troops. On the ground he mixed amongst us just like any other aircrew, planning, briefing, resting, just doing his job, but it was inspiring seeing him here. I felt respect and pride for his open concern for the soldiers out on the ground. We shared one problem: when he entered a dining hall, people would stare at him too, although for different reasons. He was a member of the royal family serving on operations; he was admired. For him, it was a stare of respect, of acknowledgment, of unveiled loyalty, and something to write home about.

This was likely to be my final tour: Merlin would soon be pulling out of Afghanistan, and my job here would be done. Back at home, everything was changing, with the RN Commando Force Sea King going out of service and the RAF trying to save money by running fewer but larger bases, and the minimum of different aircraft types. A political deal had been done and Merlin was going to the Navy. It was a crazy decision: it would have been easier, and cheaper, to share experience and skills in a joint force, rather than dismissing two squadrons of experienced RAF personnel while training replacements. As Navy crews and engineers began arriving at RAF Benson, the flying became focused on their training.

My new Flight Commander had foreseen this. Chris R-A had taken over 'B' Flight prior to our last detachment to Afghanistan. His declared mission was 'to look after his people', and I admired him for sticking to it: new commanders often said that, but their focus usually turned to further promotion. Looking after our people was exactly what was needed, when everyone was concerned about whether they would have a worthwhile job by the end of the year. When I had joined, there were over 118,000 personnel in the RAF; now it was less than 35,000. Chris's intention was to make best use of my tactics and specialist skills by loaning me back to RWOETU. I would remain squadron aircrew as part of his flight, available for flight commitments and to keep the crews tactically aware, but at all other times I would help the tactics and training (TT) desk within RWOETU. It was important for me that I remained part of the squadron: it was an essential part of my pride in what I did, and where I was. I had a loyalty to my squadron that military people will understand. Being on a squadron provides an identity to be proud of: there is respect for its past, honour in being a member, and hope for its future, all shared by a group of people with the same ethos, working as a team, enjoying camaraderie in difficult conditions, competition and banter with rivals, striving to match the highest of standards set by those who did the same before them, enjoying the good times and sharing the bad. It is a family with a purpose, and no one wants to let it down. And once you move away, you are always looking back, remembering, willing it to do well, to be safe, to go on. It never leaves you.

Mike Gallagher was in charge of TT, a very proactive, can-do character who had made this section's role the best it had ever been. He was a Puma navigator by background, and we had worked together previously, on RWOETU. But now the UK had been approached by the European Defence Agency (EDA): they liked what they saw of the way JHC trained its battlefield helicopter crews, they respected the experience of its tactics instructor core, and they wanted UK assistance to run a European version of the Helicopter Tactics Instructor Course (HTIC), to teach crews from member states the same skills, the same knowledge. There was a lot of work to do, and it fell on Mike and Rob, a Chinook pilot, to organise it – and now me, too.

In April 2013, No. 1 EDA HTIC met at RAF Linton-on-Ouse for three weeks of ground instruction and simulators. Then the students went home to collect aircraft and we all reconvened for a three-week flying phase to put it all into practice, at Vidsel, in northern Sweden. We had a mix of aircraft, from the venerable UH-1 'Huey' to the giant CH-53, crews and aircraft from Austria, Belgium, Germany and Sweden, and observers from Estonia, Hungary and Portugal. The students were all very keen to learn, and I was paired with a German 'Huey' crew as their primary instructor.

At the course graduation party, my primary student, a confident German pilot known as Till, took the 'Top Student' prize. I had never seen anyone so happy to win a prize, or more grateful for my instruction; he had continually asked hard questions, wanting to know as much as he could. We became friends, but Till wasn't the only friend I made. I had a multi-national group of friends now, and they genuinely respected and liked me, not just for what I was teaching, but as a person. Nobody questioned my suitability to be doing the job, though Till told me one evening, 'Yes, I guessed your secret the first time we met.' That was all he ever said about it, after a few drinks. It never became an issue.

From the experiences I had in Iraq and Afghanistan, and elsewhere, I always believed my circumstances were glaringly obvious, especially the minute I started talking. But I had found respect and acceptance amongst an international group, and it was really nice. I felt that I was an ambassador for military transgender service amongst the Danish, Dutch, German and US military, and beyond. Hopefully this would make a difference for transgender service in other nations' armed forces. At the very least, there was a growing number of people who saw the skills that would have been lost, had I been dismissed when I revealed who I was.

PART FOUR

SILVER LININGS

2014–2016

19

THE NEAREST SAFE PLACE

2013–2014

As 2013 approached its end, I was contacted by an American lady named Fiona Dawson, who had created a film documentary team called TransMilitary. The US still barred transgender people from serving in its armed forces and Fiona was actively campaigning against this law. She crossed the Atlantic to meet UK personnel, and visited me at home to do an interview on camera, to demonstrate that other world-class fighting forces already allowed such service, with no tangible negative effect on morale or capability, contrary to popular belief.

Of the transgender service personnel featured in her documentary, I was the eldest by far, with more military experience than the others put together, but I was the only one who proudly wore my uniform. The others preferred glamour over staying on-message! Usually, the MoD's corporate media team weren't keen on any service personnel being filmed in an unofficial capacity in uniform, but in this case, wearing civilian clothes could be misinterpreted as 'the military not wanting transgender people seen in uniform'. Fortunately, I had a new Squadron Commander, 'Diggles', and he was keenly supportive, winning permission not just for me, but for the others too. Even though

I was always self-conscious of my more masculine appearance in uniform, I felt strongly enough about accurate portrayal to go on camera wearing it; I felt it was what the USA needed to see.

2014 was supposed to be the year when I prepared myself for leaving the military, after a 35-year career. I needed to decide what job I wanted to do and where I was going to live. The military provided a resettlement package that included a three-day course, designed to assist the transition to civilian life. Unfortunately, it required attendees to have a plan for what job they wanted to do, and I didn't have a clue; the only job I knew had no civilian equivalent. I considered upgrading my PPL to a commercial licence, but that was expensive. Anyway, nothing could match what I had seen in the air. Perhaps it was time to hang up my wings and focus on other things, like finally visiting the friends and family I hadn't had a chance to see in a long time. I liked the idea of travelling the world, too, going to places I had never seen. Anywhere in a desert wasn't on my list.

Before I left, there was one last opportunity to try to get the Tri-Service Policy for Transgender Personnel Defence Instruction (DIN) sorted. It had been stalled since 2009, sat in an in-tray in the MoD. I appreciated that transgender matters were a tiny proportion of diversity and inclusion issues, considering the bigger picture of gender, sexuality, race, religion, ethnicity, disability and age, amongst many more. The fact that transgender personnel accounted for a fraction of a percentage of the military population likely kept it at the bottom of the 'to-do pile', but five years wasn't acceptable. Even simple things like terminology had changed so much in that time. Words I was getting used to had different values now, or caused offence. If I couldn't keep up with it, how could others? But this was small fry: there were administrative, logistical and medical matters to amend, update and challenge. Military medical policy regarding trans men, for instance, was erring towards discrimination. Current counsel claimed that a trans man would have too low a bone-structure density to carry the same weight that cisgender male troops did.

Cis was another new term, for people who have a gender identity that matches their sex assigned at birth. The Latin-derived prefix cis-, meaning 'on this side of', is an antonym of the Latin-derived prefix trans-, meaning over, across or on the other side of. But it still lumps everyone into different classes. Labels are awful things: they have a place in academic writings, or medical terminology, but not in everyday use. A transgender person already has a steep uphill battle without being reminded every day that they are different. While some people are proud to show their difference, many are not; to many, it is a traumatic reminder of a pre-natal quirk of fate that would for ever change the way people regarded them. A reminder that people would see them not simply as a man or a woman, but as an 'other', outside the 'normal' groups. It's why, when I arrived at my first base as Caroline, I was upset that everyone had already been briefed that 'a transgender person was arriving' – not a female, who might reveal her background only if she wanted to, or if it became necessary.

The idea that trans men couldn't be employed because of their lower bone density would only be valid if every recruit was measured against a bone-density standard, and they weren't. Some men could have a naturally lower bone density than some women, yet unknowingly be employed without restriction. Should they not be protected too? At the end of the day, if someone can meet a job's requirements, at or above the published standards, then gender, whether that be cis, trans, both or neither, should be irrelevant.

I became aware that the Army and the Navy Forum's trans reps had recently agreed a joint proposal of change to the tri-service DIN, and although it was disappointing that the RAF perspective hadn't been included, it was great that they were both responding too. It sent a far stronger message when all three forces demanded action. Because it was a policy matter, all proposals would need the support of an Equality and Diversity Policy staff officer, and I was already discussing options with the new incumbent in Headquarters Air Command.

Sarah Maskell was the new Squadron Leader in post, and although past Equality and Diversity staff officers had also pushed hard for changes, to no avail, she was keen to try. I was invited to join her as her 'specialist' at a diversity policy meeting at the MoD where the imminent release of the revised DIN was to be discussed. We met beforehand, to get to know each other in person and to join up our RAF proposals and challenges regarding the document. Apart from its out-of-date terminology, definitions and guidance, it had grown too unwieldy and confusing for its intended non-specialist reader. It needed to be broken into clear sections and annexes, and it needed an identity: it could be a technically worded policy, a medical/legal document, or a simpler-to-understand guidance document, but this current version was trying to be everything in one. If it couldn't be simplified, it would be best broken into two parts: an overall tri-service policy, complemented by single-service guidance, where it had evolved from in the first place. At the meeting, the Army, Navy and MoD agreed to all our recommendations, without addition, and that the DIN's release should be delayed again, until the accepted changes had been incorporated.

Next we had arranged to meet up with an American visitor who wanted to discuss transgender military service while he was in the UK, visiting Cambridge University. In the USA, LGB personnel had been able to serve openly for the past four years, since the repeal of 'Don't ask, don't tell', yet transgender personnel remained barred.

Professor Aaron Belkin was working on a project to persuade the US government and Department of Defense (DoD) that this was wrong. In a small café near Embankment Underground, Aaron keenly questioned Sarah on UK policy and me on my open-service experience. He was planning to hold a conference in Washington DC, bringing together nations permitting transgender service in their armed forces, and asked if we could participate. He also requested my input on a report that was being prepared for the US government and DoD by an independent national commission. Aaron was director at the Palm Center, a research initiative from the Political Science Department of San Francisco State University, and his group, chaired by a retired Major-General and a leading American civil rights attorney, with input from other high-ranking officers and noted academics, was offering 'implementation guidance for the inclusion of openly serving transgender personnel in the US military'. Over the next few months we communicated via email, regarding all manner of matters that could be argued negatively against inclusive service, such as: best practices for clothing issue, access to medication on operations, the effect of medical evaluation procedures on an individual's readiness for service, accommodation requirements, perceived influences on core values or morale, leadership concerns, peer acceptance concerns, administrative procedures, regulations and, of course, shower arrangements! The DoD argument was that transgender people couldn't serve on operations or carry a weapon for medical or psychological reasons, and therefore couldn't be in the military. The Palm Center's report would suggest otherwise. I was thrilled when Aaron credited me in the report, though my surname was spelt wrong.

The DoD and American Armed Forces resistance to transgender inclusion was the exact same argument I had heard against me being in the military, sixteen years previously, so Aaron was very keen to

invite me to the conference before my imminent retirement. Ironically, it was felt that my statement had to come from someone wearing
uniform. I had to explain that, although some veterans in the USA
still wore uniform for certain occasions, the UK had very strict rules
and veterans weren't included. For me to wear uniform to the conference meant it needed to happen within the next five months. Happily,
Aaron was keen to make that happen. Wearing uniform would add to
the image of me being a military woman, though I couldn't see why
not doing so should prevent my participation. It was my experience
that was important now. It was all about proving a transgender person
had served in a war zone and executed their job without any issue; my
experience didn't go away because I was out of uniform.

But for now, I still had time to serve. The first European HTIC
had been a rousing success, and in April 2014 we ran No. 2 Course to
the same places and the same format, though this time I instructed a
Czech Air Force crew on a Hip Mi171S helicopter, an update of an old
Soviet-design helicopter that had been a feature of many an annual
recce test. The Czech crew were just as keen to learn as the German
crew I'd instructed on No. 1 Course. They were also a good crew to
fly with, and again I was pleasantly surprised by the welcoming attitudes, even from the aircraft's two macho door-gunner crewmen,
who I needlessly worried would find my instruction awkward, though
actually the only difficulty was one of language. On 1 May, they all
kissed their female ground engineer under a tree cutting, which they
explained was a centuries-old tradition of 'kissing your love under a
blooming cherry tree or birch tree'. Legend had it that a girl who is
not kissed would wither and die in twelve months. I didn't get a kiss,
but I put that down to me not being Czech; otherwise I would find
out in twelve months! But I did get to enjoy their other tradition, the
ground-crew meeting the aircraft after a sortie with a tray of cake.

RAF engineers never did that! Once again I was proud when one of my primary students, the Czech co-pilot, won the 'Top Student' award. Two courses, two 'top students'; it was a great way to approach the end of my Air Force instructional career.

Leaving the RAF after nearly thirty-five years was going to be hard to get used to. Sadly, the traditional farewell of being 'dined out' – a final opportunity to dine formally and socialise in the officers' mess – wasn't going to happen, due to its next planned formal event being an Oktoberfest. But my flight did something that meant more to me. After they had hosted a lovely social evening, they presented flowers, a card and a wonderfully thoughtful souvenir, 'acquired' by our esteemed USAF Exchange Officer, Major Kevin Geoffroy, and engraved 'To Caz, the undisputed authority on RAF helo tactics and defensive systems. Thanks for helping keep us safe in the darkest corners of the world.' Then, because I was working with RWOETU, Mike offered to make the UK Tactics Course graduation dinner my farewell do, with a little 'encouragement' from me. It was fitting, given the twenty years I had served as a tactics instructor.

I had been saving money to celebrate my career with the holiday of a lifetime, and Val had agreed to join me. It was for fifteen days of luxury travel, including the *Orient Express* from London to Venice, four days in a luxury hotel on the shore of Lake Garda and an eight-day cruise from Venice to Athens, on board Cunard's impressive *Queen Elizabeth*, visiting archaeological delights such as Knossos in Crete and the ancient city remains of Ephesus in Turkey, a remarkable holiday and a worthy marker of significant change in my life.

Before I began my resettlement leave, Mike asked if I would lead a mentor team for a major European exercise held at Ovar Airbase, in Portugal. Exercise Hotblade 14 was sold as a 'nice easy three weeks, to wind down from military service'. It was anything but. My team included a German CH-53 pilot, Axl, and a UK Chinook crewman, Chris. The exercise was designed around multi-aircraft, multi-national missions, called COMAOs (Composite Air Operations), as big a mission as it gets in military aviation. It doesn't just involve helicopters, but fighters, bombers, transport aircraft, early warning aircraft, tankers, everything – along the lines of the 137-aircraft mission I had listened to during day one of NATO's airstrikes in Bosnia. The helicopter crews were leading this, but they had never done anything like this before. Instead of just mentoring and feeding back lessons learned, I realised we had to teach and assist, to direct, mentor and debrief, then write up post-mission debriefs, establishing the key lessons before the next day's mission, with my responsibility as the team leader adding its extra worries. It was three weeks of eighteen-hour days, with some sleep at the weekends. Axl and Chris were worth their weight in gold, and for the second week we were joined by my good friend Danny from the Helicopter Tactics Team at RAF Linton-on-Ouse. Arriving as an 'observer', he hadn't anticipated becoming so involved, but he was the kind of guy I knew would step up, and he did. It was hard work but such a great achievement, and a proud way to finish my career in tactics.

At Benson, I had one more flying task to do, my last trip in the RAF, and Merlin 'Delta' would have that honour. I was to fly her on a pair's mission up to Garelochhead on the west coast of Scotland, a long way in a helicopter, but worth it for the beautiful views near Loch Lomond. Our No. 2 hit a bird just south of Carlisle and landed safely in a field. There was nothing we could do to help, so we continued; if necessary we could check on them on the way home. Because a few of my flying currencies had expired, I was operating from the 'jump seat', but working as if in the left seat, now occupied by an RN non-handling pilot. Not being in full reach of the navigation systems made my job harder, and the weather between Carlisle and Glasgow had deteriorated, with high ground in low cloud, and poor visibility, making the navigation a challenge, but I enjoyed that.

We arrived at the troop's location on time and had just moved the first patrol group when a flashing amber light on the aircraft's main warning display drew our attention. It was a hydraulics problem, Servo Tail 2. The aircraft was advising, 'Don't panic, but I've got a problem you need to know about, in case it becomes worse.' I checked the emergency cards: 'Land as soon as practicable', meaning 'Go to the nearest aviation location, if possible', which was just as well; the barren mountainous ground wasn't the best place to land. I directed Charlie, the aircraft captain: 'Glasgow Airport is 140° at sixteen miles, in our five o'clock.' Now we monitored the hydraulic system data. There were two main systems and a back-up, but if both main systems failed it would become impossible to control the aircraft. The crewman constantly checked inside and out; hydraulic fluid has a bad habit of catching fire, and there were three hot engines on our roof, surrounding a possible leak point. As we approached the airport, another caption illuminated: Tail Valve. We upgraded our radio call to a 'PAN', declaring 'We have an emergency, we have it under control for the moment, but we need to land as soon as possible.' Glasgow Air Traffic Control gave us priority clearance direct to the airfield, where four fire engines surrounded us, just in case. Further inspection revealed Delta had had a major failure in a hydraulic component connected to the rotor controls. She was losing hydraulic fluid under pressure each time the controls were moved, so it was a good job we had landed as quickly as we did. And that was my last flight crewing a Merlin.

After two days waiting, while Delta was being repaired, I was replaced so I could return to Benson, as a passenger in an aircraft supplying a replacement crew. It was my dining-out that night, at the QHTIC graduation. We landed at 1 a.m., by which time a small reception party, anticipating my original flight returning, had drunk the 'celebration champagne', and gone home! But later that night I enjoyed a fabulous event amongst good friends, including Till, who had joined us from Germany, holding to a promise he'd made after the Tactics Course. In recognition of the centenary of the outbreak of the First World War, my farewell speech used Cecil Lewis's incredible autobiographical account, *Sagittarius Rising*, to illustrate how the WWI aerial warfare tactics of slow-moving aircraft could be seen at the heart of modern-day helicopter tactics; which received much banter from Till. Now was a good time to hang up my wings and finish my flying career – and what a career I had been fortunate enough to enjoy: over 5,000 hours of military flying, crewing, instructing or evaluating in twenty-two different aircraft types, experiencing over a dozen more, and completing seventeen operational tours.

There was just one more thing to do, before I became a veteran: the conference. I was met at Washington Dulles Airport by Fiona. It was crazy to come all this way for one day, so I had used a week of my leave to enjoy a longer stay. Fiona had kindly offered to host me during my visit, from her home, a brick-built double-fronted colonial Georgian style house, in a leafy suburb of Silver Spring, six miles north of the capital. Sharing her home was Landon, a US Navy Petty Officer, who had been quickly dismissed from service when he was formally identified as transgender three weeks into a duty tour in Afghanistan, and a shy boxer/pit bull cross called Maisie Rae, who had been abused as a bait dog before being rescued, and was now slowly rediscovering her soul, with the loving care of Fiona.

After I had settled in, Fiona showed me some of the highlights of Washington DC, initially from a 'Big Red Bus' tour. The few people who joined us on the open-top deck didn't stay long. The icy-cold October wind penetrated the thinly layered clothes I had packed for warmer weather, especially whenever the bus gathered speed, but the views were worth it. It was perhaps an eccentric British thing to do, appropriate as Fiona originally hailed from Lincolnshire. Over the following week, I ventured into Washington alone, visiting as many museums, parks and galleries as I could, while my host went about her daily business; we would meet back up for dinner.

The conference was held in the American Civil Liberties Union headquarters, but we convened first in a hotel bar, where I met trans-gender service women from Australia, New Zealand, Canada and Sweden. The ACLU is considered America's leading guardian and champion of individual rights and the conference was open to the public and the media, though it was 'ticketed' due to capacity limits. It was certainly a full house and there were several American veterans who had been required to leave the US military because they were discovered to be transgender, or had left so they could be free to tran-sition. The event consisted of several on-the-record-panels throughout the day, regarding international policy and experience. I was attending with Abbo and Sarah, who both sat on other panels regarding lead-ership and policy. I was scheduled for the penultimate discussion, on transgender service personnel 'Serving in Austere Conditions'.

The questions weren't what I was expecting, mostly about personal privacy issues, and there seemed to be a hang-up about using bath-rooms. The only issues I had experienced using communal bathrooms were caused by my own worries, not the reactions of other people, which seemed to be the argument here: how would people cope sharing ablutions with a transgender person? The same as they would with any other person, I told them, somewhat baffled. Everyone has the same right for privacy and respect. Individuals who have been uncomfortable with their bodies throughout their life aren't going to purposely seek naked attention; I always found a way to maintain my modesty, whether in the most bustling washrooms or the emptiest ones. When I'm on my own, though, using a public bathroom is a last resort for me. Visits are always rushed, cautious and in silence, worrying someone will challenge, harass or even assault me. Bizarrely, a vocal minority of people label transgender people as some kind of threat, for being 'undesirable' or 'unnatural'. These are messages usually pushed by voices within extremist religious groups, with poor records on everyday human rights, and an even poorer understanding of nature and science. If being transgender is 'unnatural', why are people born transgender? Isn't that nature at work?

But these opinionated voices prey on those who don't know, who don't understand, because the only voices they hear are the openly prejudiced ones. These voices need to be challenged. They drown out the voices of people with lived experience of being transgender, arguing, 'You're only saying that because you're transgender!'

Actually, the only reason I am saying anything is because I have lived experience of what being transgender means and how it feels, unlike those who shout the loudest. Given the extremely small percentages of trans people within the population, statistically and historically, any perceived 'menace' would more likely come from the larger 'average majority' group. People just don't want to see each other's bits when they go to a 'restroom', unless they have other issues.

During the conference, Aaron had arranged for me to be interviewed by Marco Werman for PRI's The World radio, co-produced by the BBC World Service. Marco was in New York, so the interview was conducted over a telephone link. The sound engineer set the connection up, then sat opposite throughout, monitoring audio levels, with an occasional thumbs-up to reassure me. The show manager, Jennifer, had a break-in chat first, but it didn't stop me being nervous about speaking live on radio, to a well-respected presenter with an audience in the millions. Leaning in to a large microphone from a seated position while listening through a telephone handset held tightly against my ear wasn't the most comfortable way to do an interview, either. My arm was tense and drained after a while, but I was worried more about my voice, and about saying the right thing. I had an ingrained military mentality of continually debriefing myself as I went along, realising any mistakes, looking for options to correct them, and then replaying the interview over and over in my head once it was done, searching, not so much for errors – I was discussing my own experience so I was an expert on that – but for better ways to explain something, for assumptions I had made. Just one badly emphasised word could instil negative reactions. There was always a better way to say something, but without knowing the questions beforehand, and with the time pressure of a live broadcast, I was never going to get it perfect. But Aaron thought otherwise: he was ecstatic when he listened to it, and when I got a cheering text from Steph in the UK, my worries were put aside. She had been listening to the World Service, and summoned her partner Daz, another Merlin crewman, in disbelief; it was nice of her to let me know they'd enjoyed it. I was happy, and when I did get the chance to hear it back, although my voice wasn't great, it wasn't as bad as I had anticipated. On reflection it had actually been an enjoyable experience.

I was also asked to provide a joint op-ed with Landon for CNN. The article needed to go out the same day as the media releases on the conference, to have currency, but the MoD didn't seem convinced and as a serving officer I would have to abide by their decision. Fortunately, Abbo and Aaron persuaded them of the benefits of a positive portrayal of diversity and inclusion in the UK Armed Forces, which after all was the whole purpose of the conference. The op-ed was titled 'Transgender Military Members: One Accepted, One Not' and contrasted our stories. Aaron was confident it would have a positive influence on senior commanders and the DoD. I enjoyed the conference, and meeting the people involved, but it was sad when we all split back to our home nations so quickly. I got to share the following morning exploring the Smithsonian Museum of Natural History with Donna, a genial trailblazing Army nursing officer from Australia, but the next few days I explored DC alone.

A Facebook message led me to a meeting with a friend I hadn't seen since he was a Flight Commander on 28 Squadron, several years past. 'PK' was now an RAF Wing Commander, working on exchange in the Pentagon. He chose to meet in the Poste Brasserie, which was a busy bar, but I felt at ease. It was great to meet up and renew our friendship; he was one of the few men I counted who had no problems greeting me in public with a kiss on my cheek. Once, he had taken me aside and reassured me that he unreservedly regarded me as a female in the military. His was a rare voice of acceptance, and very important to me.

Fiona hosted me for a final day of local visits, but a week wasn't enough to explore this city. I'd enjoyed a wonderful and productive visit, but the time had come for me to return home, and face up to the daunting task of leaving the RAF.

On my fifty-fifth birthday, I walked onto a base I had served at since 1993, apart from a short break to transition, and handed in all the last pieces of my military identity. I bade a few sad goodbyes, but there was no ceremony or formal farewell. I spoke to my Squadron Commander for the last time, and that was it, I was a civilian. The next day, when I needed to access my old workplace to collect a signed print that hadn't been available the day before, I was told I had to be escorted onto the base from the main guardroom. One day I had clearances above secret, and the next I wasn't trusted to walk about alone. To my friends and colleagues, my service was irreplaceable, but to the system, I was just a veteran.

20

BACK TO SCHOOL

2015–2016

2015 began with me writing letters to the President of the United States and to the US Secretary for Defense. The US cause had seemingly gone very quiet since the conference, but I still wanted to help. I wanted to use my experience, to show the way forward by positive example. But the US still only wanted a UK voice who came wearing uniform; it mattered not that those voices had no experience of serving openly on military combat operations alongside US forces. Yet the argument in the US remained a perceived unsuitability for operational service, and I was living proof that it could be done. I didn't understand their logic, so I had taken my own initiative; they were long letters, but informative ones. After three weeks, I received an answer from the office of the Secretary of Defense. It was at least a positive response, and promised that my information, and offer of advice, would be considered at the next review. Sadly, I never heard back from the office of the President.

I had been invited to remain on the RAF LGBT Forum as the veterans' representative at Abbo's request, though my first role was to help a transgender RAF reservist who was experiencing difficulties with colleagues. I had recommended Ayla as my successor as the

Forum's trans rep, a slim, androgynous 34-year-old officer who had transitioned a couple of years ago. The Army Forum had a trans rep now too, Hannah, a younger, more recently transitioned officer. Their positive experiences were an indication of how far the military had come in sixteen years in terms of acceptance and inclusion. And not just the military, either: each had transitioned in a friendly environment, with the full support of their own units, families and friends. There was much to celebrate, but this was no time for rose-tinted spectacles. I hoped they would continue to build on the solid foundations they had been given.

It came as a surprise though, with my feet barely past the threshold into life as a veteran, when the media began acclaiming both, in turn, as 'The first officer in the British Armed Forces to transition gender', or the 'first to serve openly', or 'the most senior'! The subsequent public attention was brilliant for raising the profiles of transgender people in successful employment, but their stories were good enough to stand alone – why did the media have this insatiable need for everything to be a 'first'? Media discussions suggested that the military was a perfect and easy place to transition gender, but I felt we had to be careful about suggesting that would be the same for everyone. It was certainly easier now than it had ever been. But transitioning gender isn't easy: success is totally reliant on the people surrounding the person transitioning, and there are never any guarantees those people are going to be understanding or supportive, whether in the military or not. For some people it may turn out easier than for others, but it can never be assumed to be easy. Evidence of public opinion still highlighted a need for wider education and understanding. When the Diversity Awards groups went into excited overdrive, it seemed the military's diversity spectacles were being clouded by a rose-tinted PR brush. It was right to be celebrating the military of now, but not by forgetting the how. It had been a long and difficult road to get the military to where it was with LGBT inclusion.

But there was another message in the press that riled me more. Why do reporters feel a persistent need to say that because someone is fortunate enough to be androgynous, she is more acceptable than the 'stereotypical' transgender woman? When I asked, the answer was: 'The press will be the press.' But what is an 'acceptable' female image? Is it size 8, skinny and pretty? This was dangerous ground; and the press should know better by now. Why can't people be accepted equally regardless of what they look like?

Many generations of trans women grew up in a society that was hostile to them, that turned their families and loved ones against them, that made it impossible for them to transition young except in all but the rarest of supportive circumstances. Medical transition while the body is still developing brings tremendous results in feminising or masculinising a body, bringing peace of mind to a transgender person that can literally be life-saving. But that doesn't mean it's easy for a transgender youngster of today. Social media makes bullying easy, with an invasive 24/7 reach into vulnerable and already distressed young minds, and the ability to rapidly spread gossip and rumour adds to that. Most schools still don't understand the realities of being transgender: some stand back, permitting or, even worse, encouraging mockery and the idea that exploring identity is wrong. Parents come under brutal fire for merely showing the love and support any parent should for their child, for wanting the best for them. TV documentaries reporting on young transgender lives spark feedback full of hate and anger, directed at parents for encouraging their child to 'decide to change sex'. I wonder whether the authors of these comments think it is easy for parents or guardians to have to deal with such a traumatic realisation. Those outspoken voices are fortunate they don't have to go through the same with their own children, or close relatives, to find out for themselves that it's not a 'lifestyle choice', that it's the child's whole being. And even today, children have to fight to be themselves, in a world that is supposed to be modern, forward thinking, compassionate and understanding. Should the child struggle on without support, without love? We should be celebrating that now, more than ever before, people have the opportunity to live their own lives, rather than existing in misery and at high risk of suicide, just because some vocal elements of society aren't prepared to believe people can be so different from them.

What I didn't understand about the media reporting on transgender lives in the military was why the MoD and single-service media teams were contributing to the myth that it was only in 2014 that the UK military had begun to support transgender inclusion. The politics of PR, and the constant search for a new 'first', are one thing, but why wasn't the MoD proud to show the world that in fact it had been a leading force in transgender inclusion for seventeen years by now? That transgender personnel had served openly before the bar on LGB service was lifted? That the military supported transgender personnel before many major businesses did? These younger officers had transitioned in a military that had long accepted open service, in a permissive environment. Why was it happy to disregard a significant part of military LGBT and social history?

Telling my story in the military had positively influenced people, and I had long ago resolved to follow on with that when I left the RAF, when I had the unrestricted freedom of public speech.

I had advertised myself as a public speaker with a group called Military Speakers. It lacked a positive LGBT role model, an inspirational LGBT story, so I applied and was accepted. Although the clients seemingly weren't ready for LGBT inspiration, requests from other sources began to find me, individuals and groups who wanted to hear of my experience, to learn from it, and I soon grew my own network. Some contacts became confused with my bio, after seeing articles in the media about other 'first' transgender officers, so I found myself having to explain that I was the first 'first officer', a label I'd never felt the need to claim before. I was asked to support the BAE Systems Inaugural LGBT Conference. It was a great opportunity to demonstrate the benefits of inclusion, and it led to other opportunities with other business groups. It was clear to me that big businesses were trying to redress their historically poor treatment of LGBT employees and customers. They finally saw the value in diversity, in looking after people. Equally, they would be seen positively as an employer, and recruiting from a wider population also meant a wider selection of the best people. The best people meant a healthier company: it was a win–win for business. Yet many were lagging behind the Armed Forces in so many ways, and I had much experience to offer. But a slightly different path was about to open up that would become even more rewarding.

One day, I was pleased to hear from a friend who now worked as a client manager at Stonewall. I had first met Mandy McBain six years previously, when she was an Equality and Diversity Officer in the Royal Navy and had invited me to Naval Command, to pick my brains about being transgender in the military. Mandy believed I had the perfect experience to be a Stonewall School Role Model. I liked the idea of using my experience, knowledge and background to help inspire the younger generation, but working with youngsters was something I had no experience of. I knew they were great observers: they often picked up on things quicker than adults, and they were more likely to be open and honest with their opinions, innocently or not. Not a combination I had appreciated in the past. I considered the merits for a while, until Mandy insisted that I should at least give the training day a go, and an answer was needed now to be on the first course. So I agreed.

At Stonewall's London headquarters, in a small office overlooking the South Bank, I met six other attendees and two of our trainers for the day. It was fascinating, learning about the Stonewall School Champions programme and how volunteer School Role Models fitted into the project and why. We learned some do's and don'ts of addressing youngsters of secondary school age. Then we drafted outline talks, taking it in turns to reveal our stories, each one unique and inspirational. I saw an opportunity to help youngsters, by showing them there was chance and opportunity, and not just LGBT youngsters, all youngsters, showing that difference was natural, that difference wasn't something to fear, that difference made the world better. And not just youngsters either: educating and supporting the school staff was just as important. Thus, I became a volunteer Stonewall School Role Model.

My past was catching up to me too, but in a nice way. The RAF Museum asked for an aural interview recording my service history and personal life. History needs the stories of people: personal experiences and feelings are an important part of the full picture. I warned them it might be a long interview and we laughed when I moved into their record books for the longest on record: seven hours, three minutes. I had also been invited by David 'Butty' Butterfield, an ex-RAF Phantom and helicopter engineer, to join the committee of the British F4 Phantom Aviation Group, a group of volunteers working hard to save and restore the few surviving British Phantoms, including the iconic 'Black Mike', a potentially fully functional Phantom FG1 from RAF Leuchars, one I had flown, and the last of its kind. David's support and friendship helped to introduce me back to a world I had thought lost in my past. I had been invited to attend a

Phantom aircrew reunion in London, but the reactions I had received from some people in the fast-jet air-defence world hadn't been good. I had lost some of the people I had regarded as my best friends, so it might get awkward if they also attended. This was the reason I had stayed away for so many years. But now, apparently, people had asked after me, and I was assured that I would be welcome. I had to admit, I did want to catch up with colleagues and friends I hadn't seen for nearly twenty years. The instigator of this invitation was a friend also known as 'Butty', Nigel Butterworth. I finally agreed to go, but only if Butty met me at the door on the day. And he did. Nervously, I walked into a crowded bar. Someone said hello, I was offered a drink, someone else said hello, happy smiling faces gathered around, all wanting to shake my hand. It was great to catch up with them. We had aged so much that it was like bumping into the dads of the guys I had known. Receding hair, wrinkled brows, slightly loose stomachs; nobody would guess this group had all flown supersonic fighters in ready defence of their country. I wondered what they thought of me. I bumped into a giant of a man, instantly recognisable. 'Hi Russ!' I said.

He looked at me, staring, eyes open wide, questioning. 'Do I know you?' he finally asked.

'Yes, we were on the same squadron together.'

'I don't understand… how?' I had supposed the rumour might have spread that I would be there, but he looked genuinely confused. 'We were on Phantoms together…' I didn't know if smiling was best, so I didn't.

'No… I don't understand…' Then his eyes seemed to light up as he registered who I was 'Caroline… are you Caroline?'

I got out a 'Yes' before I was grabbed in the firmest of hugs and my feet lifted from the floor, seemingly so easily. We had a lovely chat. Seeing so many accepting faces was the nicest way to close the circle on a chapter of dismissal that had been so distressing at the time. Not only did I get reacquainted with some long-lost friends, but it was also nice to meet their partners. I was so glad I had been persuaded to go, and although none of the individuals I had nervously expected to be there turned up, they might be at the next one. I would have to play that one by ear. For so many years I had expected the worst, but once again people had proven me wrong.

I had decided to move house: many of my friends in the RAF had made Lincolnshire their home, and that would cut three hours each way off any journey to visit Sandra. It made social sense to move further north, while I didn't have a job that tied me anywhere. I bought a house of two halves, one side up against the noise and bustle of a busy city-centre street, the other a quiet relaxing open area of greenery, all just a few steps away from the unspoilt medieval heart of Lincolnshire's cathedral city, a perfect place for inspiration in my new adventure: book writing. I had always been a writer at heart, from my young years of writing secret stories of 'sad boy becomes happy-ever-after girl', through the many articles I had written throughout my RAF career, and my recent articles for the Huffington Post on transgender military service, and for other media outlets, such as *Guardian* Witness, raising the profile of successful transgender inclusion wherever I could.

Val and I had booked a cruise with Cunard billed as a 175th anniversary celebration of the company's birth in Liverpool, to be marked by a meeting of all three of its liners on the River Mersey, in a spectacular bank holiday weekend of fireworks, music and 'dancing ships'. We had booked aboard the flagship, the *Queen Mary II*, the only one of the three that wasn't a cruise ship; she was designed for ocean waters, for crossing the Atlantic at speed. Though we weren't anticipating any storms on our itinerary, the weather was cold, with dull grey skies merging with dull grey seas. *Queen Mary II* berthed overnight in

Liverpool and we enjoyed a whistle-stop Beatles tour before returning to the ship for the evening's celebrations, which weren't a disappointment. The following day, to the music of a Beatles tribute band, The Beatles Experience, we sailed to the mouth of the River Mersey. Small white dots on the horizon grew to be the *Queen Elizabeth* and the *Queen Victoria*, and we turned into place as the vanguard, our escorting fire-boat firing jets of water left and right in salute. The excitement on all three ships was clearly visible at every guardrail, every balcony, on every level, with waves and cheers, but the beaches and promenades were alive too, thousands and thousands of people, from the water's tidal edge backwards, as far as the eye could see, all waving, a moving background set against familiar sights from a distant childhood.

A ferry across the Mersey, the MV *Snowdrop*, dazzling in her new zig-zags of colour, a celebration of art in war, a disruptive pattern camouflage in contrasting shades of grey, brought to life in bright yellow, blue and red, with black and white geometric patterns, linking the scheme to its First World War heritage; the entrance to the Birkenhead docks, where I had rowed; the Wallasey Town Hall, near where I was born; and of course the Three Graces of Liverpool, proudly symbolic buildings of the city from where I joined the RAF, all distant memories, rekindled briefly as I enjoyed the sights and sounds of three giant ships performing a gentle 'coordinated ballet' before posing in a spearhead formation. Then the quiet rumble as *Queen Mary II* accelerated away, taking us to enjoy at least a little bit of sun and warmth, in the Channel Islands. It was a privilege to be on board for this prestigious event, and it must have been an awesome sight from the shoreline, but I didn't realise I would be back here before the year was out.

Dr Emma Vickers, a senior lecturer in history at Liverpool's John Moore University, was interviewing transgender veterans for a series of academic articles, looking at the experiences of transgender service personnel before 'the change in policy', with a focus on perceptions of self, coping strategies and gender identity. Most of her interviewees had either been dismissed from service after being outed or left to move their lives forward, without the trauma of being humiliated and dismissed in an uncontrollable manner. She was keen to also capture life after the policy change, and that was what I could offer: acceptance and inclusion following humiliation and rejection.

The assignment involved a photographer from Liverpool, Stephen King, who met with me to discuss his part in the project. Arts Council funding was enabling the project to be presented as part of Homotopia in Liverpool, and Outburst in Belfast. It was the first commission exploring the intersection between gender identity and military service. It appealed to me, because history is important; losing sight of history means lessons learned once can be forgotten, not just regarding transgender people, but for any minority or persecuted group. When people forget why things had to change for the better, they make it possible for the bad things to creep back unsighted. Society is, after all, a collection of minority groups, some fortuitously adding to each other, forming a majority. The project was called 'Dry Your Eyes, Princess', based on a derogatory term unofficially used within the Armed Forces, to mock personnel and suggest they toughen up.

Stephen analysed and reinterpreted Emma's notes into images, portraits, reflections that hinted at a key moment that linked the individual's military career with a personal connection. We drove around Lincolnshire looking for the 'perfect field' for his interpretation of my story. I was escorted into the middle of a field of crops, dressed for an interview at home, clumping through cold sticky mud in leather court shoes, holding up my No. 1 uniform jacket, at arm's length, the weight of the jacket and medals slowly draining my arm of strength. The background of crops rolled into a big open sky, his interpretation of standing alone through difficult times, before finding success as a female in the military, symbolised by my jacket and medals.

The exhibition ran for two months around Christmas, in the Museum of Liverpool, my portrait singled out in media publicity because of my local connection. Positive reviews of my launch day film interview with Homotopia gave me the confidence to do more. As the exhibition closed, a local business, Pink Tie Promotions, arranged a public discussion panel with four of the portrait subjects. The aim was to put into context the academic narrative and photographic interpretation through exploring our personal experiences, and to provide an opportunity to discuss best practice, by revealing some of the issues and challenges facing organisational managers, individuals and families through our stories. Again, it was the historical aspect that appealed. Here was a spectrum of experience of being transgender in the Armed Forces, the negative as well as the positive, an important part of military social history. I was honoured when the museum said they had chosen my portrait to keep, as a record of the exhibition.

One of my fellow panellists was Abi, formerly known as Jan, the ex-Army captain who had been the subject of a 2008 TV documentary. I was taken pleasantly by surprise when she publicly apologised for her inaction in the past. Troops she had commanded several years before she herself had transitioned gender were amongst those who had openly mocked me, when I flew them in Bosnia. She felt guilty about not showing support, or at least chastising them. Later she discussed how her role as 'the first Army officer to transition' was being overlooked, with someone else currently being credited. I smiled as I related how her own documentary had claimed she was 'the first transgender officer in the Armed Forces', the same claim being repeated, the media demonstrating its short-term memory and its need for 'firsts'.

2016 had barely begun when Sandra gave me the news that no one wants to hear. Just before Christmas she had become concerned about a strange feeling in her tummy area, following a gentle push from a granddaughter. An ultrasound found shadows on her kidneys, initially assessed as kidney stones, but a CT scan gave worrying results. When initial assessments were presented as 'a distortion of the womb', she wasn't convinced. Fortunately, her gynaecologist agreed and arranged for an MRI scan. Then followed a rollercoaster of emotions, for us all, but I couldn't imagine how hard it would be for her. She had been given the all-clear once before, after a bowel cancer diagnosis three years previously. Now it looked like the cancer was back, this time as a tumour on her lymph node. Sandra was my closest family, and had stood by me when I needed her to; I would find it hard to lose her. I was stunned, then outraged, when the oncologist casually gave her no hope, but she has always been a strong and determined sister, a fighter, and I was so grateful for that, and proud. It was that determination that had convinced medical professionals all was not well during her previous encounter with cancer.

Ironically, the doctor's fatalistic approach triggered anger, and she used that anger, insisting on chemotherapy. With wonderful support from her family and the nursing staff, and her own sheer determination, the results began to swing positively. It would be foolish to assume the defeat is permanent, and regular scans and tests will maintain a watchful eye, but for the moment everyone is remaining positive. Sandra is leading the way, and a smile has returned to my beautiful sister's face.

After the success in Liverpool, Emma asked if I would participate in another panel discussion, this time for an event she was chairing at the Imperial War Museum (North), in Manchester, as part of the second National Festival of LGBT History, exploring the researching of LGBT histories in the British Armed Forces and Merchant Navy. The event was hosted by the museum and organised by Schools OUT UK, a registered UK charity that works towards the equality, safety and visibility of LGBT people in education, and sponsors LGBT History Month events in the UK. I listened as professional historians from the UK and the USA spoke about their own research and offered advice on how others could proceed. Researching military LGBT history apparently wasn't as easy as it sounded: although gay interactions had been recorded since the nineteenth century, many official accounts had been destroyed during the World War Two bombing of London. Living history was difficult to capture, seemingly because of perceived breaches of loyalty to service, unit, or colleagues, or through individuals not wanting to recall past experiences they thought best forgotten.

I was part of a three-member panel revealing more modern history, by recounting our own stories. With me was Elaine Chambers, an Army nursing officer, who happened to be a lesbian, who was exposed, investigated and forced to resign her commission, ending all hopes of her military career in caring for others. The third member was Ed Hall, whose career as a Royal Navy officer came to an equally abrupt end when he was outed as a gay man. They had become part of a legal challenge group that had influenced the repeal of the ban on LGB service in 2000. The audience was captivated, and the day inspired me to write an article for the Huffington Post to capture the history I had experienced. More interviews followed, including with Anna Walker, a *Reader's Digest* digital editor who aspired to profile transgender role models for the over-50s, and groups like Mike Young's Aircrew Interview were interested in the role I played in military aviation, the aircraft I flew, and the personal aspects that humanised the story, recording it for YouTube audiences.

When I'd met Schools OUT UK's Jeff Evans, he liked the idea that I was working on a book that covered a unique part of UK military LGBT history, and he asked Emma to put me in touch with a publisher. Their encouragement was pivotal, but once again I waited in nervous anticipation while a publisher considered the detail I had sent. I received a call from the managing editor, Olivia Beattie; she said they liked it, and would take it on! I couldn't believe it, I was absolutely thrilled, not for me alone, but for those people who had encouraged me to do this, to contribute a story that could raise awareness, and give others hope, reassurance and inspiration, or insight, or even pride in themselves.

Civilian life was good. I had no regrets; I was getting time to enjoy the things I wanted to. I had even joined an award-winning rail travel company as a tour manager. I was worried that they might not employ me as a transgender woman, because I would be on the front line of their customer service. But these were my own worries. Nobody asked the question at interview, and I felt no need to volunteer such personal history, though it was readily available from a simple internet search anyway. It was hard work, but fun too. I took a group of thirty-eight customers on a ten-day tour of the Scottish Highlands, and a group of twenty-six on a ten-day tour of northern Italy, in the Lake Garda area. It was a great way to travel and meet people, but unfortunately 2016 proved to be an incredibly busy year, so I took a break, intending to return.

I had been asked to work alongside an EDA-sponsored team, teaching helicopter tactics to European military crews as a civilian contractor, and it was an offer I just couldn't refuse. My experience teaching on the first two European Helicopter Tactics Instructor Courses had stood me in good stead; I was invited to re-join them for No. 4 Course. Mike Gallagher was now the chief instructor, in an RAF post responsible for solely managing and running the European courses. The course had interest from the UK too, with Chinook or Puma helicopter crews now joining as trainee instructors. I had expected some nations to find it difficult receiving instruction on these skills from a civilian aviator, let alone a transgender woman, but I was wrong. They all demonstrated open respect for my experience; I was a veteran not a civilian, and they never questioned my suitability. For me, it was a symbol of wider international acceptance, hopefully a positive experience that would benefit transgender personnel in their own armed forces. But it also meant that my extensive experience in this role was not just fading into the past, that I could share the matters I enjoyed teaching, that I could continue my contribution now, to the safety not just of UK crews on operations, but of European crews and assets too. It was a wonderful gift to be able to share. I never believed the day would come when I did this from within my own business. The team I now worked with was of course key to this, and it was great to be working alongside some familiar RAF and Army faces, from my flying days, especially Danny, Mike and Roj, an ex-Merlin crewman who had also recently retired, but also international friends, from Austria, Germany and Sweden, people who always made me smile with their greetings.

I was also being well looked after by my friends, but I was still missing that one special relationship. In 2012, I had met a second person through the online dating agency I had been a member of for twelve years. I had remained honest with my details and he saw no problem with that. We met a couple of times, for lunch and a walk alongside the Thames, but then he decided he couldn't take the relationship further, because he was worried what his family would think. I thought that if you wanted a relationship with someone, then that should be your focus, not worrying about what others would think. That kind of worry is what destroyed my family. But it wasn't up to me, so we parted as quickly as we'd met. I resigned myself to being single for the rest of my life. If I couldn't attract a partner by now, then I never would. It did upset me, it reinforced what I already knew, and I'd lost count of the number of times I'd gone to bed feeling low. Sleep brought better dreams.

But, as my life as a veteran begins, those long-term fears have become unexpectedly complicated. The timing is bad, just before going away for two months, to help manage and instruct on the 2016 European Helicopter Tactics Instructor Course, but someone else who can see past my background has contacted me. Steve seems keen, but my worries have changed; now the danger is not from him worrying about telling people, but from me worrying about my feelings. It has taken too long, and I have grown used to expecting a forever-single future. Going through what most people experience in their teenage years while in my mid-fifties is a bewilderingly testing inconvenience. I don't have the experimentation or inexperience of youth to bounce back from, and I ask too many questions of myself, thinking things through too much. Why would he be interested in me? Even the evidently simple act of kissing someone becomes a tangled thought process: why would you do that? What is the function of kissing? It just looks wrong. I've had a lifetime of becoming uncomfortable at witnessing anything but the briefest moment of lips meeting lips. Perhaps initially from jealousy, then the realisation that nobody wanted to kiss me, then the pain of seeing something so common being so unreachable. And now, a fear of not liking it, of doing it wrong! And what could follow is even more of a minefield of inexperience and worry. Simple things to anyone but me; I worry now that it may be too late. I am finally happy being me, I have survived difficult times without a companion; is it something I need any more? For the moment, I don't know.

For now, of all the things that have happened since I left the military, the one that has had the most impact is being a volunteer Stonewall

School Role Model (SRM). My first few months were incredibly busy, and I was finding the role far more rewarding than I had anticipated. During my first school visit I was accompanied; after that I went on my own. To begin with, the limited number of SRMs meant travel far and wide, but as more schools sought to become School Champions, the number of SRMs grew. My journeys took me south to the London area, north to Newcastle, west to Huddersfield. My busiest month occurred in February, when many schools requested a visit to coincide with projects involving LGBT History Month. It was heart-warming to see the education and inclusion processes they had developed or envisaged. Some schools had diversity groups, set up by pupils with the caring supervision of staff, and I often got chance to chat with these groups over lunch. I met youngsters who were confident in themselves, who felt secure, who had ambitions and hopes, a far cry from my school days.

If I give hope to just one individual, then it is a priceless contribution, but the feedback I was getting exceeded that. At one school, the day following my talk, a year 11 pupil asked his teacher if he could speak to the class. He apologised to his peers for his past attitude, for bullying LGBT pupils. He felt ashamed, he hadn't realised what being LGBT meant, or what impact bullying truly had. The fact that he had the strength to stand up and apologise in front of his peers revealed so much good about his true character. Being an ally is far more valuable than someone might believe, and it's rewarding for both parties. At another school I met a mum anxious about her transgender son, starting out in his new life, fretting that she would do or say the wrong thing, but she had already done so much more than she would ever realise, in just extending her love and support to her child unconditionally. Jude and I chatted, then she kindly offered support to me too, but she had already done that, by extending friendship!

Why do LGBT people need open voices of support, and special protection through law? Surely the laws preventing general discrimination and harassment are enough? Unfortunately, all the evidence still suggests otherwise: many people retain long-standing fears, ingrained intolerance or a naive misunderstanding. Their prejudice is fuelled by a narrow-minded media, blinkered religious groups, and bullies of the past; the relic of a society with a fear of change. Change is emerging, but it still has a lot of fences to climb over. The law helps, but a speed limit doesn't stop people speeding; understanding why it's there does.

If only all schools, and all parents and guardians, could see how these forward-looking projects make everyone so much happier and inclusive, not just LGBT students or staff, but any child who is a minority, or feels alone, or believes they are different in some way, for whatever reason. And not just them, either. When I started visiting schools, it struck me how all the children got behind this: they were keen to show how they wanted to respect difference, to embrace it, to stand against bullies, to support their friends. I was seeing this in one form or another wherever I went, even Oriel College at Oxford University, a place I had been warned was 'old-fashioned in its ideas on diversity', but which received my presentation positively. A teachers' meet in Nottingham and another in Sheffield were equally warm in their reception. The world is growing to be a better place, though that doesn't mean it is there just yet. There are still people who don't appreciate learning, knowing, understanding others, though these people are few and far between. Most people have good hearts, it's just a case of helping the 'unsure ones' to see the danger of being influenced by the few bad apples that burn themselves up with spite, envy or just plain nastiness. That is what diversity education is all about: working together, respecting difference, just being nice when there's no reason not to be. Perhaps it's a world beyond reach for some time yet, but there's no reason this generation shouldn't be proud of the start it has made. That is what my book is about. The world I lived in as a youngster was a hostile one for me; it should be a safe place for any child to realise how precious it is to be different, to be proud of themselves, of their friends and their family, not to live in fear, to be strong, to live their lives, and to experience respect in doing so.

My journey only happened because of the people who surrounded me when I finally gained the courage to reveal myself, far too many to name. Most of them know, but some may never get to know, to realise how on one day, in one place, they said something that made a huge difference. I may never know either, about the people who stood up for me when I wasn't there, but thank you. People have a positive influence just by standing up for someone, for something, when they're not there or able to do so themselves. One action of respect always generates more, however unintentionally. If the reader takes nothing away from this book other than this one thought, they will be making the world a better place for everyone. Respect others for who they are, don't dislike someone for something you don't really know much about, or don't understand. Don't rely on something you heard that someone else heard: read about it, learn about the realities of being in that person's shoes, then make an informed judgement; there can be nothing fairer to ask of anyone than that. And, if there is one key lesson I have learned in my lifetime, it is: whoever you are, believe in you, trust in you, be you; there can be no stronger foundation for life.

If you need to speak to someone about gender identity issues, advice and support are available from the following groups and resources:

Schools-out.org.uk
Schools OUT UK works towards equality, safety and visibility in education for all lesbian, gay, bisexual and trans people.

gendertrust.org.uk
The Gender Trust is a listening ear, a caring support and an information centre for anyone with any question or problem concerning their gender identity, or whose loved one is struggling with gender identity issues.

gires.org.uk
Gender Identity Research and Education Society has information available for the families of trans people and for trans parents seeking custody of or access to their children.

Genderedintelligence.co.uk
Gendered Intelligence is a not-for-profit community interest company, established in 2008. They work predominantly with the trans community and those who impact on trans lives; they particularly specialise in supporting young trans people aged 8–25.

mermaidsuk.org.uk
Mermaids supports children and young people up to nineteen years old suffering from gender identity issues, as well as their families and professionals involved in their care.

stonewall.org.uk
Stonewall School Champions Programme. Schools that participate in Stonewall's Train the Trainer courses are also automatically enrolled in the Stonewall School Champion programme.